BUGSY!

The life and times of Bugs Stevens three-time NASCAR National Modified Champion

with Bones Bourcier

Coastal 181

PUBLISHER

For the record...

For too long, auto racing has been guilty of neglecting its history. At most short tracks, records either aren't kept or aren't updated; statistics slip through the cracks; memories fade. But as near as our research could determine, Bugs Stevens won at least one modified feature race—and in almost every case, far more—at the following tracks:

MASSACHUSETTS: Seekonk Speedway, Norwood Arena, Westboro Speedway; CONNECTICUT: Stafford Motor Speedway, Thompson Speedway, Waterford Speedbowl; NEW HAMPSHIRE: Monadnock Speedway, Star Speedway; VERMONT: Catamount Stadium; MAINE: Oxford Plains Speedway; NEW YORK: Albany-Saratoga Speedway, Utica-Rome Speedway, Airborne (Plattsburgh) Speedway, Shangri-La Speedway; NEW JERSEY: Trenton Fairgrounds Speedway; PENNSYLVANIA: Pocono International Raceway; VIRGINA: Martinsville Speedway; FLORIDA: New Smyrna Speedway.

His resumé also includes track championships at Stafford (one on dirt, three on pavement), Thompson, Seekonk, Norwood, Westboro, and Albany-Saratoga.

Credits
Front cover photo: Mike Adaskaveg
Back cover photos: background, Mike Adaskaveg; insets, John Grady

ISBN: 0-9709854-3-6

For additional information contact:

LEW BOYD
Coastal 181.com
29 Water Street
Newburyport, MA 01950
All rights reserved.

No part of this book may be reproduced in any form, or by any means, without permission in writing from the publisher.

The author and publisher shall not be held liable for any incidental or consequential damages that might result from the content of this book.

First printing, July 2002

Printed in the United States of America

Contents

		Preface	v
Introduction	vi	One Cool Customer	vi
Pete Zanardi on Bugsy	2	Being Bugsy	4
Dave Stevens on Bugsy	16	The Early Days	18
Pete Hamilton on Bugsy	34	The Championship Years	36
Gene Bergin on Bugsy	54	Tracks	56
"Humpy" Wheeler on Bugsy	74	The Big Leagues	76
Bill Slater on Bugsy	88	Fast Times	90
Val LeSieur on Bugsy	106	The Seventies	108
Ron Bouchard on Bugsy	134	Etiquette	136
Geoff Bodine on Bugsy	146	Rivals	148
Sonny Koszela on Bugsy	166	Just a Jockey	168
Richie Evans on Bugsy	182	It's a Mental Thing	184
George Summers on Bugsy	198	The Home Stretch	200
Doris Berghman on Bugsy	218	Growing Old, Yes; Growing Up, No	220

Preface

BUGSY! *The Life and Times of Bugs Stevens* is the third in a series of books we are producing on the evolution of regional oval track racing in the United States. The first two, *They Called Me 'the Shoe'* and FONDA! *An Illustrated and Documented History of the Legendary Fonda Speedway* have proven that there is huge interest in the subject.

As is the case with most every champion in the pioneering days of racing, Bugs Stevens is certainly made of uncommon clay. The pages that follow will paint the picture of an incessantly playful guy who had an extraordinary talent behind the wheel. Interestingly, along the way it becomes clear that Bugsy is something else as well—a thinking man whose centered and homespun wisdom and philosophy carry messages for us all.

We are very pleased that Bones Bourcier was available to undertake this project. One of the finest motorsports journalists, Bones has had a long and close personal relationship with The Bug. Bones' sensitivity and clairvoyance guide this story through the amazing ups and downs of one of America's greatest short track racers.

Three folks, Val LeSieur, Mike Adaskaveg, and RA Silvia have once again demonstrated their enormous commitment to racing and were there to help us in any way at any time. Val opened the considerable files at *Speedway Scene*, a Northeastern race paper that has covered the flight of The Bug for nearly thirty years. Mike Adaskaveg's brilliant images speak to his virtuosity as a news and racing photographer, and we are unendingly grateful to him. RA Silvia, New England's racing historian and resident good guy, allowed us full access to the volumes and volumes of materials in his incredible, self-funded museum.

Special thanks also go to Skip Welch, Bill Balser, John Grady, Tom Ormsby, Danny Pardi, and to all Bugsy's contemporaries who took the time to write so passionately about him in the chapter introductions and to all other photographers whose pictures appear in the book.

Jim Rigney and his team of designers and production editors deserve special thanks for their fine work on this book. Jim's uncompromising love of motorsports and his commitment to preserving auto racing history are reflected in the pages of this book.

Sandra Rigney is to be complimented for her interior design of the book. Her choice of the casual and somewhat whimsical script typeface mirrors the personality of The Bugman. The page layout is clean, orderly, and easy to read.

We thank Joyce Wells for her superb cover design. Joyce has never seen a live car race, but her talent as a designer and her ability to communicate messages with strong graphic images and text is demonstrated here.

Another special thanks goes to MaryRose Moskell. She's the friendly voice on the other end of the phone when you order books from Coastal, and her value goes well beyond that single responsibility. She is the heart of the operation—be it selling books, arranging meetings and conferences or brainstorming the latest marketing plans—MaryRose is always there with a creative and innovative solution and a friendly smile.

JIM RIGNEY
Editor

LEW BOYD
Publisher, Coastal 181

One Cool Customer

I ALWAYS THOUGHT he was the coolest guy in the place, no matter where he was. Bugsy Stevens just had something about him, something that set him apart. Even his peers—Richie Evans, Eddie Flemke, Ron Bouchard, George Summers and a handful more—talked about Bugsy differently, maybe a touch more fondly, than they talked about other drivers. If you want to call it a star quality, I won't argue.

Elsewhere in this book, 1970 Daytona 500 winner Pete Hamilton—a Stevens contemporary in the coupe era—admits that in their younger years he thought Bugsy "epitomized what a race driver should be, what he should look like and act like." Funny, but I always thought the same thing. Maybe it was the journalist in me, but I always enjoyed *characters*. For me, the most entertaining driver was one who combined raw ability behind the wheel with a devil-may-care spirit, a sense of humor, and a roguish need to flirt with the edges of social correctness. And that about summed up Carl Berghman, better known by his *nomme de guerre*, Bugs Stevens.

Said Ronnie Bouchard, "You never had to worry about Bugsy not having a good time. No matter what, that was going to happen."

Nobody was immune from getting dragged along for the ride, as hard-charging Gene Bergin was reminded one summer night at Stafford Motor Speedway.

"I'm sitting in my car, ready for my heat race," Bergin recalled. "Bugsy leans into my window. He's smoking his cigar, and he's holding up this pack of firecrackers. I looked at him, and I said, 'Bugsy, you wouldn't . . . '

"Well, guess again. He lit that fuse with his cigar, and the next thing I know, it's *pop-pop-pop-pop* . . . I'll bet there were 50 of those things that went off. The whole inside of the car is full of smoke, and there's all this paper flying around, and I can't just jump out of the car because I'm strapped in.

"That was Bugsy."

And this was Bugsy: It's 1980 at the Westboro Speedway, and the modifieds are rolling out of the pits to start their feature. Stevens, aboard Joe Brady's car, stops at the flagstand and gestures to Dick Brooks, the veteran starter. Brooks, figuring that Stevens needs clarification of his starting position, scrambles off his perch and walks to the driver's door. At which point, to Brooks's surprise, Stevens hands him a burlap sack.

(Mike Adaskaveg Photo)

When you're handed a burlap sack, you open it. And when you're a live chicken trapped in a burlap sack and suddenly sensing freedom, you fly out and scramble around with great commotion, to the shock of one flagman and the infinite delight of a few thousand fans.

But in this racket, nobody gets to be a hero—nobody takes on that star quality—simply by being a cut-up. If you're the funniest guy at the track and you run 15th every week, all you are is a guy who runs 15th. Well, Bugsy didn't run 15th very often. Bugsy won.

Godamighty, did Bugsy win: three NASCAR national modified titles, seven Martinsville victories, all those Stafford scores—73 of 'em, big and small—and checkered flags at big, fast joints like Trenton and little bullrings like Seekonk Speedway, just down the road from his Massachusetts home.

So, how best to look at Bugs Stevens? As a character, or as a champion?

Well, how about both?

I blend the two, seeing different parts of him at different times, and inevitably I come to this conclusion: That the man whose life story you are about to read is one of the real giants of American short-track racing.

Working with Bugsy on this book has been an absolute joy. For one thing, it put me back in touch with so many names out of my own past. The interviews we did for our chapter introductions, the digging for buried facts, the searches for photographs, all were labors of love. Doris, Bugsy's saintly wife of more than 40 years, was her usual cheerful self throughout, and stealing a little bit of time with the Berghman family is always a joy. One Florida noon I even had lunch with Bugsy and legendary modified owner Bob Judkins, although I couldn't help thinking that most of the other 60-somethings in the restaurant would have fainted had they been told just a few tidbits from the zany, dramatic, thrill-a-minute lives these two men had led.

In the course of putting together this book, I grinned a lot.

But it was not all light duty, because we covered some serious topics. I have talked to Bugsy a dozen times over the years about the racing deaths of his friends Fred DeSarro and Richie Evans, and I wasn't looking forward to doing it again, but it had to be done. At other points his voice rose in anger and frustration as he rued the spiraling costs of racing and the steady, undeniable decline of what he called the ethics of racing, the unwritten codes of conduct he and his rivals drove by. He is a man who has earned the right to his opinions, even though he sometimes seemed hesitant to trumpet them, declaring more than once, "Don't let me get off on these tangents."

In the end, the best part of doing the book was just getting to hang out with The Bugman again. Even the outtakes from our taping sessions bring a smile. There we were one night, me on the living room sofa at his home in Massachusetts, him in the kitchen, staring into the refrigerator.

"You want a soda?" he asked.

"No thanks, Bugs."

"Beer?"

"Nope."

"How about a highball?"

"No."

Closing the fridge now and heading back into the living room, Bugs Stevens said, "You know where you find good highballs, don't you?"

I fell for it. "Where?"

"On a giraffe," he shrugged, and then he plopped down onto the sofa to start the interview.

Funny. Funny and cool.

Same old Bugsy.

BONES BOURCIER
Indianapolis, Indiana

(Mike Adaskaveg Photo)

Pete Zanardi on Bugsy

Pete Zanardi and Bugs Stevens, NEAR Hall of Fame dinner, 1998.
(Courtesy of Speedway Illustrated)

Pete Zanardi, veteran sportswriter: "When you talk about how Bugsy *became* Bugsy, it's that old argument: Do the times make the man, or does the man make the times?

"One thing that helped him was that he was so damn competitive. He never wanted to be beaten. He didn't like to be beaten in an argument; he didn't like to be beaten at drinking beer. One time, I wrote that Ronnie Bouchard was the best driver I had ever seen at Stafford, just in terms of the way he rode that outside groove, and Bugsy let me know that he didn't appreciate that.

"He's also brighter than the average bear. So his intelligence and his competitive nature—the mind and body working together in the classic Greek sense—are what made him a great race driver.

"But if you want to know what made Bugsy Stevens such a legend, I'd say Bugsy Stevens did. He catered to the fans. He played that game better than anyone. In my time, Bill Slater was the first race driver who understood how to play to the fans; Bill was the guy who dressed neatly with the white shirt and the black pants, who gave people rides in his race car. Well, Bugsy took that a little bit further. He always seemed to know exactly what he should do in a certain situation, while at the same time keeping that cavalier image that he had.

"He was well aware that this thing between him and the fans was a great relationship. He was getting as much out of it as he was putting into it.

"Bugsy had a way of knowing what was going on at all times. Journalistically, you went to him because if you needed a good line, he gave you a good line. You knew you were going to get great quotes, and you were going to cut right to the heart of the matter. He would save you time; he knew what you wanted, and what would make your story better.

"Oh, sometimes he'd play games with you. I'd ask him a question, and he'd

Being Bugsy

say, 'Have you been watching the stock market? Have you noticed what the goddam market is doing?' But most of the time, he knew what I was after.

"He had been a high school athlete of great acclaim, and later on he'd played sports in college and in the service. So when he got to Norwood Arena in the sixties and started winning races, that wasn't the first time people were writing about him, or paying attention to him. It wasn't new to him. He already understood what sportswriters were all about.

"After he won his three NASCAR championships, he started catching on elsewhere. Whenever he went to Martinsville, the writers from the Roanoke and Greensboro papers wrote about Bugsy, and he became a national figure.

"I think he knew what he meant to the sport. He knew that people really respected him, and he understood that what he did and what he said had a lot to do with where the sport was going to go.

"What has helped Bugsy's name endure is that, for some reason, nostalgia has really started to catch on in auto racing, so people are curious about him. And he is so important to those of us who watched him, and were there.

"I went to see him in Florida a few years back, looking for a quote for a story I was doing about Norwood Arena. I spent all day with him, and he never gave me the quote. He just wouldn't do it. Well, [my wife] Jane had an interesting point. She felt that by not cooperating with me, Bugsy was trying to say that this relationship—the relationship between him and me—should be on another level now. In other words, I shouldn't have been there *working*.

"See, the previous time I had visited him, he and Gene Bergin and I had gone out on Bugsy's boat, shrimping in the river. It was a great experience for me; I mean, I'm out there with two of the greatest race drivers I've ever seen, and there was nothing professional involved. We were just three old men, having fun and talking. Now I'm back again, trying to interview Bugsy for this Norwood story, and the way Jane described it, it was like he was telling me, 'Hey, it's over. You're not here as a writer, and I'm not here as a race driver. We should just be sitting around, drinking beer, going out to eat.' I think she hit it right on the nose; what he was saying was, 'We're in a different situation now.'

"Yes, Bugsy was the perfect guy for his time. And I know this: He was the perfect guy for me. It would have been a whole lot less of a career for me had he not been a part of it. There was a lot of trust between us, I think, and I hope I'm not talking out of school.

"I value his friendship immensely. One of my proudest moments was inducting him into the [New England Auto Racers] Hall of Fame. There were probably other guys who could have done that, but I would have fought like hell if they tried to take that way from me.

"You're asking me what made Bugsy? I wish I knew, so we could bottle it."

Being Bugsy

Being Bugsy

THIS IS ALL HINDSIGHT. Everything in these pages is coming from a guy who's trying to look back and try to piece together a puzzle that took thirty years to build the first time around. Some of the pieces got away over the years, which is why this book isn't the exact chronological story of my life. It jumps around a bit, because my memory jumps around a bit.

It would take a guy with a really sound mind to remember all the things that have happened to me, and I've never been accused of having a sound mind. My wife Doris says I don't have enough brain cells to remember very much, and she might be right; I'm sure I left some of 'em behind at this party or that party, and maybe a few of those brain cells went to sleep for good after I hit the wall at Stafford or Thompson or who knows where.

Besides, I'm not sure that you need every last detail to make this an interesting story. I mean, I've never been a stat guy; never kept

(Dick Berggren Photo)

records, and never really paid much attention whenever anybody showed 'em to me. In fact, if you run across any numbers in here that seem impressive, that only means we probably had to look 'em up.

I have no idea how many races I've won. The best I can do is a ballpark guess, and I'd put that guess somewhere between 300 and 400. I know that at some point in 1971, after I'd split with Lenny Boehler and was in my first season driving for Sonny Koszela, I scored my one 100th NASCAR victory. So when you factor in all the winning I had done up to that point in non-NASCAR races, and all the racing I did after that—in and out of NASCAR—the total would have to be up over 300. But, again, I have no way to know for sure. I raced at a lot of tracks and for a lot of promoters who didn't bother keeping records, so I don't even know where you'd start to figure it out.

It's the same with trying to decide which victory was my biggest. I mean, I won seven times at Martinsville, and there used to be a lot of glory in winning a modified race at that joint. And I clinched my first NASCAR championship in 1967 with a win on the old mile track at Trenton, so that was an awfully special day, too. But there's so been many good ones. I won the only Thompson 500 ever run, and I've won Stafford's two biggest races, the 200 and the Spring Sizzler.

But most of my wins came in regular shows all over the Northeast, 30 or 35 laps long, and in a lot of ways those were tougher than the special events. In New England, the weekly features were lined up according to a handicapping system: the more money you'd won lately, the farther back you started. And we were successful enough that it seemed like we *always* started toward the back, seven or eight rows deep.

So, no, I don't remember a lot of little details, but I remember passing cars. Lots and lots of cars.

God, we had some great races.

I'm not sure exactly what my driving style was. I do know that I always spent a lot of time looking at the feature lineup, trying to figure out what might happen. I'd check out the guys starting ahead of me, think about what I could do to get by 'em, and calculate how much time I needed. Of course, a lot of that scheming went straight to hell once the green flag waved, because there's only so much you can plan for. Still, it never hurts to do your homework.

A long time ago, one of the veteran guys—and I'm sorry, but I honestly can't remember who it was, although it may have been Hop Harrington—taught me a great lesson. He said, "When you're not out there on that race track, sit up in the grandstands and study the other drivers as they practice. Study 'em all. That way, you'll know how they're going to react when you're around 'em." I did that, and I kept right on doing it for years and years. I'd check out which groove the various guys preferred, and I noticed where their cars seemed to slip a little. I filed everything away. That's what I mean by homework.

A lot of people said and wrote that I was an aggressive racer, and I guess I was when I had to be. But if you look at my record in the big races, I was usually around at the end of those big races, so being aggressive certainly didn't mean being reckless or wild.

My philosophy was, drive as hard as you can while still managing to stay out of trouble. There were plenty of races at Martinsville and Trenton, and some of the longer events at Stafford or Thompson, where I didn't worry about running in the top five or even the top ten for the first half of the race. I'd ride along, reminding myself to save the car, save the tires, save the brakes, save the engine. I was in the show to win it, and that meant getting to the finish. That sort of thinking won me a lot of races.

I always believed in racing hard, but I was also pretty good at sticking around to the finish. I ended up taking home a lot of big trophies that way. (Bill Haynes Photo/ Courtesy of Speedway Scene)

In a crazy way, a lot of that thinking went back to my late father, who wasn't a racing guy at all. When I was growing up in Rehoboth, Massachusetts, he had a lot of different jobs, and for a long time he was a house painter. Some of the projects were so big that they'd take a few weeks or a month to complete; he'd sand those houses right down to the bare wood, and start from there. He was very fussy about his work, very thorough, and very good. Well, there were times when he'd get through with a house, having done a beautiful job, and then he'd get stiffed on the payment. The homeowner would either pay late, or wouldn't be able to come up with the cash at all. That bothered the hell out of my father, because he was the kind of old-school Yankee who really worried about money.

For years I heard, "If this guy doesn't pay me soon, we're not going to make the mortgage payment. We won't be able to buy food."

That drilled into my head a very insecure feeling that I've never been able to shake. Even as I got older and had some success, in business and in my racing, that insecurity stayed with me. In fact, right to this day it's there. And so while I was racing, I was always focusing on survival, keeping in mind that I had to finish, because finishing meant money.

In the course of all this, I became very good at seeing the big picture. Once I really started to hit my stride, I could be thrashing around in the middle of a tight pack and still nothing escaped me. Anything that went on out there, I took it in. And it all came out of that need to get to the finish.

I think that fear of dropping out also helped me develop my ability to miss crashes. I'd avoid a big wreck, and all the guys in the pits would tell me, "Man, what a job you did, getting through that mess." Of course, I'd stand there and take all their compliments, but inside I knew that I hadn't done anything but react naturally, dodging the wreck because I knew that wrecking would put me out of the race.

But none of this happened overnight. It was the product of a lot of nights, a lot of laps. So I guess you could say that I never consciously developed a style. My style developed itself.

Racing has given me everything I have. Well, "given" is the wrong word, because I feel like I've paid my dues. But had I not ever gotten the itch to drive race cars, my life would sure look a lot different today.

You can start with my business, Freetown Auto Salvage. I was working for an insurance company as a claims adjuster when I started driving for Lenny Boehler in 1964. Lenny lived out in Freetown, to the east of Rehoboth, and as I drove the back roads to his shop I'd pass this closed-up junkyard. For the longest time, I'd daydream to myself about reopening that place, because I figured that if it was run properly a salvage yard might be a good business. The more times I went past that yard, the more serious I got.

I was a little hesitant to do it myself, so over a period of time I talked Lenny into coming along as my partner. We pooled together whatever money we had, which wasn't much, and borrowed some more, and together we opened Freetown Auto in 1966. Later on, thanks to some stuff we'll get into in another chapter, I ended up buying out Lenny's share five years later. I've been the sole owner ever since.

I think I did a pretty good job with the yard, because it has grown considerably, but it was anything but easy. I mean, I ate, slept, and drank that business for a long time. There were times when, no matter what else I had going on in my life, the yard *had* to come first, and in those cases it did.

But if it hadn't been for racing, that salvage yard wouldn't exist, at least not with my name on it.

Best of all, in a roundabout way racing ended up putting me together with my wife Doris. She's from the coal country down in western Virginia, the two of us met when we were both in the Air Force, stationed in Texas. She was working at the base hospital, and I was there on temporary assignment. One day I was eating lunch in the cafeteria, and I happened to look up just as these two young women walked past, looking really nice in their hospital uniforms. One of them was Doris. The way she tells it, I flirted with her a time or two, and it all took off from there.

But what really solidified the relationship, I guess, was the way I made her a partner-in-crime in my young racing career. I had been messing around with a jalopy car at a local short track, and one day as I was fiddling around with the engine, which was running, I managed to catch my elbow in the fan. It gave me a pretty good gash, and I made it worse by not taking care of the wound. It got infected and swelled up to a huge size. They admitted me to a room on the seventh or eighth floor of the base hospital for treatment, but the problem was, I wanted to go racing the next night.

I was stuck in there wearing hospital clothes, and there I was no way I could walk out wearing those things. So I had some of my buddies sneak my Air Force uniform into the hospital and hang it down the hall, in the visitor's bathroom. Then I told Doris to make sure she was sitting in her car outside, with the engine running, at exactly 4:30 the next afternoon.

Everybody came through perfectly. My pals had the clothes right

where I told them to, and I ditched the hospital gown and changed into my uniform. When I got downstairs, there was Doris, waiting in her car. She rode me back to the barracks, and when I got there I made another quick change, this time into my civilian clothes, as if I was just another guy heading into town for dinner or something. Then I took off for the race track, with Doris right along for the ride.

By midnight I was back at the base hospital, changing back into the gown in the visitor's bathroom, and nobody even noticed I was gone. And Doris has been with me ever since.

It can't be easy to be the wife—or the husband, as the case may be—of anybody who's supposed to be a big shot at whatever it is they do. Because, see, when you're on top, everybody wants a piece of you, everybody wants to pull you here or there, and everybody wants to *be* with you, so your spouse has to be willing to share you with those people.

It takes a special person to do that, and in our marriage Doris has gone above and beyond the call of duty. What's helped us, I think, is that she has as big a fun-loving personality as I do. She's not as outgoing as I am, and she doesn't necessarily have to be in the middle of whatever's going on, like I always seemed to be, but Doris likes to be around when there's a good time happening. She enjoys people, just like I do.

If I hadn't married her, I'm sure I'd have been divorced a dozen times by now. Obviously, since Doris had a little bit of a hand in us having a family of our own, I've got to thank racing for that, too.

My wife Doris didn't have it easy. She put up with me being gone, put up with me being hurt ... basically, she put up with me! Here's the two of us with Anthony and Irene Venditti on a night when their track, Seekonk Speedway, honored me in 1982. (John Mercury photo/ Courtesy of Speedway Scene*)*

Here a picture of the whole family at my daughter Zoe's place on July 1, 2002. From the left: Rick and Debra Hanatow, Carl Berghman, Doris, me, Tyler Fitzpatrick, Bob and Zoe Kelliher with Wes, Lea Fitzpatrick, Dave and Cyndi Berghman with Talia.
(Karl Fredrickson Photo)

We've got four great kids: Carl, Zoe Ann, David and Debbie, in that order. They all lead their own individual lives, and each of them is pretty independent, and I say that as a compliment.

Carl was born in Texas while I was in the service, and, although he was too young to realize it at the time, he went to his fair share of hole-in-the-wall bullring tracks down there. These days, Carl runs the salvage yard, and does a great job of it.

Zoe was the first of our kids born in Massachusetts. I think she's got a lot of my blood in her, because she's as competitive as I am. She was a great athlete in school, and today she lives not far from Doris and me, over toward Freetown, with her husband Bob and her three children, Lea, Tyler and Wes.

David was the kind of kid who didn't take anything seriously— school, life, anything—for a long time. It was getting to the point where I was really worried about him going the wrong way, because he was running with a wild crowd. Of course, his old man had done a little bit of that, too, so I could see how that happened. But when he was 14, I got him a hobby-level stock car, and at 15 he drove his first race at Seekonk Speedway. He fell in love with that right away, and I think racing put a real work ethic into him. Today he's in a modified, running with the NASCAR touring series under his given name, David Berghman, and doing a good job. He and his wife Cyndi and their daughter Talia live down in Fall River.

Debra is our youngest, and the feistiest. She likes to do everything her own way, which shows that she inherited some of my determination. Her big sister owns a nail salon in Swanse, and Deb looks after that. She and her husband, Rick Hanatow, who's done quite a bit of racing at Seekonk himself, bought a piece of land from me and they're going to do some farming, and she's stubborn enough to do that.

Like I said, all four of our kids do their own thing, and I'm proud of all of 'em.

Where would I even start thanking them, and especially Doris, for putting up with me all these years? You think it could have been easy having a wacko like me heading up the household?

Looking back, I was pretty much an absentee husband and father, and I'm tempted to say I'd do that differently if I got another chance. But, let's be honest: When you're pursuing something you love the way I loved racing, and you're trying to get to the top and then *stay* on top, it's probably inevitable that your family life is going to take a beating. In my busiest years, we raced from Daytona in February until Martinsville in October, and when I wasn't on the road I was trying to run my business. With a schedule like that, there's not much time left over for the wife and the kids. But, you know, I'm sure the same thing happens to hockey players, football players, maybe even corporate executives. I see a lot of that in David. He's got a nice shop, and he's so into that race car that he might be there until 2:30 in the morning. I understand that devotion, that drive.

For a lot of years I was only a part-time father, which is the price you pay if you're trying to be successful. That's my daughter Deb and I, chatting through the Seekonk pit fence in the late 1970s. (Herb Dodge Photo/Courtesy of Speedway Scene)

11

Here's three NASCAR modified championships and two NASCAR presidents. That's me with Big Bill France and Bill Jr. at Martinsville, way back when. (Balser & Son Photo/ Courtesy of Speedway Scene*)*

All things considered, we came through it all right. We're a close family, I'd say, although not in the traditional sense. We keep up with one another by telephone—everybody knows what everybody else is up to—but we're not a socializing, Sunday dinner-type family. I'd just as soon be at the salvage yard on a Sunday afternoon, or out clearing some land, as sitting down for a big get-together. I've got to admit, though, now that we've got grandkids, I find myself making time for a little more of that stuff.

So, as you can see, racing opened up a lot of doors for me. Hell, it was my whole life from 1954, when I first sat in a race car, until 1987, when I stepped out of a NASCAR modified for the last time, and then through my semi-retirement years playing around with pro stock cars at Seekonk.

Racing allowed me to start a business. Racing allowed me to start a family. And what racing did, mostly, was allow me to be *somebody*.

Up until then, I had basically been Carl Berghman, farm kid from Rehoboth. In fact, if it wasn't for racing, I'd probably have spent just about my entire life—except for my military years—on the same street.

The Berghmans were farming people, just like everybody in our part of town. The whole area was dairy farms and vegetable fields and some chicken coops. Up and down our street for miles, all you had were farmers. There were a couple of great old barns that have been knocked down since then, and the whole town really had a rural feel to it.

I've lived most of my life in the house I live in today, just up the road from the place I lived as a kid. My father was a farmer for a while, too, although after a time the family sold off a bunch of their property and he took a job as a machinist in a textile factory in East Providence, Rhode Island.

I was born in 1934—May 11—and my sister Nancy came along five years later, and Rehoboth was pretty much our world. Oh, we did live in East Providence for a year or so during World War II; I'm not clear exactly why, because I was just a kid, but I think it had something to do with gasoline rationing. But in 1944 he bought this house, and we were right back in Rehoboth.

It was a pretty quiet life, compared to way most kids live today. We didn't own a television; in fact, I was probably 15 or 16 years old before I ever even *saw* a television set. A guy down the road, another farmer named Harold, had a little TV with a nine-inch screen, and once the neighborhood kids saw that thing, you couldn't keep us away. We'd all go down there on Friday nights—seven or eight of us, at least—to watch Milton Berle and wrestling. That was a big, big deal.

But, you know, there's a difference between a quiet life and a boring life. I mean, I remember my childhood as being a really fun time.

I guess maybe growing up in that environment helped make me the joker I am to this day. I had to make my own entertainment, and I always figured out a way to do that. My friends all said I was nuts, a candidate for the "bughouse," which is what people used to call the mental hospital, and by the time I was in high school my reputation as a lunatic had given me a nickname: "Bughouse" was shortened to "Bugs" and "Bugsy," and I was Bugsy Berghman for quite a while around Rehoboth.

It's hard to believe sometimes how far my life has come. It's like, How'd I get from *there* all the way to *here*? I mean, I know how hard I worked to get the business up and running, and I know how dedicated I was to racing, and I know how much effort it took to win all the races and championships. But I really don't know how I got to be this . . . this *figure*.

How'd I get to the point where I'd end up writing a book? I just don't know.

I have no way of knowing for sure exactly why I caught on with race fans the way I did, or why that feeling lasted as long as it has. I guess part of it was that I honestly *liked* people. Even today, if you've got a frown on your face, I'll try to make you smile. I think that probably put a few people in my corner. And I'm sure a lot of it has to do with the fact that I managed to win races over a pretty good span of time, from the early 1960s right through the '70s and into the '80s, up and down the East Coast. When you're winning, everybody loves you, and I won for a long time.

Whatever it was, I'm glad it happened. Although, I've got to say, it does feel funny sometimes, the way people still come up to me at race tracks, wanting to talk. They treat me like I'm some big deal, and it's been a while since I've done anything worth making a fuss about. But I take that as a good sign. To me, it means that at some point in their lives I made a good impression on them, and I'm happy about that.

There are some race drivers—some athletes, period—who tell you that it's not their job to be role models. Well, frankly, I don't think they have a choice. If you've got young people around you, watching every move you make, you're a role model. You end up setting an example whether you want to or not.

I wasn't a saint, by any means, and we'll get into more about that as this book rolls along. But when it came to being around kids and showing them a positive public image of what a race driver could be, I think I did my job.

I've said this before, but it's something I believe strongly: As you age, you get to the point in your life where your ego starts to take a back seat, and you can look back objectively at what you've done. By then, you are what you are, and if you're lucky—like I am—you're pretty much satisfied with what you've done. Yes, you might think once in a while about what else you *could* have done, and you might wonder if you should have done some things a little differently. But for the most part, you're happy with the way things have gone. That's me. I wouldn't trade lives—or careers, if we're talking about racing—with anybody.

So settle back, and I'll explain, as best I can, how it all went. I don't have a college degree in linguistics, and I don't always look at things from the most educated, intelligent point of view. But I believe I can tell you a few stories about racing, how it was and how it is.

If nothing else, we'll have some fun trying to rebuild that puzzle.

(Mike Adaskaveg Photo)

Dave Stevens on Bugsy

Dave Stevens and Bugs Stevens, Freetown, MA, 2002. (Karl Fredrickson Photo)

Dave Stevens, longtime friend: "I've known Carl—that's what I still call him about half the time—since we were kids. Fifth grade? Seventh grade? We were both from Rehoboth, and we just kind of became friendly. I don't know how it happened, really, but it did. I grew up on a farm, and he grew up working on a farm, so we had that in common. Later on, he was an athlete and I wasn't, but we both were into cars, for some reason. The two of us were talking about hot rods even before we were old enough to drive.

"Right from the beginning, he was a character. I'll tell you what he was like growing up: *He was wild*. It's not that he did anything really crazy. It was just the usual school-kid stuff, but he did maybe more than his share. How should I put this? Well, let's just say that he and the school principal were very familiar with each other. Even at that age, he didn't like to deal with authority.

The Early Days

"By the time we got out of school, there was a small group of us who were pretty good buddies. The military draft was still a big thing back then, and of course we were all eligible. This one fellow Noel Turgeon and I, we decided that we would volunteer for the Army. I mean, we were ready to go. Then Bugsy and another fellow decided that they were going to go into the Air Force, and they talked us into going along with them. We basically told the Army, 'No thanks. We're going into the Air Force instead.' And Carl and I ended up stationed together in San Antonio for the next several years.

"Down there in San Antonio, of course, is where we both got involved in racing. We used to go to this small track there in town, and he got it into his head that he wanted to race, so he got his hands on an old car and we all worked on it. That was his start, really. But to us, racing was just a way to have fun. They didn't pay you enough to even cover your expenses, but, boy, we sure had some fun. In fact, I had so much fun that I ended up getting a car of my own and racing it.

"It's funny, but we both stayed down there in Texas for a while after we got out of the service. His job took him to Brownsville, and I stayed in San Antonio for a couple of years, and then the way it worked out, we both decided to come home to Massachusetts at just about the same time. It wasn't anything we'd planned, but there we were, back in Rehoboth.

"My racing was over with by then. I got married, and I worked as a mechanic, and my life went in a different direction. But Bugsy, obviously, kept on going. So after we'd been back here for a couple of years, we kind of drifted apart. He was so deeply into the racing thing, and I didn't travel in those same circles. I'd keep up with what he was doing—I'd go and watch him at Seekonk, and maybe at Thompson—but for several years we didn't have much to do with each other. It's only been fairly recently that we've gotten back together.

"And it's not that we see each other that often today. It's only three or four times a year, because we both spend about half the year in Florida and we're on opposite coasts down there. But with old friends, you don't have to see each other that much. We're as close as we were when we were kids, even though we don't see each other that often.

"It's been fun to watch how his life has gone. He's done very well, in racing and out of racing. But, you know, I can't say that surprised me."

The Early Days

The Early Days

THE FIRST TIME I ever drove a race car was in 1954 at Seekonk Speedway. At the time, Seekonk was running what used to be called "cutdowns." They were basically coupes that had been chopped up and lightened so much that they weren't really stock cars anymore. A buddy of mine named Thurston Grant had just built one, and he let me try it out. He knew I'd wanted to try driving, because I wasn't shy about letting him know that. I ran around that place for three or four laps with no safety gear—believe it or not, I don't even think I wore a helmet—and I actually got going pretty fast.

I had always enjoyed living on the edge. Growing up, my younger sister Nancy used to joke that I had suicidal tendencies. She'd say, "You always want to do the craziest things." But to me, this wasn't crazy. That race car didn't scare me. It never even made me uncomfortable. As soon as I hit the gas, I knew inside that this was something I could do.

It was everything I wanted.

I was 20 years old, and I knew right then which way my life was headed.

All my life to that point, I had turned everything into a competition. It didn't matter what I was doing, I wanted to do it right, to do it the best I could. And, hopefully, to do it better than the next guy.

I was even that way when I was working. My first job was at the farm next door to where I live now. They had sixty cows, and I'd help milk 'em. I was 10 years old, and from 6:00 to 7:30 a.m.—when it was time for school—I'd be lugging around milk pails so heavy I could just about carry 'em. But I wasn't going to let those pails get the best of me. You see what I mean? Competition.

After school I'd get right back to the farm and work until 6:00 p.m., shoveling the cow shit. I also did a few other odd jobs, like every kid in a farm town like ours. I cleaned chicken houses up and down the road; in fact, we had our own chicken house in the back yard for a while. And I'd help my father do the cleaning and maintenance at the Rehoboth Congregational Church near our house, and at Goff

This is me and my father, in a shot from the 1970s. He was never a racing guy, but he did have a huge influence on my life and my racing style.
(Courtesy of Speedway Scene)

Memorial Hall, a meeting house just up the street. We'd get those places ready for whatever functions they were having, and I took a lot of pride in doing it right.

And I always wanted to do things *fast*. I used to ride my bicycle from Rehoboth to East Providence just to go roller skating. I'd ride there as fast as I could, skate as fast as I could, and ride home as fast as I could.

From the time I was a kid, I was steering tractors and farm trucks, and I was always trying to go quicker. I drove all the other workers crazy; one of their jobs was to pitch hay up onto a flatbed truck, and whenever I drove that thing we got up and down those rows a whole lot faster than they wanted to. If I had a dollar for every time I heard those guys holler at me—"Slow this goddam thing down!"—I'd have been a rich little guy, that's for sure. When I finally got my driver's license, things only got worse. I was a terror out on Route 44, the main drag through town.

I got into trouble for speeding with every single thing I ever drove.

I liked the thrill of going fast. But it was more than just a love of speed; it was another way to push myself, to turn whatever I was doing into a contest. That was my mindset.

Not surprisingly, organized sports were a big part of my life. I was a good athlete, but I'm not sure if I had any great natural talent. What I mean is, I always felt like I had to try hard to excel at whatever I did. So it's difficult to know if I succeeded because I had a gift for sports, or because I *drove* myself to succeed.

I was probably in fourth or fifth grade when I started playing Little

Just a farm kid from Rehoboth. These look like school photos from my growing-up years.
(Berghman Family Collection)

League baseball, and then all through my school years I played every sport there was. At Dighton High School I pitched and played outfield for the baseball team, played both offense and defense in football, played guard on the basketball team, and even ran track.

Basketball was my only real weak link, because I never could develop a good shooting hand. In track I set a new school record in the 220 meter run as a sophomore, and always placed well in the 100-yard dash and even the shot put. And football was my favorite sport. As a halfback I ran for 16 touchdowns as a junior and 21 as a senior, and I was the leading scorer on our state championship team in 1951.

But baseball was probably the sport where I showed the most potential. I had a great record as a pitcher—struck out 70 batters in 52 innings as a senior—and also led the team in hitting with a .378 batting average. Even while I was at Dighton High, we had scouts from some of the pro teams taking a look at me; I'd hear rumors that they were going to show up at a game and, sure enough, I'd see these guys sitting alone in a corner of the grandstands, keeping charts on me.

Right around that same time, I also played a couple seasons on a summertime semi-pro baseball league in Taunton. That was fun, but those older guys hated me. They were pretty good ballplayers with a lot of pride in what they did, and here I was, this blond-headed kid who could throw the ball 900 miles per hour—*zing!*—right past 'em.

What kind of slowed my baseball dreams a bit was an injury I suffered in my senior year. It actually happened during football season, on a defensive play; I tackled the runner, and we went down hard. But it was a great tackle, because I had to dive over a blocker to get at the guy with the ball. Anyway, I found out years later that I had messed up my rotator cuff. In those days, nobody really knew what the hell a rotator cuff was, but what I did know was that my shoulder hurt like hell for a long time. It recovered enough for me to have a strong pitching season as a senior, and for me to get more than 20 offers of baseball scholarships; eventually I went to Dean Academy and Junior College in Franklin, Massachusetts, where I had a pretty good record. But in my mind, the arm was at its best before that football injury.

In the end, though, everything worked out. I found myself another activity I was pretty good at.

For a while, I played every sport there was. I have to say, I had a pretty good record as an athlete in school. (Berghman Family Collection)

To be honest, I'd had racing on my brain for a long, long time.

When I was a teenager, every Saturday I'd see this big old flatbed truck roll past our farm with a stock car on the back. It was a coupe, a 1934 Ford, and Freddy Schulz raced it at Seekonk. Now, everybody who knows racing in New England has heard of Freddy; he won a ton of races all over New England, from the days of the jalopies and the cutdowns in the fifties right up through the modifieds of the late seventies. I probably ended up racing against him a hundred times myself. But when I was a kid on the farm, it just blew me away to see that car go by on its way to the race track every week.

If I close my eyes, I can still see that coupe. It was maroon and white, with a big fat exhaust that looked like a stove pipe running up the side.

Seekonk Speedway was only four or five miles from the farm, so it was probably inevitable that I'd get there sooner or later. I can't say for sure, but I believe that the first time I ever went to the races, me and a couple of friends rode our bicycles over there. And once I went, man, I was hooked.

Schulz was one of the big stars at Seekonk back then. Hop Harrington was another one. Then there were guys like Jim Holt, Paul Carr, Billy Tibberts, and Henri "Red" Barbeau. Just like it's always been, Seekonk was a fun place to watch a Saturday-night race.

For several years, I never got any closer to the action than the grandstands. Then a neighbor from up the road named Walter Goff—who much later became a good friend of mine—put together a race car. Well, I'd ride my bike over there just to stand around and watch them work on that thing. At some point, I graduated from watching to doing whatever I could to help. I guess that would have been my first real involvement in the sport.

I was out of high school and into my first year at Dean when my pal Thurston Grant started putting together his cutdown, the one I ended up trying out that night in 1954. I probably would have been a race driver from that moment on, if it hadn't been for a little something called the United States Air Force.

Not long after I had warmed up Thurston's car, some friends and I got word through the grapevine that our numbers were about ready to come up in the military draft. That was a serious thing back then; don't forget, the Korean War had just ended in July of '53.

If you got drafted, you went wherever Uncle Sam told you to go, period. They chose the branch of the service, they chose the training camp. I knew some guys who ended up in Army training at Fort Drum, near Watertown, New York, way up in the snow country. I never liked the cold, and the thought of being stuck someplace like that was on my mind. On the other hand, most of the Air Force camps were in warm sunny places, because they relied on having good weather for flight training.

I said, "Look, instead of maybe letting the Army get us and send us wherever they want, let's enlist in the Air Force." And that's what a few of us did.

I spent the next six years in Texas. I was stationed in Lackland Air Force Base in San Antonio, which was like a whole different country to a dumb Yankee farm boy like me. They put us through 12 weeks of boot camp, which I didn't mind. It wasn't easy, by any means, but it wasn't as bad as people lead you to believe, either.

I wanted to be a pilot, because it seemed like the speed and the challenge would be right up my alley. Unfortunately, I flunked all the written exams. There was too much math for me—a pilot has to do a lot of calculations, I guess—and all through life that was always my worst subject.

So instead I became a drill instructor. Well, they called us "tactical instructors," but that was just a fancy title. I taught classes, led guys on hikes, organized bivouacs out into the boonies for a couple weeks at a time. I was right there with 'em, crawling under barbed wire with people shooting at us, just like you see in the movies.

I loved being a drill instructor. I mean, I really got into it. I took a lot of pride in having the best-disciplined troops on the base, having the shoes on my guys shine the brightest, having the best barracks. I got promoted as high as staff sergeant, which was a pretty fair amount of responsibility.

For fun, I played on the Lackland baseball team, in a league that put us up against teams from other military installations. That was great, because I got to pitch against several guys who had actually played pro ball. I also played some semi-pro ball for two different breweries, Lone Star and Falstaff, in separate leagues. That was a pretty nice racket.

It probably wasn't until my second year in Texas that I discovered they had another sport down there.

Pan American Speedway in San Antonio was a little bullring, a quarter-mile asphalt oval where they ran stock cars—jalopies, really—on Saturday nights. It had a wall around the outside, and a little rail made of pipe around the inside, just like you'd see at a dog track. A few of the guys on the Lackland base were race fans, and I went over there with them a few times.

This must have been some kind of publicity shot. I played baseball for the traveling team from Lackland Air Force Base, which was a great experience. (Berghman Family Collection)

What kind of got me to the next step was the fact that I used to take some of the other drill instructors for rides, and I guess I scared the hell out of them because I always went fast. For me, that was just standard procedure, but it really made an impression on them.

They said, "We've got to get you a race car."

I told them, "Well, actually, I tried that a little bit back home …"

Before long, they got me hooked up with somebody who gave me a little bit of garage space, and that's where my first race car came together. It wasn't anything fancy, that's for sure. It was a hobby division car, a 1937 Ford coupe we built out of a street car. Dave Stevens, one of the guys from back home who had enlisted with me—Dave's another farm kid from North Rehoboth—helped me put it together.

It took us exactly one day.

That's the truth. We gutted that old shitbox, welded together three driveshafts to form one roll bar—up one side, across the top behind my head, and down the other side—and that was it. We were ready to race.

Now, that one roll bar didn't offer a lot of support. People say, "Didn't you worry about tipping over?" Well, the answer is, No. I didn't worry about a damn thing back then.

My first year was 1957, and I really didn't have a clue what I was doing. But by the second year, I did well enough to get a little bit of attention. Which, to tell you the truth, was exactly what I *didn't* want.

I've told the story a million times about how I went from being Carl Berghman to being Bugs Stevens, but it seems like every time somebody re-tells it, they put a little different spin on it. Once and for all, this is how it happened.

After a while, it wasn't any big secret that I was racing; a lot of people around the base knew it. Obviously, some of the guys who went to Pan American recognized me, especially once I started having some success. Then some of the guys on the baseball team started griping amongst themselves that whenever we had a Saturday game, they needed to find another pitcher because I was off racing. This was starting to get me a little nervous, because driving race cars wasn't a hobby the Air Force—or any branch of the service—wanted its personnel to participate in.

Luckily, my commanding officer, who came from Springfield, Massachusetts, was a good guy. Before I got into too much hot water, he called me into his office and said, "I'm getting a lot of flack from my superiors. They've been getting reports that you've been racing."

Check out this hot-shot racer. That's me in my early days in Texas, wearing an old Cromwell helmet, ready for battle. (Berghman Family Collection)

I shrugged and played dumb.

He said, "Here's what's probably going to happen. If you keep racing, they'll take away a stripe and knock you back a rank."

I said, "Geez, what am I supposed to do?

He said, "I would advise you not to race until you get out of the service."

Well, that didn't seem like a good option to me. I talked it over with my buddy Dave Stevens, who had also started racing, and found out he was in the same mess. In the end, we figured we might be able to mix the Air Force people up by running under assumed names. Dave's middle name was Mitchell, so the next time he went to Pan American Speedway he entered as "Dave Mitchell."

I took the nickname I'd had since high school, paired it up with Dave's last name to really confuse the issue, and I became "Bugs Stevens."

By the way, Dave Stevens was a guy who could have been a good race driver if he had stuck with it. He wasn't as crazy as I was, but he had a lot of natural ability and he was a super mechanic. I guess he just didn't have the raw love of the sport that I had.

In any case, Dave Mitchell didn't go quite as far in racing as Bugs Stevens did.

By the middle of the 1958 season, racing had really gotten its teeth

Pretty fancy tow rig, huh? We're on our way to Corpus Christi, or Houston, or who knows where. (Berghman Family Collection)

into me. Running once a week at Pan American Speedway wasn't enough anymore, and I started traveling. I'd haul just about anyplace we heard there was a race.

I raced all over Texas. I ran at a bunch of dirt tracks whose names I can't remember, but I ran a few places that people might know: Corpus Christi Speedway, Playland Park in Houston. One night at Playland Park, they had a doubleheader: stock cars and midgets. I sat in the grandstands to watch the midgets run. There were a bunch of drivers' wives sitting there, and I got a kick out of watching them root for their husbands. One of those husbands turned out to be a pretty good race driver. His name was A.J. Foyt. It's funny, because A.J. is still my all-time hero because of his versitility and his style—for years I tried to mimic how he sat straight up in those midgets—and yet one of my biggest memories of him is actually his wife, cheering him on.

By now I had a pretty supportive wife behind me, too. Not only did Doris go to the races with me, but she spent a lot of time helping me work on that old hobby car. I had a one-bay garage with a dirt floor, and most nights during the week that's where you could find Doris and me.

Then, come the weekend, we'd full that car full of tools and whatever spare parts we had, and head toward one race track or another. For a while I didn't even own a trailer, but that was no problem. We'd just flat-tow that sonofabitch down the road.

I remember this: from San Antonio to Playland Park was 329 miles. And we covered just about that whole distance at 80 or 90 miles per hour.

Looking back, for as little as we had and as little as I knew, we did well. I mean, we were almost always competitive. I didn't win a lot, but I won some, and we were generally somewhere in the top five. I'm

It's hard to believe the miles we covered, and how fast we covered them, towing down the road like this. But if you want to race badly enough, you'll do what it takes! (Berghman Family Collection)

sure that as a driver I was getting better all the time, but I wasn't conscious of it at the time. I just went with the flow.

I never did expect that the flow might end up taking me back home. I mean, while I was in Texas I never had given much thought to coming back to New England. I was pretty happy down there. Even when my four-year stint in the Air Force ended, I figured I'd stay put.

I took a job as a collector for a finance company, and I liked the work, which amounted to chasing the local deadbeats for money. Then in 1960, the company transferred me from San Antonio to Brownsville, just north of the border on the Gulf of Mexico. I took my race car with me, and before long I got hooked up with an older guy who had a shop.

One thing had improved: I wasn't flat-towing to the race tracks anymore. I had a small trailer, and on Saturdays we'd hook it to the back of a Chevy El Camino which was actually a company car. By now, Doris and I had one child—Carl, the first of our two boys—and the three of us would set sail, heading for Corpus Christi.

It was about a three-hour ride from Brownsville, two-and-half if you really hauled ass, and I *always* hauled ass. One time I got hustling a little too hard, and I spun that rig, trailer and all, with Doris and Carl on board. That wasn't too smart, I know, but, hell, it happened.

You know what actually got me back home? Doris and I came back to Massachusetts on a short vacation that summer, and I discovered that it was easy to race three nights a week without even travel-

27

ing too far from Rehoboth. In my mind, that long ride to Corpus Christi run didn't look so appealing anymore.

As soon as I got home to Brownsville, I sold my race car. Then I turned in my resignation at the finance company, handed over the keys to that El Camino, and said, "Adios."

That was that. Goodbye, Texas.

We must have made quite a sight as we headed north. I was steering the family car, a 1954 Plymouth, and behind us on my little trailer was just about everything I had that was of any value: one racing engine, some tires, a couple of transmissions, Carl's crib, and Doris's washing machine.

Almost as soon as I was back in Rehoboth I reconnected with Thurston Grant, the guy who had let me warm up that cutdown at Seekonk Speedway in 1954. Within two weeks, we were building me a race car. Thurston and I were basically partners in the thing.

I made my Seekonk debut in 1961. At the time, the weekly headline division—"Class A" was how D. Anthony Venditti, the Seekonk promoter, referred to it—consisted of coupes and sedans with flathead engines. My car was a 1946 Ford, white, number 28.

Seekonk had a pretty hot little group of drivers. Red Barbeau was still a regular winner, and there were a handful of guys—George Summers, Billy Clarke, Dave Humphrey and the Astle brothers, Deke and Freddy—who eventually went beyond Seekonk, just like I did. But the really hot driver that year was Joe Rosenfield, a big, burly guy who did a lot of winning at that track. Joe won four features, including the last three in a row, and beat Barbeau to win the points championship.

I ended up twelfth in the standings. It was a decent season, especially considering how competitive things were at Seekonk, but I certainly wasn't an instant phenomenon.

The next year, 1962, was a little bit better. I was starting to run up front on a more regular basis; I've got an old scrapbook that shows me finishing in the top five eight times: two seconds, a third, and five fifths. And we finished fifth in the points, behind Rosenfield (again), Clarke, Bobby Sprague and Summers. Still, I didn't feel like we were in a position to challenge for the win very often. The problem was, we had a good car, but some of those guys had *great* cars.

What finally help get us going was the arrival of a guy named Skid Sorterup, an old-timer who had a reputation as a terrific mechanic; he'd had several good years with a really good local racer named Don Hall. Anyway, Skid decided to help us. He came up to Thurston's garage and really did a number on our old coupe. He cut it here,

trimmed it there, lightened everything up, and basically made a real race car out of it. After that, we started flying.

Seekonk is a tight little place, and in those days, with those big coupes and their skinny tires, the only real groove was right around the bottom. Well, Skip got our car handling so good that I could run anywhere I wanted to. While everybody else was plugging up the bottom lane, I'd just jump to the outside. I was really quick up there. *Too* quick, I guess. Because, see, before long all the other hot dogs noticed how easy it was for me to pass out there, and they moved up, too. But that was okay; it made me feel good to know that we were doing something worth copying.

I finally won a Seekonk Speedway feature on June 8, 1963. Here's something that will show you how good that car was handling: I started outside the tenth row in a 25-lap feature, and I passed George Murray for the lead on lap eight. He did get me back a little bit later, on a restart, but nothing was going to stop me that night. The top five was me, Billy Clarke, George Murray, Red Barbeau and Dave Dias.

How's this for a souvenir: My very first competition license from Seekonk Speedway, signed by Irene Venditti, whose husband built and ran the track. (Berghman Family Collection)

Cool and casual, ready to go racing. This was taken outside Thurston Grant's shop. (Berghman Family Collection)

29

Thurston Grant was my partner in the first car I ran at Seekonk, and I owe a lot of my success to him. (Berghman Family Collection)

Once we got some of the excess weight trimmed away, that number 28 was a good car for its time. I'm pretty sure that's George Murray, one of Seekonk's big stars for years, in the number 5. (RA Silvia Collection)

Later on in '68, Thurston and I hit a little bit of a dry spell. In fact, we almost split up. A buddy of mine named Manny Santos and I bought a car with an Oldsmobile engine—the first overhead valve engine at Seekonk, I think, because they had just made 'em legal—and I almost quit Thurston to drive that car instead. But I stuck with Thurston, and we put Deke Astle in the other car. That thing had all

30

That's Deke Astle in a car I owned in partnership with Manny Santos. It had one of the first overhead valve engines at Seekonk, maybe the first.
(RA Silvia Collection)

kinds of horsepower, but we could never get it to handle, and Deke crashed it a few times.

So the car I was driving wasn't going well, and the car I owned wasn't going well. It was not the happiest time. That continued into 1964, when my number 28 was still struggling.

And that's when Lenny Boehler came long.

Boehler was a guy who had been around a while. He had built and owned a few cars, racing mostly with Tony Cortes, a local driver who lived near Boehler over in Freetown. In 1963 and part of '64, Lenny had Don Hall and Eddie Hoyle, two really good shoes, in his cars. The word around the area was that Boehler was a pretty smart guy, but he was in the same boat I was in: he wasn't winning.

In the spring of 1964, the two of us were talking one day about engines, and I gave him the part number of a camshaft that had worked wonders for me down in Texas. Lenny went out and got one of those cams, and it really helped, and after that encounter we started talking a little bit more.

When you look back on it today, it's amazing to think what that one camshaft led to.

Like I said, both of us were in a frame of mind where we weren't satisfied with the way our racing was going. Lenny had been running some of the bigger modified races in the area, and one Sunday he went over to Thompson Speedway with Hoyle in the car. Well, they didn't qualify for the feature. That was a bad break for Eddie, but a good break for me.

The next time Boehler competed at Thompson, I drove. I hadn't ever been there, but we won the first time out. It was June 14, 1964.

The next time we went back there, we won again.

Lenny and I were an instant hit.

I still did my own thing on Saturday nights of Seekonk for the rest of that season, but Lenny and I ran a few more races, enough to know that we wanted to do something together on a regular basis. When the 1965 season opened, we were a team.

And a pretty good team, at that. We concentrated on Seekonk, and we won the track championship. That was a huge thrill for me; not only was it my first real racing title of any kind, but the guys I beat—in order, George Summers, Deke Astle, Joe Rosenfield and Bobby Sprague—were the same guys I had been chasing around since I'd come back from Texas.

Seekonk ran 21 Class A features that season. Boehler and I won nine of 'em. The next-highest win total belonged to Summers, who had four.

And Lenny and I were just getting to know each other.

The biggest show in the world back then for the modifieds was the Race of Champions at Langhorne, Pennsylvania. They held it in the fall, after all the weekly tracks had closed up for the summer, and every big dog in the game showed up. Lenny and I went there for the first time in 1965.

Langhorne, which was a one-mile oval, was by far the biggest track I had ever been on, but for some reason I felt right at home there. In fact, there were times during the race when we were as quick as anybody.

Bill Slater, who had been a big star around Connecticut and Massachusetts for several years by then, won the Race of Champions that year. Later on, he said, "Geez, Bugsy, you must have passed me five times. But every time I came around the corner, you'd be sitting in the infield!" Slater was exaggerating a little bit, but he was basically right: I did pass him a few times, but I spun out twice. Both times, I either nicked a lapped car or got nicked myself. Still, I finished third, so it was still a pretty good day for a new kid on the block.

From the time Lenny and I had won those races at Thompson in '64, I'd had no lack of confidence in my own ability. Our season at

Seekonk in 1965 had backed that up. Finishing third at Langhorne was just more proof.

Don't get me wrong, I wasn't overly cocky, or anything like that. My eyes were still open wide, just seeing all these new places and competing at what was obviously going to be a higher level of modified racing.

But by the fall of 1965, I knew I was on the right track.

I could run with anybody, anywhere.

For me, 1965 was an amazing year. In my first full season driving for Lenny Boehler, I won nine out of the 21 races at Seekonk and locked up my first track championship. (RA Silvia Collection)

Pete Hamilton on Bugsy

Championship Years

Pete Hamilton, 1970 Daytona 500 winner and 1967 NASCAR national sportsman champion: "I'm not sure if people today realize what a grind it was, chasing those [NASCAR] points back then. In 1967, the year that Bugsy and I both won championships—he won the modifieds, and I won the sportsman title—I towed to 121 events. I think we may have gotten rained out 15 times, but the rest of those nights we raced. In those days, you usually had the race driver and his mechanic, and that was it. We spent a lot of our lives sitting in the cabs of our tow vehicles.

"Don't forget, basically every track in the country that was NASCAR-sanctioned held races that counted toward those championships. Bugsy and I both ran at Daytona; we both ran at Baton Rouge, Louisiana. I raced at Jefferson, Georgia, and Macon, Georgia, and you can almost go right up the East Coast from there: Richmond, Trenton, Albany-Saratoga, Utica-Rome, and of course all the New England tracks.

"I didn't go up and down the road with Bugsy, or anything like that. Eddie Flemke and I were a lot closer than Bugsy and I were, so Eddie and I would travel together, starting off on Thursdays at Catamount in Vermont and continuing on through the weekend. But in that season, I would say that Bugsy and I certainly raced together over 50 percent of the time. There were nights when he'd go to one track and I'd go off in another direction, but most of the time we raced together.

"The modifieds and the sportsman cars were identical, except for a couple of things. If you had a sportsman, you ran a small block engine with a carburetor instead of the big blocks and fuel injectors the modifieds used. I ran a little 327. There was no weight penalty for running a big block—in fact, I don't recall anybody ever weighing our cars back then, if you can imagine that—but the weight of the big block engine itself was over 100 pounds heavier than the small block, so it was easier to get a sportsman to handle. The sportsman car was better on most of the bullrings, and even on some of the bigger tracks. At Stafford, we were always as quick as the modifieds because it was a flat track and handling was so important. At Thompson, a good shoe in the right modified could beat you up over a long distance because of the straightaway speed, but in a 30-lapper a sportsman was just fine, and we won our share of races there. Hell, I took a sportsman car to Trenton, which was a one-mile track, and ran as fast as any modified there, just because we got through the corners so damn much faster. A real good-handling modified would beat the shit out of a sportsman car, but there just weren't that many of them.

"The other problem with the big blocks was that they weren't as developed as the little engines were, in terms of the high-performance parts that

Pete Hamilton and Bugs Stevens, Daytona International Speedway, 1969. (Bones Bourcier Collection)

were available. Although, I'd have to say, that might not have effected Bugsy as much, because Lenny Boehler probably got more out of his engines than most guys did, even though he did it on a pretty tight budget.

"Bugsy was exceptional when it came to chasing those championships. I think that's because he was more of a smart driver than he was a fast driver. Don't get me wrong, he could put the pedal to the metal as hard as anybody, but he was just so good at saving his car. There were other guys who might have been more spectacular, who slipped and slid around a little more —Fats Caruso was that way—and yet Bugsy was always there when it counted.

"But, you know, speaking for myself—and I believe I can speak for Bugsy, too—there wasn't a lot of backing off involved. Ninety percent of the races we ran were short shows, 25 or 35 laps, with handicapped starts, and you had to get to the front.

"I think that in those days, Bugsy epitomized what a race driver should be, what he should look like and act like, both on and off the track. That was a rough-and-tumble time, and it took tough drivers; there was no power steering, no air-conditioned helmets, no lots of stuff. It was a different period, and in that period he was the perfect example of a race driver, or at least a whole lot better than a guy like me. For one thing, I wasn't quite as physically imposing as Bugsy. Plus, Bugsy always had a little bit of an aura about him, even at the point when he hadn't won many races yet. He wasn't cocky, but he was *close* to cocky. All that stuff added up.

"I very much looked up to him."

Championship Years

The Championship Years

For 30-odd years now, people have been talking about my championship years. I got that a lot when I raced—"Tell us about your championship years"—and I still get it today.

They're talking about 1967-69, when I won the NASCAR modified championship three years in a row with Lenny Boehler's car. What made it such a big deal, I guess, was the fact that nobody had ever won that thing three straight times. Of course, Jerry Cook and Richie Evans blew that all to hell in the seventies and eighties, and Richie ended up winning it eight straight times before he died. But a three-peat in those days was pretty much unheard of.

What most people don't remember is that we came awfully close to making it four straight.

All that championship stuff actually started in 1966, with Boehler and I getting out of Seekonk. We'd done well enough in our travels in '64 and '65 that we knew we could handle anything the modified division threw at us. When we'd won those Thompson features, and when we'd done so well at Langhorne, we'd been going up against all the best NASCAR modified guys. It made sense to us that if we could compete with them at those places, running NASCAR only part-time, we could compete against them on a regular basis.

So in '66 we stepped things up a little bit. Seekonk wasn't a NASCAR track, so we moved our Saturday-night racing to the Norwood Arena, and we also started running Thompson every time they had a show, which meant most Sundays.

I figured we'd do all right. We did a little bit better than that. Even after everything that came later, I'd have to look at 1966 as one of the biggest years of my life.

Norwood is gone now—it closed in 1972—but in the middle sixties it was one of the hottest modified tracks around. It had a great location, just south of Boston on Route 1, so the crowds were terrific, and just about every big name in New England modified racing ran there: Bill Slater, Eddie Flemke, Gene Bergin, Ernie Gahan, Leo Cleary, Freddy Schulz, Pete Hamilton, Don MacTavish and a bunch

Going to Norwood Arena with Boehler opened a whole new world for me. We won the track championship there in 1966. I'm guessing that's Leo Cleary in Joe Brady's 41 alongside me. (Balser & Son Photo)

more. I knew we were going to be all right when we showed up on opening night in '66 and finished third behind Schulz and Fred DeSarro, who was kind of like me, a young guy getting established. Flemke was fourth.

We ended up winning three Norwood features that season, and when we weren't up front we weren't far behind. We had a ton of top-five finishes, and something like 24 top-tens. With that kind of consistency, we ended up winning the track championship, which was a pretty good pat on the back for Lenny and me. Norwood was in its heyday, and it wasn't the kind of place where you expected a couple of new guys to blow in and win the title. But that's what we did.

We also won the track championship at Thompson that year, but I'd already had enough success there with Boehler's car that nothing we did in '66 was going to surprise anybody.

But what was a shocker, I guess, was the third championship I won that season, on the dirt at Stafford Springs. Stafford was running Friday nights and it was NASCAR sanctioned, but it's not like I went there specifically to chase points. Honestly, the whole Stafford thing happened almost by accident.

Jack Koszela—Sonny's dad, who everybody called "Pop"—owned the car, a big old number 15 coupe. Ernie Gahan and Bill Slater had each won races for Jack, but he was between drivers, so he basically gave me that car to run, with the idea that I was responsible for maintaining it and getting it to and from the race track. Whenever I wasn't off driving for Boehler, me and my pal Jimmy King and the Rogers

I had a lot of fun running "Pop" Koszela's old dirt coupe at Stafford in 1966. (Tom Ormsby Collection)

brothers, Jim and Bob, would work on the Koszela car, and then on Friday afternoons we'd load it into the back of a dump truck—*a dump truck!*—and haul over to Connecticut.

I didn't win any features on the dirt at Stafford, but we were competitive enough and consistent enough to clinch the title in the last race of the year. In fact, I ended by beating Maynard Forrette by just one point, and Forrette was one of the toughest dirt modified guys in the Northeast.

So it was a pretty amazing summer: three tracks, three track championships.

I also mixed in a bunch of other shows. If there was a midweek event someplace, or a special show in the spring or the fall, Boehler and I were usually there. We went to Trenton and timed second-quick on that big mile, and in October I set a new track record at Martinsville, my first time there; Bobby Allison started next to me on the front row.

The point is, we were running a lot of NASCAR races, and that put us in great position in the points. Don't forget, in those days the NASCAR modified championship wasn't decided by a *tour*; you didn't just run twenty-two or twenty-three races and add up the points from those. For years, right up into the 1980s, every single event you ran—provided it was at a NASCAR-sanctioned track—counted toward the title.

Actually, it wasn't *that* simple. The regular weekly shows, all those 30 and 35 lappers, had one points structure; then every track was allowed a certain number of races that paid double points; and on top of that, a handful of the biggest races, which were designated "national championship" events, had a different points structure altogether.

The way I went racing in 1966, running so many weekly shows between Boehler's car and Koszela's, and then hitting every big race Lenny and I could make it to, was perfect for that old points system.

It wasn't like I'd *planned* it that way, because we had never consciously tried to chase points. Hell, '66 was the year Lenny and I opened up our salvage yard, so between the business and the race cars we had enough to worry about. The way I remember it, we were just about at the end of the season—I mean, with just a few races to go—when people started pointing out that I was third in the NASCAR standings, behind Ernie Gahan and Ray Hendrick.

Anyway, I looked into that a little bit, and, sure enough, we were right there. We weren't exactly in the thick of things—Ernie and Ray were way out front—but we stood a fighting chance. At that point, Boehler and decided we'd be crazy *not* to do whatever we could to try and win the thing, and we did close the gap over the next couple of races.

The season finale was a modified/sportsman show at Atlanta Motor Speedway, which at that time was still a true oval, a mile and a half around, way bigger than any race track I'd ever run before. Obviously, our coupes weren't going to get the job at that place, so Lenny and I went down there with a full-bodied '64 Ford we bought from Roy Hallquist, a great racer from Connecticut who won a ton of late model races on Harvey Tattersall's old United Stock Car circuit.

Late model racing wasn't our thing, and superspeedway racing wasn't *my* thing just yet—although I learned to love it later—so we didn't exactly set the world on fire down there. Still, we had a better day than Hendrick, who dropped out early, or Gahan, who struggled all day in some old bucket of a car; in fact, I remember lapping Ernie a couple of times. When the smoke cleared, I had gone right past Ray into second in the standings behind Ernie, who won the 1966 NASCAR modified title.

I remember both Lenny and I feeling a strong sense of accomplishment that day. That season was the first time either one of us had really hit the road, and we damn near won the national championship without even knowing we were close to it.

And here's how close we were: there was one point in that Atlanta race when Gahan's car got sideways right in front of me, and I had to really jump out of the throttle to avoid him. Ernie saved the car, and we both kept rolling along. If I'd given him just the slightest little tap, and maybe spun him down into the infield just to get him out of my way, who knows how the point tally might have ended up?

I'd never have done that, of course. Taking advantage of a guy in trouble wasn't ever my style, so I don't regret the way that whole thing played out. But when you look back on it now, I was maybe one little tap away from winning *four* straight NASCAR championships.

Coming so close to that title in 1966 must have really woke up Lenny and me, because it was almost automatic that we were going to go after those points seriously in '67. I mean, it's not like we set the title as a do-or-die goal, but for a while that winter we went wacky about it, looking at schedules and trying to figure out all the angles that went into chasing points in those days.

Under that old points system, you really had to work to stay on top of everything that was going on. You had to weigh a lot of things out. For example, if you were running really well at one of your home tracks, well enough that you could almost bank on a win, was it worth giving that up for one week to travel to a double-points race at a strange place? You had to make those kinds of decisions all the time.

This is a neat picture. That's Jimmy Costello, one of the top flagmen in New England, handing me the checkered flag after a Thompson win with Lenny's coupe.
(Balser & Son Photo)

Later on, Jerry Cook had that stuff down to a science, but Lenny and I played those same games.

The other thing that was difficult was, a lot of times you weren't actually racing head-to-head against the guys you were fighting for the championship. You could be running on Friday nights at Stafford while your number one rival was at the Albany-Saratoga Speedway up in Malta, New York; or on Saturday night you'd be at Norwood, and he'd be on the dirt at Fonda, New York, or down on Long Island at Islip Speedway. Hell, there were even tracks in places like Baton Rouge, Louisiana, and Midfield, Alabama, that awarded points toward the modified championship. Because of that, you never really knew right away where you stood; you didn't just add up the points while you loaded up your race car. It might be Monday or Tuesday before you knew what kind of weekend the opposition had.

In 1967, there were no Internet sites you could use to look this stuff up. E-mail did not exist. Nobody had ever heard of cell phones. If you needed to know exactly where you ranked in the points, you called NASCAR headquarters in Daytona Beach. And, even though it sounds funny to think about it now, we never did that very much. That was a long-distance call, and, as everybody in modified racing knows, Lenny Boehler was a pretty frugal guy. He hated the idea of making those toll calls.

Our regular circuit that year would have been Stafford—which, by the way, had just been paved—on Friday nights, Norwood Arena on Saturday nights, and Thompson on Sundays. We expanded on that as soon as we found out they were running NASCAR modifieds every Thursday night at Catamount Stadium up in Milton, Vermont; as a matter of fact, we ended up winning the Catamount track championship.

Those four tracks made up the biggest chunk of our schedule, but by no means our *whole* schedule. If there was a NASCAR modified show going on someplace, we weren't sitting home, that's for sure. We hauled out into New York State quite a bit for big events at Albany-Saratoga, Plattsburgh and Utica-Rome, and we went south quite a bit, too, into Maryland, Virginia and North Carolina. I ran a few tracks I can still see in my head, but I've forgotten the names of. Hey, it's tough getting old.

What I *do* remember is how tough it was going to some of those places for the first time. I don't care what track you're talking about, when you go into somebody's backyard—the place where he's run every week for *years*—he's got an automatic advantage on you. That had to be the toughest thing about chasing points, at least that first time around.

We ran decent all year, obviously, but we really didn't get hot until

I guess I just won something big at Norwood Arena, because I've got the checkered flag and that's Carl Merrill, the NASCAR chief steward at Norwood, on my left, and Eddie Flemke on my right. Eddie must have run second.
(Balser & Son Photo)

late spring. In fact, we didn't win a NASCAR show until the middle of May, at Thompson. In the early part of the season, the modified points leader was Freddy Fryar, a short-track hero out of Baton Rouge. He ran weekly at a couple of tracks in Louisiana, and also over in Alabama. But once our season really got rolling up north, Don MacTavish and I reeled him in.

MacTavish was another young guy out of Massachusetts. He came from Dover, up toward Boston, and I had seen quite a bit of him at Norwood Arena and a bunch of other places. He was a great driver who had great equipment, and he had something else going for him: the previous year, 1966, he had won the NASCAR national sportsman championship. Back then, a sportsman car was kind of like what we call an SK modified today, basically a modified coupe with a limited engine; the full-bore modifieds ran big blocks, sometimes with fuel injection, and the sportsman cars ran small blocks and carburetors. On the way to that sportsman championship, Mac had run 106 NASCAR events, so he knew all the tricks a title contender needed to know.

I saw quite a bit of MacTavish in that summer of '67, while Freddy Fryar and I didn't race against each other ten times all year. And yet there we were, the three of us, battling for the same championship.

I took over the points lead in July, and Lenny and I basically held onto it from there. But MacTavish made it tough on us, I remember that. In September, he won four races over the Labor Day weekend, and that had us sweating a little.

Then we went to Trenton for a 200-mile national championship show on the old mile track. Lenny and I had been really fast there the previous year—timed second, finished in the top 10—and we were even better in '67. Donnie Allison and I battled for the win, and I got him right at the end. Donnie was driving the Tant-Mitchell 11, which was easily the hottest of the southern modifieds in that period.

Anyway, that victory clinched us the 1967 NASCAR modified championship over MacTavish and Fryar.

To that point, the Trenton 200 was easily the biggest win of my life. Even today, I'd have to say it's awfully high on the list. It's not every day that you win at a place like Trenton, beat a car like that number 11 coupe, and clinch a national championship.

I felt a whole range of emotions that afternoon. I was happy, I was tired, I was proud. Lenny Boehler never was the kind of guy who like to show what he was thinking, but it was obviously that he was right there with me: happy, tired, proud.

It was a great way to end a great year.

Chasing points in those days was a hell of a grind. When I think back on what Boehler and I put ourselves through in those years—especially in 1967, when it was all so new to us—I'm amazed.

For the entire time he raced, Lenny always operated with a small, tight crew. That's just the way he was; he didn't get wrapped up in having a big crowd around. He always built his own cars, and in those championship years he was building our engines, too. Of course, modified engines back then weren't nearly as sophisticated as they became later on. That year, we ran two engines, a 327-cubic-inch small block and the other a big-block something over 427 inches; only Lenny knew for sure exactly how big it was. Both of them were fuel-injected. Lenny had a close friend named Bob Roy who used to handle his machine work—honing the blocks, cleaning up the clearances—and then he'd do the assembly himself. Lenny would run an engine for half a season and then yank it out for a rebuild, and in 1967 a rebuild consisted basically of throwing in a new set of piston rings and dropping the engine back in.

Generally, at the shop there'd be just Lenny and a few buddies of ours: Tommy Sherman, Earl Kindberg, Ted Cox, Brian Daggett, Lou LaChapelle. They'd go to whatever races they could. When we went on the road, though, it was tough, because these were working guys, and anybody with a regular job can't put up for very long with a schedule like we had. There were plenty of times when our entire crew consisted of Lenny and me. The good thing was, if we got into a real jam at the track, we could usually rely on somebody from another team to pitch in; most racing people are good like that.

But regardless of who was with us, and regardless of whether we were at the shop or at the speedway, Boehler was very definitely the guy in charge. Lenny was The Man.

As lucky as I was to have Lenny on my side in racing, he was probably lucky to have me on his side in our business. I put as much effort into Freetown Auto as he put into those coupes. No matter where we might be racing on a particular night, I was almost always at the salvage yard the next day to open the place up. That meant a lot of bleary-eyed mornings; I'd blow out of Plattsburgh, New York, tear up the highway all the way home, and roll into my driveway in Rehoboth at five a.m. Then I'd lay down for a little while, and be at the yard by eight.

It was a physically demanding life, that's for sure. All that travel was draining enough, and, don't forget, you had to be a pretty fit guy to drive those coupes. You needed strong arms and a solid upper body, because those big 'ole cars never let you relax. Between the straight-axle front ends and the crude suspension systems and the small brakes, those things didn't want to turn and they didn't want to stop. You really had to drive your tail off; every lap, you had to be right on top of the thing.

I was a lot more devoted to racing back then than a lot of people might believe. I mean, people talk about the hell-raising that always went on when I was around—and don't worry, we'll get into that subject later on in the book—but I also dedicated myself to being in the best physical condition I could.

All through my days playing sports in high school and at Dean Academy, my coaches had drilled into my brain the fact that when you get tired, your reflexes slow up. That's something you can't prevent; it just happens. So the trick is not to get tired.

I busted my ass in the gym every chance I could, working out hard, all to be ready for battle when they threw that green flag. I'd be in that gym, throwing weights around, taking steam baths to get ready for the grind, and the whole time I'd be telling myself, "That race car isn't going to beat *me*."

Lenny Boehler never had a big crowd around him. He did his own thing, built his own cars, assembled his own engines. Once we hit our stride, we were a heck of a team. (Dick Berggren Photo)

There were certain perks that went along with winning a NASCAR championship, even then. There was a point fund, of course, but there was more to the title than money. You'd get free stuff—tires, shocks, rear ends, stuff like that—from manufacturers who wanted to advertise that you ran their products, and as the national champion you could always count on some show-up cash from every promoter who was running a modified race. Hell, with so many tracks running modifieds back then, it was easy to play one promoter against the other, and run at whatever track gave us the best deal.

Once we looked at all that, it was pretty much a foregone conclusion that Lenny and I would go after the championship again in 1968. Both of us had been worn down by the travel, but we figured that if we concentrated on running well close to home and traveled only when it was necessary, we could be in the hunt again.

And we were right. Looking back, '68 might have been the best year I ever had. If it wasn't the best, it was definitely the most successful from the standpoint of sheer winning. Just looking at the numbers from our NASCAR starts, we won 29 out of the 72 shows we ran, which is a pretty fair percentage. We also won track championships at both Stafford and Thompson, and if you were a serious points-chaser it was awfully tough to win individual tracks, because you could almost count on being away from your home track once or twice for a national championship event or a double-points race someplace else.

We got off on the right foot by winning the Dogwood 300 at

The old NASCAR points system encouraged drivers to be conservative, but I always tended to run for the wins and let the points fall accordingly. Obviously, that strategy worked out pretty well.
(Balser & Son Photo)

Martinsville in March, and from there we just kept up the pace. Most of our 29 wins came in regular weekly shows, but we did win a couple of national championship races at Stafford.

That 1968 season was the perfect example of the old saying about how if you win enough races, the points will take care of themselves. One of the problems with that old NASCAR points structure was that a guy could easily beat you for the championship simply by running more often, or by putting together more top-ten finishes even if you had the fastest car all year long. It almost *encouraged* a guy to be conservative, and there were quite a few guys over the years who approached the whole thing that way. Well, I can honestly say that I never stroked it, not once, anytime I was chasing points. I raced for the win every time out, and we watched the points just pile up in our column.

Nobody ever won the NASCAR modified championship by a bigger margin than Lenny and I did that year; we had 6452 points to Fred DeSarro's 4522.

Our battle with Freddy was a little bit like the one with MacTavish the previous year. No, it wasn't as close as Don and I had been in 1966, but Freddy was another guy from around home, a Norwood guy who was starting to branch out a little bit more. Generally speaking, wherever I raced, *he* raced. I saw an awful lot of him in 1968, that's for sure. But, again, behind us were a couple of guys we saw mostly at the big spring and fall races: Perk Brown and Billy Hensley, two Virginia boys, ended up third and fourth.

Lenny and I had several great seasons together—we were together from 1964 through 1970—but I don't know if we were ever better than we were in '68. As a chassis man, he always seemed to have that car set up perfectly, and mechanically it was bulletproof; we ran the same big block engine all year long.

And the driver was doing his job, too. By 1968, I had been to most of the modified tracks enough times to figure them out, and I had the kind of confidence that always comes from winning races and championships.

It never really mattered where we went. Come race time, the Boehler coupe and I were going to be in the picture.

People ask me all the time whether that traveling life was fun, and I never know for sure how to answer them. I mean, yes, we had a lot of laughs, and both Lenny and I were doing something we loved. But I don't think we were ever really *aware* that we were living this romantic gypsy lifestyle; we were probably numb. We were too busy thinking about getting to the next race to understand what was going into it.

Look at the World of Outlaws sprint car guys today. Sure, when you stand back and look at the lives they lead, it seems like it'd be an awful lot of fun. But you ask anybody who's actually living that life year after year, and he's probably working too hard to stop and think about all the fun he's supposed to be having.

I know this: life on the road wasn't easy. It wasn't fancy hotels and room service, not by a long shot. We stayed in the cheapest little places we could find, or we slept in the truck on the side of the road. Then again, our schedule was so crazy that I did a lot of my sleeping on the way from one race track to the next one. Even now, when somebody mentions those championship years, you know what I think of? Snoozing in the truck, and rolling down the highway.

Sleep and drive, drive and sleep. All those miles.

I think about the hours we spent running up and down the Massachusetts Turnpike, the New York Thruway, even I-95 headed to Virginia or the Carolinas, and I get tired just remembering it. But that's what chasing a title is all about: you go where the points are.

Sometimes when the schedule got really crazy, we'd actually send our two race cars in different directions, one on Lenny's ramp truck and the other on a truck and trailer, and I'd fly between tracks if I had to. There was always somebody who knew somebody else who had a small private plane if we needed one. But more often than not, we'd just go roaring down the highway.

On a lot of those longer road trips, it was just Lenny and me hauling down the road, and Lenny drove about 90 percent of the time. We had a pretty simple arrangement: if he was too tired to see, I'd drive. But as long as he was halfway awake, he was steering that truck down the road.

One night we were hauling home from Catamount, and Lenny was wiped out from working his tail off on that race car, so I was driving the truck. I was rolling down the highway at about 90 miles an hour, flying down the side of some big Vermont mountain, and a deer ran right out in front of us. Well, neither one of us had a chance; I didn't have a chance to swerve, and that deer didn't have a chance against the plow rig on the front of that truck. Oh, it was a hell of a wreck. To this day, I don't know how I got that truck stopped safely, but I did. But, God, what a mess that deer made.

It was quite a while before Boehler slept on a ride home after that.

Oh, yeah, all that traveling is a ball. Just not while you're doing it.

While I'm on the subject of hectic schedules, I ought to point out that Lenny and I also ran a lot of non-NASCAR events. In the summer months we'd run with the old All Star League, a midweek series promoted by Larry Mendelsohn, a guy out of Long Island whose main job was operating Islip Speedway; that All Star schedule might have you at Riverside Park one week, on the dirt at Fonda the next week, and Albany-Saratoga the following week.

And Boehler and I ran a bunch of open-competition races at the Lebanon Valley dirt track in New York. Those were tough, tough races, because you'd have the very best dirt guys from all over the East Coast, and, let's face it, Lenny and I were asphalt guys. Sure, I'd won that championship at Stafford on the dirt in 1966, but as tough as those Stafford fields were, they were nothing compared to those 100-lap opens at the Valley.

Still, we did all right. One night I was leading with just a handful of laps to go, and to tell you the truth I wasn't even aware that I was out front until a caution flag waved and they lined me up first on a restart. I was wearing a pair of old World War II-style aviator goggles, but the strap had broken and that left me with no eye protection whatsoever. Whatever they used to help bind the dirt surface together—calcium, maybe—was just blinding me; I mean, my eyes were burning like you had poured salt into 'em. That's an awfully fast track to run when you can't see worth a damn. Anyway, just after the restart Dutch Hoag went sailing past me, and that was the end of that.

But it was another good memory, another adventure.

I look a little tired in this picture. Chasing points in the late 1960s would do that to you. (John Grady Photo)

For some reason, I don't remember as much about 1969—you know, the ins and outs of how the season went—as I do about our first two championship years. Maybe because we'd already done it twice, it didn't leave as much of an impression in my mind. Don't get me wrong: anytime you win a title like that, it's special. I guess it's just that after you've won something once, the second time has less of an impact, and then the third time it's lesser still.

The thing that does stand out, like I said earlier, was the fuss everybody made about the '69 championship being my third straight. At the time, that was really significant, and I was like any race driver: if you want to make a big deal out of me, I'll go along with it.

Boehler and I started 1969 the same way we started '68: not obsessed with winning another championship, but knowing inside that if we were in the hunt once the season really got rolling, we'd probably chase it again.

The crazy thing was, we did manage to stay in the hunt, but this time around we were the hunter instead of the hunted. In the last half of the '67 season, we made Don MacTavish chase us; in '68, Freddy DeSarro chased us from a long way back. But in 1969, we never once led the NASCAR points until a week before the end of the season. They held a 500-lap race at Thompson Speedway that fall, and Lenny

49

and I went there running a close second in the standings. Jerry Cook was the guy on top.

Cook was a steady racer who had won some track championships out in New York, and had been a fixture in the modifieds and the sportsman coupes for several years. He won his share of races, but he was more the kind of guy who would wear you down over the course of a long season; every night, Cookie would always be there, banging out those top-fives and top-tens. Like I said, he was steady.

I guess you could say that if you really wanted to examine driving styles, at least among the guys who won races, Jerry was at one extreme, on the conservative side. At the other extreme you had some of the crazier guys from down South; those guys cared only about running up front. The way they looked at it, if you were leading by half a lap and you crashed, that was beautiful. You'd proven to everybody that you were fast, and that was all that counted.

Me? I think my own style was somewhere in the middle. I always went out there thinking I could win, and I approached each race that way, but I figured you could win as many races with your head as you could with your right foot. I'm not talking about stroking; in my day, the worst thing you could call somebody was a stroker. Stroking is when you're hanging back, running at 80 percent, just looking to slide into a good finish, and I never did that. But unless I was in a hot battle for the lead, I'd back things down to about 95 percent, which was good enough to stay in the fight but still left me and my equipment a

Thompson Speedway, wide open on the backstretch in Lenny's coupe. That was a great feeling.
(Dick Berggren Photo)

little bit of breathing room. And when it was time to race, *really* race, I was always ready to go.

Looking back, I think my style was perfect for that old points system. I won more than the conservative guys did, and I sure crashed a hell of a lot less than some of those Rebels did.

Anyway, heading into Thompson, we had run 66 NASCAR modified races, and Lenny and I had won nineteen of them, so we didn't have any problems in the speed department. We won a 100-lapper at Martinsville in September, won a couple of national championship races at Stafford and another up at Plattsburgh, and had a bunch of victories at Thompson, where I won the track championship for the third time. But all summer long, Cook had been more consistent, and that's what had him out front.

In the end, though, it was another win that gave me that 1969 championship. They ran that 500-lapper on a day that was really warm, especially for that time of the year, and I did my usual deal: saving a little something in reserve, and then gassing it when it counted.

That was the only Thompson 500 ever run, and I beat Eddie Flemke to win it.

I don't remember where Cookie ended up, but when we left Thompson that night I had the points lead for the first time all year long. All we had left was the season finale at Martinsville. Ray Hendrick, one of those mash-the-gas Southern guys, won the race, but Lenny and I won the modified championship. Again.

That ended up being my last run at the NASCAR title, with or without Lenny Boehler. There were a lot of different reasons for that. Lenny's first wife, Joanne, had been sick for a while, and she passed away after the 1969 season. That got Lenny a little bit sideways, just like it would anybody, and I don't think he had a clear idea what he wanted to do for a while. I'd had a few people ask me about running Winston Cup cars, and Lenny and I started talking about the possibility of doing that together, or maybe running some late model sportsman races—what we now call the Busch Series—as a team.

At any rate, I didn't think Lenny had the focus it took to chase another championship. I'm not sure I did, either.

Aside from all that, I was really starting to take a hard look at the economics of that thing. I knew as well as anybody how much time and effort and money went into going after the championship, and I just didn't think it was worth it anymore. It was an expensive deal in '67, it was a more expensive deal in '68, it was worse still in '69. And if you paid attention, you could see that it sure wasn't going to get any

Championships come with all kinds of perks. That's Governor Frank Sargent on the right, presenting me with a special citation from the Commonwealth of Massachusetts after my third straight NASCAR modified title in 1969.
(Dick Berggren Photo)

better. Engine parts, in particular, were costing a lot of money, and that was hurting the backyard operators like Lenny.

At the same time, some of the guys who had sponsors were starting to raise the bar for the rest of us. That happens every few years in racing: a couple of teams show up with better funding, and either you go out and find some extra funding of your own or you get left behind. I remember Jerry Cook coming along with Hollebrand Trucking, the outfit that backed him all through *his* championship years, and that made a real impression on me. Aside from whatever financial backing Cookie got, you just knew that getting up and down the road was never going to be a problem for a team sponsored by a trucking company. It sounds crazy now, but even simple transportation was an obstacle back then; it was tough on Lenny to keep his truck maintained, never mind the race car.

Little by little, I was watching our advantages slip away. I remember talking with Lenny at one point in '69, and telling him, "Buddy, it's getting to the point where we'll just be banging our heads against the wall." And Boehler knew what I meant. So even before his wife passed away, and even before we looked really hard at other kinds of racing, we had reasons for backing away from chasing those points.

I'm not sure any of those reasons was *the* single factor. But if you put 'em all into a basket and shook it up, you had a pretty good list of reasons not to do it.

And, hell, maybe my biggest reason was simply that I'd already won the thing three times. Been there, done that. Leave it to somebody else now.

You know what I'm proud of? To me, the cars we were running at the close of the sixties, at the end of that three-year title run, might have been the most *modified* modifieds we've ever seen. What I mean is, the cars were getting lighter, the tires had gotten lower and wider and better, the suspensions let us corner faster, and those big blocks—with fuel injection and a tank full of alcohol—gave you every last bit of horsepower you needed.

Sure, today's cars are faster overall, and with all the technology that's available, they *should* be. But they sure don't pack the punch you got when you stuck a big block into one of Boehler's flyweight frames. At some of the faster tracks, you'd swear that if you put wings on the sides of one of those coupes, you could fly it right out of the damn track.

That might have been the ultimate racing. You sucked in a deep breath, and you pushed the pedal. It took balls.

To me, that little period—1968, '69, right in there—was a high point for NASCAR modified racing. It *must* be a high point, because when you talk to people from New England who've been around racing from the fifties onward, they love to reminisce about those injected coupes from the tail end of the sixties. They appreciate, I suppose, how wild those cars were, and how good the action was.

So when I look at it that way, I might have been the champion at just the right time. The *best* time.

This was some of the best racing there ever was: Fuel-injected big blocks in lightweight coupes on a fast track like Thompson. That's Bob Garbarino's V4 beside me, probably with Leo Cleary driving. (Balser & Son Photo)

53

Gene Bergin on Bugsy

Gene Bergin, legendary modified driver: "Some guys just adapt better to different race tracks than other guys. They just understand that it takes different things to go fast and win at each place. It might be a natural skill, but I also think it's something you can learn. Either way, you have to have it, or you're in trouble.

"The good drivers—Bugsy, Eddie Flemke, Leo Cleary, Fats Caruso, Pete Hamilton—made that adjustment. It's like a lineman in a football game; he's going to line up according to what the other team is doing, and he's going to do it in a way that gives him a little bit of an advantage over the other player. Well, those good drivers would do that. They would look at each track, and really study ways to get around it.

"I'm sure that when Bugsy looked at a race track, it made him stop and think. Like, 'Hey, this is Islip Speedway, and I can't run Islip Speedway exactly like I'd run Norwood Arena.'

"I had my own way of adapting. I wouldn't tell this to too many people, because they'd think I was crazy, but it worked for me. There were times when we'd be at, say, Thompson Speedway, and I'd be driving both a modified and a midget. When you do that, you're getting out of a 1,000-pound car, the midget, and into a 2,500-pound car. Well, I'd look at those two cars and I'd say to myself, 'Gene, this car over here is a midget, and you have to drive it this way. That car over there is a modified stock car, and you have to drive it that way.' Because, see, they react differently, and you can get away with things in one car that you can't get away with in the other. Well, it's the same thing with race tracks. There are things you do at one place but not at the other.

"Myself, I liked the bigger tracks. To me, they were so much easier. I enjoyed going to Trenton; I enjoyed going to Langhorne. Now, Langhorne was a very difficult race track, believe you me, and a lot of guys never adapted to it, but I liked it. For some reason or another, I could get the feel of a fast race track quicker than I would at a smaller place.

"Bugsy was strong everywhere. I don't think he had any weaknesses. You could be at the fastest track there was, and he'd be as cool as he was at a little quarter-mile. I know, because I chased that man lap after lap at Trenton, and I've seen the control he had. I also banged wheels with him at the bullrings, and on the half-miles at Stafford, Thompson, and Martinsville.

"He drove me crazy, boy, down at Martinsville [in 1972]. I was driving the number 1 car for Dick Armstrong, and I chased Bugsy for 50 laps. I had the faster car, and I could crawl all over his back end, but he knew how to slow me down. When I went to the outside, he was there, and when I went to pass him on the inside, he was there, too. And yet he wasn't being dirty about it! He gave me room, gave me a lane, but he was always where I wanted to be, and that

Ron Bouchard, Gene Bergin, and Bugs Stevens, Manadnock Speedway, 1978. (Courtesy of Speedway Scene)

slowed me down. I had the better car, and yet he beat me. He did it by maintaining that high level of thinking for a long time.

"With Bugsy, you couldn't push him into a turn and make him run harder than he wanted to. He backed off here, and he accelerated there, and that was that. He ran his own race. And that's something special, that ability.

"I don't think I had two bad words with Bugsy, and we ran hundreds of races together. I know this: I finished second to that guy a lot of nights. To win as many races for as long a time as he did, I know how tough that is. Just to be that competitive, and keep that same frame of mind every week, is hard.

"You know one of the things that really stands out about Bugsy, in my memory? We were up at Norwood on a Saturday night. This was when he and Lenny were chasing points, winning those championships. I was in the dressing room, putting on my uniform. Well, in walked Bugsy. He sat down, and he just looked so tired. I said, 'Geez, Bugsy, are you sick? What's the matter?'

"He told me that already that week, he'd run someplace on Thursday night, and then on Friday night he'd been down South, running a 200-lapper someplace. Now he was at Norwood. I don't remember how he did that night, but I'll never forget how tired he was. The heart the guy showed was really special to me. Because, see, he had made it to Norwood, and he was there to *race*. He was going to run as hard as he could, and he wasn't going to back off. You appreciate a guy like that.

"I loved racing against Bugsy. He's not only a great driver, but a great person, too. I'm proud to have known him. And I'm even prouder to be able to say that I've beaten him a few times."

Tracks

55

Tracks

I ALWAYS THOUGHT the ideal modified track was just under a half-mile around. To me, a small half was the perfect size for a good Saturday-night shootout.

See, a half-mile oval is a whisker too big, and a quarter-mile is a whisker too small, because they present different sets of problems. On a half-mile, the guys with the best equipment and the most expensive engines will go to the front every time, so the little guy doesn't stand a very good chance. On the other end of the spectrum, at a little bullring you leave more up to the driver, which is good, but you also end up with so much beating and banging that it takes away from the racing.

A place that measures, oh, four-tenths or three-eighths, whatever you'd want to call it, gives you all the characteristics you want in a good short track. Number one, if we're looking at this sport as entertainment—and that's what it is—a track like I'm describing is still small enough to keep a bit of the old crash-bang action, and, let's face it, that's a part of this sport. It's also small enough to make corner speed more important than straightaway speed, so you're making it a mechanic's game and a driver's game, which is how racing should be, I think. At the same time, a nice three-eighths-miler gives you enough room to maneuver.

And a track that size generally won't be too tough on equipment, either. It won't stretch the motors as bad as a fast half-mile, and the drivers probably won't beat up the cars like they would on a quarter.

As for what else you'd want in an ideal track, you need *some* banking, but not much. A little bit of a bank lets you get a good second groove going, but you don't want the turns so steep that it gets too fast and becomes a one-lane race track.

And here's a couple more things: most times you'll find that tracks that are more corner than straightaway—in other words, the ones that are almost circular—have the best racing, so you'd want to lay it out with that in mind. And make it nice and wide, so the right two guys can run side-by-side all night long.

Yeah, give me a round little track any night of the week.

But you know something? All this daydreaming about a perfect track is fun, but it doesn't amount to anything, because you won't find

Probably the closest thing to an ideal track, in my mind, was Oxford Plains up in Maine. I won a couple of races there, including this one in 1981. (Clint Lawton Photo/Courtesy of Speedway Scene*)*

many places that match that description. One of the places that came close was Oxford Plains, up in Maine. That place was just the right size, it was fairly round and just slightly banked, and you could run two-abreast pretty easily. In fact, if that place was a *tiny* bit wider, it would have been almost just right. Unfortunately, I never got there much, because Oxford was primarily a late model track. I did win a NASCAR national championship modified race there with Lenny Boehler's coupe, and a 100-lapper with Dick Armstrong's car in '81, which made me like the place even more.

Still, the bottom line is, wherever the next big race is, that's where you go. In my day, that might have been Islip Speedway, a tiny Long Island bullring just one-fifth of a mile around, or it might have been the Trenton Fairgrounds, a 1.5-mile track with a long front straightaway and a right-turn dogleg in the middle of the backstretch. It might have even been a half-mile dirt track.

I don't know how many tracks I ran, but there were dozens of 'em.

None of them were perfect, and every damn one of 'em was a challenge.

When I first got away from Seekonk a little bit and started traveling around with Boehler, it felt like I was seeing at least one new track every week. For a young driver, that's an exciting time.

Whenever we'd pull into a place I hadn't seen before, as soon as we

Every track has its challenges, and the good drivers just overcome them. This is me at Albany-Saratoga, a neat little joint, with Sonny Koszela's coupe in the early 1970s. (Mike Adaskaveg Photo)

got into the pit area I'd walk over to take a good look at the track. If I had the chance, I'd even walk around and study it up close. I picked up that habit when I first started going to Martinsville, and I kind of took it to a lot of the other places we went. I'd always say I was looking for stray nuts and bolts—stuff that could cut a tire—but there was more to it than that. It was a great way to better understand exactly where the bumps were, how the seams laid in the pavement, where there might be a little ridge or something between the lanes of asphalt.

Each speedway has its own characteristics, but there's usually something about a new one that you can compare to someplace else you've been. You catch yourself thinking, Okay, the groove at this place is up high, like at Thompson, or you tell yourself, Hey, this joint is shaped a little bit like Norwood. You sort of program that stuff into your brain. I'm not smart enough to understand how that works, but it *does* work.

When it came time for the first warm-up session at a track I was seeing for the first time, I'd always start at a moderate pace and built up from there. Actually, I was never one to go balls-out right away, anyway, even if it was a track I ran every week. You need to be sure you've warmed the tires, warmed the engine. I mean, it doesn't pay a dime to break the track record in practice. But if I was at a new place, I might be a little extra careful for a few laps.

If there was one guy there who was the big local hot dog, sometimes I'd check out where he was running, just to figure out what he was doing. But normally, I'd try and find the groove myself. On an asphalt track, it's usually pretty easy to see where the fast lane is, just by the way the rubber lays down; it's like following footprints. Then I'd move around and experiment with different lines, because if everybody else is running decent in that one fast groove, you won't be able to pass 'em unless you get *out* of that groove. Sometimes when you try that, you find a spot that works just right for you.

Generally, if you gave me ten or fifteen hard laps, that was enough. I was in the ballpark.

Now, I'll admit, it wasn't that way everywhere. I think the hardest place to figure out, at least for me, was Fonda. It wasn't that Fonda was dirt, because I'd been pretty successful at Stafford before they paved it. I guess it's because Fonda was the kind of place where you needed to build up a rhythm, and since I seldom ran there I never got that rhythm down perfectly. I ran decent there occasionally, but I never felt like I had it quite figured out. And I could probably say the same thing about Oswego Speedway; I ran there only a few times, and I'd always end up chasing guys like Maynard Troyer and Richie Evans and Roger Treichler, who had a ton of laps at that track.

Still, I must have been pretty good at figuring out new places, because we ended up winning at so many of them. But, you know, that was just part of the job. I was no different than a guy who worked pumping gas at one filling station, and then moved across the street to another filling station. It was automatic. I figured 'em out because I *had* to.

❖ ❖ ❖ ❖ ❖

Seekonk Speedway is a place where the groove is basically a big circle. I loved the place for sentimental reasons, and because it was just a ball to drive. (RA Silvia Collection)

Martinsville was always a tough place to race, because you funneled from very fast straightaways into very tight turns. That's me in the Garbarino 4, alongside Reggie Ruggiero in 1983.
(Johnny Mercury Photo/ Courtesy of Speedway Scene)

I've been asked a million times to name my favorite track, and, honestly, it kind of changes from time to time. I guess it depends on how you want to look at it. I mean, Seekonk will always be special to me, because it's where I was brought up. We used to joke that driving at Seekonk was like testing at a skid pad, one of those circular things you see at an automotive proving grounds. On a skid pad, the goal is to go faster and faster until either the front end pushes or the back end breaks loose; at that point you adjust the car to get rid of that problem, and then you start the whole process again. Well, Seekonk gave you that same challenge. You'd just run that circle a hard as you could without the car slipping. And, of course, you had to do that while you were fighting your way past twenty other cars.

If you want to be sentimental about things, sure, Seekonk is right up there in my book.

And Martinsville is close to my heart, too. I won seven races there between 1968 and 1977, and in that period a victory at Martinsville was a huge thing to have on your résumé. You'd get a grandfather clock for winning a race there, and there wasn't a modified driver alive who didn't want one of those things.

Martinsville was a track I took to instantly. I always felt like I had it figured out as well as the next cat did, no matter who he was. It's basically two drag strips with a hairpin turn on each end. There wasn't any real secret to going fast there, but there *was* one major requirement: big balls. I mean, big enough to toss 'em right up on the dashboard. You'd drive into those corners so deep that you were sure you couldn't stop, sure you were over your head, and then you found yourself in a turn where you had to be so *precise*. On the inside there was a big high curb, and you didn't want to bounce off that thing; on the outside there were always a bunch of marble19—loose rubber and dust and junk—and if you hit that stuff you were probably going to end up in the fence.

In the older cars, Martinsville was a real test for a driver. It got easier as the cars improved and handled better, and I'm sure it's easier still today, because the brakes and tires and suspensions are more efficient than ever. Thirty years ago, that joint was a real bear, and I loved it anyway.

But I guess if I had to pick out one track as my all-time favorite, it would have to be the place where I had the most success, and the most good memories. And that, of course, would be Stafford.

I'm not sure exactly why I did so well there, besides the fact that I usually had great cars. But I had that track down pat for a long, long time.

Stafford was a difficult place to learn, one of those tracks that is trickier than it looks, because it's not a true oval. If you looked at it from above, you'd find that both ends of the track are very different. Turns three and four make a nice round arc, a typical oval-track corner, but the other end, particularly turn one, is sort of squared off. In fact, I first noticed that one day when I looked at an aerial photograph that was hanging in the track office. Naturally, with that first turn being so unique, it became the key to getting around the place. A lot of guys were slow to catch on to that secret.

If I had to name one track as my favorite, it would have to be Stafford. I've still got the all-time win record there, with 73 features. (Rene Dugas Photo/Courtesy of Speedway Scene)

When Richie Evans first started showing up at Stafford in the early seventies, he struggled, like most drivers did. Finally Richie said to me, "There's something you're doing in that first turn. I'm gonna follow you around." I mean, he'd pick my brain about that place all the time. Obviously, he figured it out eventually, and once that happened he was a hard sucker to beat there. But I had Richie and just about everybody else covered at Stafford for a long, long time. Ronnie Bouchard was tough there, and so were Geoff Bodine and Fred DeSarro and a few other guys, but if my car was right they had to beat me if they were going to win.

Richie was right about one thing: I did have a little turn-one secret. When I ran down the front straightaway, I'd hold my car up against the outside wall long after the other guys had already turned into the corner. Then I'd cut it hard left, squaring off the corner because, like I said, that's what it was: square. By running it that way, I could get right back into the gas for an instant, like I was making another short little straightaway between the first and second turns.

Running that unique line is what led to that trademark pass I used all the time in turn one. While the other guy's car was sliding up the track because he'd turned in so early, I'd drive right through the hole he left on the inside. You had to time everything exactly, but if you did it right that move was almost unstoppable. In the seventies, they started calling it "the bottom shot," because that's how it looked: I'd just slingshot right past the other guy on the bottom. I was on the gas, and he wasn't, and I'd be past him in a flash. Most times, the other guy

Anytime I saw daylight on the inside of turns one and two at Stafford, I was gone. That's Ronnie Bouchard upstairs in Bob Johnson's Pinto, probably in 1973. (Rene Dugas Photo/Courtesy of Speedway Scene*)*

never saw you coming. Hell, he never even dreamed that you *might* be coming.

I must have used that move a thousand times. Everybody says I invented it, and I'm not sure about that. But I definitely helped *perfect* it. It won me a lot of races, that's for sure.

Probably the best bottom shot of them all came one night in 1977, when I got past Bodine for the lead on the last lap. To this day, I'm sure Geoff had no idea I was inside him until it was too late. That's one of my favorite Stafford memories, but I've got so many good ones. I won the Spring Sizzler there in '74, and some of the big 100-lappers. And I won the track championship four times; I'm the only guy to ever win the title there on dirt *and* asphalt, which is something special.

What's sad to me is that a couple of the crashes I had at Stafford, wrecks that didn't do my body any good, probably affect the way I'll always remember that track. When I was driving for Lenny Boehler, I took a hell of a tumble there. I was lapping Tommy Sutcliffe going into turn one, and he moved wide, and I went right up over his tire. I rode the top of that fence, end for end, all the way into turn two. That cracked a vertebra in my upper back. Years later, in 1982, I was going into that same first turn with Bob Garbarino's car and my left-rear tire came off its bead at top speed and spun me into the concrete wall. That one was a hellacious crash; it left me with a compression fracture of two vertebrae in my lower back, and came damn close to crippling me.

Those injuries didn't necessarily make me love Stafford any less, but in some way they changed the way I looked at the place. It's a hard thing for me to explain, but it's there. Any yet Stafford is still special to me. It always will be.

I'm pretty lucky, I guess, because I've got fond memories of just about every track I've raced at.

Thompson was a place where I had good years and bad years, but if you look at the big picture I did awfully well there. It's the first track where Boehler and I ever won together, so it was definitely important to my career. Lenny had that joint figured out as well as anybody ever did, and we took a bunch of victories there, including that Thompson 500 back in 1969. And we had a lot of success there separately, too; Lenny and Freddy DeSarro practically owned that joint for a while in the seventies, but I won some, too, first with Sonny Koszela and later on with Joe Brady.

For years, Thompson used high sandbanks as a retaining barrier, and in those days the fast groove was way up high. I mean, you'd run

For a long time, the fast lane at Thompson was right around the top. This was 1978, and I'm running high in Joe Brady's car while Freddy Schulz is trying the bottom.
(Mike Adaskaveg Photo)

right up at the top of the turns, almost up into that sand. But that all changed when they put a concrete wall around the track in 1982. The groove moved down; it wasn't that anybody was afraid of the walls, it was just that now all the loose rubber and dirt collected up in the outside lanes instead of blowing off the track like it always had.

Thompson was a great track to drive, a fast track. It was quite a ride in those old coupes, sitting way up high, with all that horsepower—injectors, big-block engines, alcohol fuel—pulling you out of the banked turns and down those long straightaways. Even later on, as the cars changed, it was still a fun place. I had some really good races there with Freddy, with Eddie Flemke, with Leo Cleary, with George

This is what Thompson was all about: Speed. That's Eddie Flemke in the Garuti & Arute 14 out front, and me right behind in the Boehler 3.
(Balser & Son Photo)

Winning at Norwood was a big, big deal in the late 1960s, because the best modified guys in New England ran there every Saturday night.
(Balser & Son Photo)

Summers, with Ronnie and Kenny Bouchard, with everybody. It was the fastest place we ran on a regular basis, and that made it special.

Norwood Arena, on the other hand, wasn't very fast compared to Thompson, but it was an awfully exciting. During the years I spent there, from about 1966 through 1969, they packed that place with fans every Saturday night, so it felt like a big deal. Norwood's layout was a lot like Seekonk's, but with a bit more banking. To look at it in a photograph, you wouldn't say it was as round as Seekonk, but you basically drove it as if it was a circle. It was a fun joint, your classic bullring.

In the seventies, I ran quite a bit at Westboro Speedway, driving for Joe Brady on Friday nights; for a while, Bobby Santos and I were teammates in Joe's cars. Later on, once Stafford switched to Friday nights, Brady and I ran a bunch of Saturday-night races at Westboro. No matter what night we ran, we won our share there. That was a rough little place with fairly high banks, and it was really bumpy. It was a fun track to drive, because those bumps would move the car around under you, but it was also a pretty dangerous place. See, Westboro had wooden guardrails, and I always hated those damn things. I'd seen too many guys get hurt when wooden rails came apart and speared right through their cars. In the sixties, Thompson had a wooden guardrail, and one wreck there showed me how much trouble that wood could cause. I bumped wheels with a guy, and evidently it cracked something in my front end because on the next straightaway my car took a hard right. I took out maybe a hundred yards of that fence, and when the crashing stopped I looked down and discovered that this huge length of lumber—a 2X6, a 2X8, whatever it was—had

Westboro Speedway was fast, bumpy, scary, and a lot of fun all at the same time. I won a bunch of open-competition races there, including this one in the Koszela coupe.
(Elman B. Myers Photo/Courtesy of Speedway Scene*)*

gone right through the firewall of my car and right between my legs, just under the seat. Westboro was a lot slower than Thompson, of course, but I still never liked the idea of relying on those wooden guardrails.

One night I was warming up at Westboro in Bobby Judkins's car, and just as I was passing a guy on the outside going into turn three I saw his right-front wheel wiggle a bit. I knew right then that he was in over his head, but it was too late for me to get away from him. My left-side tires rode up over his right-sides, and away I went. But instead of slamming that wooden rail, I cleared it altogether. Before the wreck was through, my car tore down a length of the chain-link fence and landed right next to some guys working in the pits. Like I said, Westboro was wild.

There were a lot of small tracks like that all over New England, places where I had a ball but never got to run too much. We'd get into our regular Friday-Saturday-Sunday patterns every year, and that just didn't leave a lot of time for some of these other joints. But there'd always be a time when one of our regular tracks wasn't running, and we'd sneak off to one of those other places for an open-competition show.

The Waterford Speedbowl was a good example. In the seventies, they'd open up with a 100-lapper called the Blast-Off, and in the summer they might run a couple of midweek events. I always looked forward to those races, because I liked Waterford. It was one of those tracks where you really had to *drive* the place: work the corners, try different grooves, fight the traffic. I won there with Bobby Judkins, Sonny Koszela, and Joe Brady.

The old Lee Speedway in New Hampshire was another place where the driver really had to hustle. We ran there for a short time in the NASCAR modifieds in the early seventies, and even though it was totally weird—a triangular deal that had an elevation change or two—Lee was a gas once you figured it out. Just up the road from Lee was the Star Speedway, a great quarter-miler banked just enough to let you put on a really good side-by-side race. Judkins and I won a Yankee All-Star League race there in 1976, and I always felt like I had a good feel for the place. And Monadnock Speedway, on the other side of New Hampshire near the Vermont line, was another tricky little track I loved. It had lots of banking in turns one and two, a little bit less in three, and then it flattened out as you went through turn four. I won some races there with Brady's car in the late seventies, and it was always a place I looked forward to running.

When Boehler and I were chasing NASCAR points, we hauled out to Catamount Stadium in Vermont on a fairly regular basis. Ken Squier, who everybody knows from his television work, was the promoter up there, and he was a good guy to run for. Catamount was a nice track, maybe a third-miler, and we won some races there.

I ran all over New York State for years, with Lenny and later with Sonny Koszela. We raced a lot at the Albany-Saratoga Speedway, at Utica-Rome, at Plattsburgh, and at the track they used to call Shangri-La Speedway, and we won at all those places.

Utica-Rome was a tight little bullring, a tough place to pass. Because of that, it wasn't the most enjoyable place to run, but it was

There were some places where I loved to win just because I considered them drivers' tracks. One was the Waterford Speedbowl. That's me and the Brady Bunch Pinto in '78. (Courtesy of Speedway Scene)

Albany-Saratoga was a pretty small race track, but it definitely was roomy enough to race on. This shot is from 1973. That's Eddie Flemke in the Judkins 2X and Jerry Cook on the bottom, and I'm working the outside.
(Mike Adaskaveg Photo)

part of our circuit back then so you did your best to get going well there. Albany-Saratoga wasn't much bigger, bit it *felt* roomier; it didn't have any fences, except along the front straightaway, and it just seemed like you had more elbow room. Plattsburgh, which was a short half-miler, was kind of quirky, because it had tight turns and a little bit of an uphill-downhill layout. And Shangri-La was just plain flat; it was one of the toughest places in the world to pass a guy, because if you wanted to get him on the outside you were going to have to hang out there all night and work him an inch at a time.

Still, all those places were a picnic compared to Islip, on Long Island. Geez, what a crazy place that was. It was the smallest place I've ever run a modified, and, to be honest, you had just enough time to burp the throttle, and already you were at the next corner. It was, *brrrrp*, turn, *brrrrp*, turn, *brrrrp*, turn. I raced there quite a bit, and I always ran pretty well, but it wasn't an enjoyable place to drive since you spent so much time banging bumpers. I had a hard time adapting to that, because for a while it felt like everybody else hit me more than I hit them. In the end, I figured out that you had to run those guys the way *they* ran *you*. I didn't intentionally run into anybody, but let's just say that I stopped trying so hard *not* to run into them. That was the law of the jungle at Islip.

Freeport Stadium, which isn't there anymore, was another tough Long Island track. It was run by the Campi family, which operated the big Cremosa Cheese company in town, and Sonny and I would go down there for big races like the Cremosa 100. Freeport was a shade bigger than Islip, so at least you had time to catch your breath once in a while. But Freeport was still a tough sonofabitch to get around. If you got out of there in one piece—and I had some decent runs there—you felt like you'd done good.

I've run several tracks down South, aside from Martinsville. Most of them I only ran once or twice and, to be honest, I don't remember all that much about 'em. But I ran a few times at Hickory, North Carolina, and I really enjoyed that place. I was running good there one day in 1977 with Joe Brady's car, maybe even good enough to win, until Geoff Bodine and I crashed in the pits, of all things. And I remember having a great run at Orange County, a beautiful track in Rougemont, North Carolina, when I finished second to Jeff Fuller. It's funny, but I first started going to all those Southern tracks in the late sixties, and twenty years later it was still fun to go down there and race.

In 1978, I won a feature at the New Smyrna Speedway in Florida, as part of the World Series program they hold every February during Speedweeks. It wasn't any big deal, just a 25-lapper, but once I won there I was able to say I'd won from Maine to Florida. New Smyrna is exactly what Martinsville would be if you banked Martinsville's turns: it's got a narrow groove, it's hard to run any way but single-file, and it's *fast*. It was tough to pass there, but it definitely had some speed to it.

There are a few tracks I've missed in this list, I'm sure, because my memory ain't what it used to be. I'm lucky I remembered this many.

But you know something? No matter where we were, I showed up ready. Strap in. Let's go.

This is going to sound crazy, because I started off this chapter talking about how the perfect track was small and not too fast, but I enjoyed the places where could really wring out a race car. You know, the *really* fast places.

I loved Trenton. I mean, absolutely loved it. I ran there when it was a one-mile oval, and I ran there after they added that dogleg in 1972, which lengthened it by another half-mile or so. The outer boundaries didn't change; the turns stayed the same, which meant that whether you're talking about the oval or the dogleg track, turns one and two were tighter and flatter, and turns three and four were like one big, fast sweeper.

One of the trickiest modified tracks ever, was Trenton, once it was lengthened in 1972. That's me in Sonny Koszela's Ford in '78, setting myself up for that crazy right-hand dogleg turn on the backstretch.
(Mike Adaskaveg Photo)

But the dogleg did more than just make the track longer; it made Trenton a completely different race track. As an oval, Trenton was fast but not too tricky, but with that right-hander it was insane. People don't realize what a sharp turn that dogleg actually was. It was also pretty blind, so you had to pray that there wasn't a car sitting there when you got to the other side. It probably wasn't the safest place to run modifieds, but I guess I never gave that much of a thought back then.

Man, that place would thrill you. The dogleg was weird, sure, but once you figured it out you'd just whistle through there and then sail right around turns three and four, with the throttle just about flat all the way. And that big 'ole sweeping corner was just bumpy enough to take your breath; the car would skate around and change lanes a little bit. I'm telling you, I had a ball there.

I won a 200-lapper at Trenton in 1967, when it was a mile, and came up just short twice on the extended track: in the '74 Race of Champions, which I lost by a couple of feet to Freddy DeSarro, and in the '78 Dogleg 200, when I ran out of gas with two laps to go while Richie Evans and I were fighting for the lead.

Langhorne Speedway, where they used to run the Race of Champions before they moved it to Trenton, was another place that kept you on your toes. It was a mile-long circle, and it scared the hell

A lot of guys were spooked by the big track at Pocono, but, man, I loved the speed. Here I'm hiking back after bouncing off the wall in Joe Brady's car in 1979. We'd been running well until somebody dumped a bunch of oil in front of us. (Courtesy of Speedway Scene*)*

out of some guys, but I took to it right away. I felt the same way when they ran the ROC on the 2.5-mile Pocono superspeedway for a few years in the late seventies; a lot of guys were against that move because the track was so fast, but I was comfortable right away. The first time I ran there was in 1977, with Sonny Koszela's Pinto, and right off the trailer we were absolutely flying. We were as quick as anybody there, and some of the guys had showed up with tricked-up, aerodynamic cars that should have left us in the dust. But as soon as I had convinced myself that we'd be in good shape, we blew the engine, and that was that. I ran the big Pocono track again in '79 with Joe Brady's car, and we were having a pretty decent run until I got into the oil from somebody else's blown engine and smacked the wall.

We also ran a few modified races on what everybody called the "little" track at Pocono, which wasn't very little; it was a three-quarter-mile, and it was fast. It had flat, sweeping turns, so you needed to have a good chassis, and naturally you needed a strong engine because the straightaways were long, by our standards. But you also needed a driver who would hang it out, because there were a couple of bumps there that would really thrill you.

We had a race there in 1973, the Coke 250, that ended up being a hell of a mess. When it was over I was sure I had won it, but at the same time Richie Evans was pretty sure that *he'd* won it. At first they

Pocono again, but this time on the infield three-quarter. This was the day I beat Richie Evans in the 1973 Coke 250, but almost lost the thing because the scoring was screwed up.
(R.N. Masser, Jr. Photo/Courtesy of Speedway Illustrated)

gave it to Richie, which I knew was wrong. What happened was, early on the penalized me a lap for passing under the yellow flag, which I hadn't done. Anyway, for most of the race I ran right with the leaders, and when I passed them all, Richie included, the scoreboard read like I was only getting my lap back. Five hours later, after I was long gone and Richie had gone through all the victory lane stuff, they finally figured out that I had actually won the thing.

I had another up-and-down day there in 1981, when they held the Race of Champions on the shorter Pocono track. I was driving Dick Armstrong's car, and it was on rails. I was biding my time early on, but I could tell that I had the best car there; I mean, I *knew* I was going to win that day. Then somebody gave me a hard shot from behind in traffic—Jerry Cook, I think it was—and that jolt broke my car's rear-end gears. That's a rare thing, but it happens. Just like that, we were out.

So even though I liked the three-quarter-miler at Pocono, I don't have fond memories of the place. Too many crazy things happened to me there.

But I guess the craziest place I ever ran a modified was on the road course at Daytona. NASCAR had the division there three times, from 1974 through '76, and I ran two of 'em. The one that really stands out was 1975, when I had a great run go bad in a hurry with the Koszela Vega. I had just passed Bobby Allison for the lead going through turn one when, *zing*, my RPMs shot right to the moon. Broken clutch. Done.

Looking back, it was kind of a strange thing to be running modifieds, cars built for Saturday-night ovals, on a big winding track that was half road course and half superspeedway. But, hell, I loved it. It

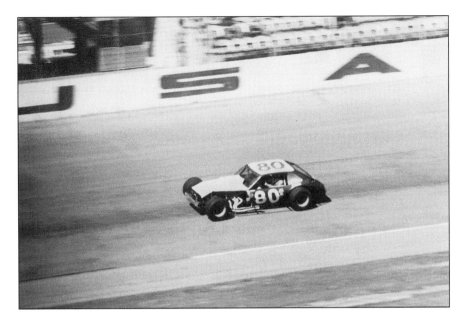

We used to run modifieds on the road course at Daytona, and the speeds we'd hit in the tri-oval might have been the highest we reached anywhere. Talk about crazy!
(Courtesy of Speedway Scene)

was different, and it was a challenge. And, of course, you had to really grit your teeth there, because the top speeds were quicker than anyplace else we raced at that time.

Maybe what I'm trying to say here is that a short, round track is perfect for staging a good modified race, but the perfect track for me, based on the joy I got from really standing on the gas, was anyplace big and fast.

Plus, I always felt like I had an edge at those places. Part of that, let's face it, was a bravery thing. At Trenton or Daytona or the big track at Pocono, a lot depended on how much courage you had. I think that's why, even though there were lots of guys who rolled into those places with great motors and great cars, the same small group always seemed to be up front. There were some drivers who just weren't comfortable there, and you could see that.

I looked at all those fast tracks with the same basic philosophy I used at the small ones, which is this: When it comes right down to it, it doesn't matter much if you like the track or not. If that's where you've got to run, you'd better *learn* to like it.

Otherwise, you're going to get your doors blown off. And I never liked getting my doors blown off.

"Humpy" Wheeler on Bugsy

H.A. "Humpy" Wheeler, president, Lowe's Motor Speedway, Charlotte, NC: "Bugsy was one of the best race drivers I've ever seen. That modified division during his day was one of the toughest in the country. They ran a variety of tracks, from Islip to Trenton, and the competition was fierce.

"In 1970, I was with one of the major tire companies, and we brought Bugs in to run a test for us [with a Winston Cup car], just out of curiosity. The late Ronny Householder was in charge of Chrysler's racing teams, and he scowled at the thought of putting this interloper into one of his cars. But before the day was over, Bugs had broken the track record.

"(Later) he got a ride for World 600 at Charlotte. He finished sixth. It was a strong showing.

"I told Bugs he really was nuts if he didn't move down here and go racing at the highest level of NASCAR. I told him that he obviously had the talent. 'You don't understand,' he told me. 'I can't. It's my junkyard.'

"I got to checking around, and Bugs owned one of the best-operated junkyards in the country, back home in Massachusetts. It was so successful that he couldn't take the cut in income that running down here would have meant (in the early 1970s).

"The problem he had, back in his time, was that it was difficult for well-established guys like him to break away from their local racing, where the bucks were good, and come down here and eat beans for a couple of years until they became one of the frontrunners in Winston Cup. I liken him in this respect to Dick Trickle; they were both great drivers in their day who definitely would have made it on the top levels [under different circumstances].

"And so the ride Bugsy might have been put in (a Cotton Owens Plymouth) went instead to another New England driver, Pete Hamilton (who scored 11 top-five finishes with it in 1971).

"With Bugsy's color—he reminds me of a cigar-chomping cross between actors Aldo Ray and Mickey Rooney—and his driving ability, I have no doubt that he could have become one of the sport's biggest stars. A smash. I think he definitely could have cracked the top seven or eight, all-time, in Winston Cup.

"Oh, I wish we had him today, with his flair for showmanship and his rugged appeal to fans."

The Big Leagues

"Humpy" Wheeler, Lowes Motor Speedway, 2000. *(Courtesy of* Speedway Illustrated*)*

The Big Leagues

The Big Leagues

AFTER I WON those three NASCAR modified championships, my old Seekonk Speedway rival and friend Bobby Sprague introduced me to Ralph Moody. Well, let's back up a minute; whenever I tell these old stories, I have to remember that a lot of people who follow racing today don't know all the names and places we're talking about.

Ralph Moody was half of Holman-Moody, which through the sixties and early seventies was basically the stock car racing arm of the Ford Motor Company. Holman-Moody was housed in a huge complex in Charlotte; if you passed by the place and didn't know a thing about it, you'd have wondered what kind of industry might be housed in a facility that large. It looked nothing at all like a race shop, until you started snooping around. Then you'd see frames and roll cages being built in one area, and engines being built in another, and the cars of all the Ford factory drivers—David Pearson, A.J. Foyt, Parnelli Jones, Fred Lorenzen, Dick Hutcherson, Mario Andretti—being worked on in another section.

John Holman was Ralph Moody's partner. Holman was the business brain, and Ralph was the racing brain. The two of them had built an empire; they found the mechanics, they developed and nurtured the drivers, they guided the whole NASCAR effort for Ford.

Ralph originally came out of Massachusetts, and from the thirties right up through the fifties he was a crackerjack driver in midgets and the jalopy-type stock cars that eventually turned into modifieds. Once he stopped driving, he earned himself a great reputation as a car builder and a chassis man. When it came to anything related to stock cars, Ralph Moody was a craftsman.

It's kind of a complicated thing, but Ralph had kept an eye on me for a few years. He still had some family in New England, including a sister who followed short-track racing and had become a fan of mine. I never even met the lady, to the best of my knowledge, but apparently she bragged me up to her brother. Then I guess Ralph asked some of his old racing buddies from back home about me, and he heard some good things.

Anyway, after that 1969 championship Ralph told me I ought to move down to Charlotte. He said he'd give me a job sweeping floors and doing odd jobs at Holman-Moody until a Winston Cup ride became available. What he was doing, really, was opening the door to the big time. Not offering me a sure thing, by any means, but opening the door at least a crack for me.

Ralph Moody was the first guy down there who paid any real attention to me, and he was *somebody*, so I gave a lot of weight to what he said. But at that point in my life, I was still very big into that whole security thing. Again, it all goes back to my childhood, to my father, and me hearing him constantly worry about money. His voice still rang in my head: "*The bills have to be paid. What about the mortgage? The bills have to be paid ...*"

Even back then, the Winston Cup guys made bigger money than us short-trackers, no question. But there wasn't the giant gap you see today between what they make and what a modified guy makes. Today, a guy who runs in the middle of the Winston Cup pack every Sunday is a millionaire, and the best short-track guys would eat beans every night if they depended on their winnings. But in 1970, the money the average Cup guy was earning wasn't *that* much bigger than what we could make racing close to home, certainly not so much bigger that you'd just throw away everything you'd worked for.

My salvage business was just a few years old, and doing very well. On top of that, I had been racing four nights a week in the modifieds, and winning my share, so I was making good money. I'll bet I was putting a grand a week into my pocket just out of the racing. That was pretty strong money in 1969, 1970. Doris and I had three children by then—Carl, ZoeAnn, and David—so there were plenty of bills to pay, but I was doing all right.

To accept Ralph's offer, I'd have been giving up a lot in exchange for a minimum-wage job at Holman-Moody, and a chance, just a *chance*, that some seat might open up down the road. And here came Dad's voice again: "*How are you going to afford a mortgage? Who buys the food for the wife and kids?*"

In the end, it just didn't seem worth it to me to take that shot. I told Ralph Moody thanks, but no thanks.

It's funny, because all my life I've been taking risks: steering tractors on the farm when I was just a boy, playing football, driving those early race cars with their flimsy roll cages. I never thought I was scared of anything. But going out on a limb financially scared the hell out of me. The salvage yard and the modifieds were a sure thing, so that's the way I went.

Of course, if the money had been like it is today in Winston Cup, I'd have jumped at Ralph's offer in a heartbeat. Sure thing or not, I'd have been gone like a rocket.

This was in a time when a lot of guys from the Northeast were just starting to look South, toward Winston Cup and Daytona. Don MacTavish and Pete Hamilton had both made that move, and I think their initial success opened a few eyes in our neck of the woods. Pete won the NASCAR national sportsman championship in 1967, and immediately jumped to Winston Cup and was the Rookie of the Year in 1968; Mac had mixed a bunch of late model races into his modified schedule in '68, and he was obviously going places.

I watched what those guys were doing in that period, and I was really happy for both of them. They were two guys I'd raced with quite a bit, and we were all friends. Not that we hung out constantly, but we were definitely friends.

Peter was a Boston boy, an educated guy who came from an educated family; his father was the dean of the business school at Northeastern University in Boston. He came up through the hobby cars at Norwood, and once he started running modifieds he was sort of taken in by Eddie Flemke; I used to say that Pete was one of Eddie's disciples, because Eddie really took the kid under his wing. Pete was a quiet young guy who was more into focusing on his race car than on socializing, but I liked him.

Don MacTavish also took his racing very seriously, but he was more of a party guy than Pete was. Donnie and I had a few beers together when the two of us were chasing points all over the country.

Those two guys were very focused on pointing their careers toward Winston Cup. I could tell just from talking to them that they were really into climbing that ladder. They gave that stuff a lot more thought than I was giving it in the late sixties, I know that. But, like I said, I respected both of them, and in my heart I wished them well.

It's crazy, considering how close their careers seemed to be running, the way things worked out so differently for the two of them. Hamilton got hooked up with Petty Enterprises and won the Daytona 500 in 1970, and that put him on the map forever. MacTavish was on his way to being a star, too, when he showed up at Daytona in 1969 for the Permatex 300 late model sportsman race. Then he ended up getting into a horrible crash, and, bang, he was gone.

One guy dies, the other guy becomes a star. Like I said: crazy.

The whole time Hamilton and MacTavish were getting their careers rolling down South, I'd watch how they did and try to gauge myself against them. I'd think, OK, if they're doing this or that, that means *I* could do this or that, too. I wasn't jealous or envious in any way, but I'd watch those guys, and I was pretty confident that I could do the things they were doing. It was just something I'd think about.

You've got to understand, by then Lenny and I had done a little bit of superspeedway racing, and we had learned a little bit about late model-type cars. We'd hung onto that old Ford we brought to Atlanta at the end of 1966, and Lenny made some modifications to it. Every year between 1967 and 1969, we hauled that thing down to Daytona to run the Permatex race.

The first time we went down there, we thought we were pretty slick. I mean, Boehler and I figured we knew everything. Then Ralph Moody came strolling along, and he showed exactly how much we *didn't* know about racing at Daytona. He taught us a few things about the chassis, gave us some tips about the engine—I remember him explaining to Lenny which jets to run in the carburetor—and even passed on a few secrets about aerodynamics. Those old cars were so big and boxy compared to the Winston Cup and Busch cars today, but there were things the smart guys would do to help them cut through the wind. They'd play with the angle of their windshields, change the rooflines, and do all kinds of subtle things that would get you thrown out of the NASCAR inspection line today.

When you spend enough time around tracks where every little thing counts, like Ralph had, you learn all those tricks. I'll give you a couple of examples.

The safety straps we had to run outside the windshield were held in place by these aluminum bolts that had tiny little heads on them. Well, Ralph took one look at those bolts and shook his head. He made us go out and get some new bolts with smaller heads, and even that

Here's a couple 1969 snapshots of the old Ford that Lenny Boehler and I ran in a few of those Daytona Permatex 300 races. Check out our sponsors: Freetown Auto and Norwood Arena! (RA Silvia Collection)

wasn't enough; once the bolts were in, he had us grind the heads down to almost nothing. Less wind resistance, he said. Now, you look at a big 1964 Ford back in the days when the bodies were almost completely stock, and you'd think the last thing in the world you'd worry about was streamlining the bolts on the windshield straps. But Moody figured every little bit helped, and of course he was absolutely correct.

Later on, between practice sessions, Ralph came over again. Keep in mind, he was pretty busy with everything he had going on in the Winston Cup garage, but he kept walking over to check on us. He said, "If you boys want to go faster yet, have somebody wax that car all day. I mean, wax it *good*. Then rub some talcum powder all over the body. It'll make the car slicker."

It sounded crazy, but you know something? It worked. All the Winston Cup teams powdered up their cars back then.

Hell, Ralph even helped me as a driver. I had run a few practice laps, and my speeds weren't exactly setting the woods on fire. I figured it was the car. Moody figured it was me. Turned out he was right.

You ask anybody about his first few laps around Daytona, and he'll tell you the same thing: You look down those long straightaways, and you don't think there's any way you can make it around that next corner without backing out of the throttle. Even if you've been told that it's easy to run the place flat out, it's almost impossible to believe that. So you lift a bit. *Everybody* does. It's human instinct. If a driver tells you he ran around Daytona on his first hot lap and never backed off, he's lying. I wasn't lifting much, but I *was* lifting.

Well, I was getting ready to go out and practice some more, and Moody pulled me aside.

"Tell me the truth, Bugs," he said. "Are you lifting out there?"

I said, "Nope. I'm just *feathering* it just a bit."

Ralph said, "Well, stop that. You don't feather anything around here. Once you shift into fourth gear going out of the pits, get wide open and *stay* wide open."

Then he said, "If you have to, take your left foot and put it over your right foot and *hold* it down. And don't you lift off that throttle until you see me holding up a pit board telling you to come in."

So that's what I did: I got that Ford running wide open, and then I literally slid my left foot over my right and kept it there for a whole lap. That throttle never left the floorboard. Just like that, I had figured out Daytona.

It's funny how the mind works. Once you convince yourself that you really *can* go around that joint wide open, it's a breeze. It's automatic.

I ended up finishing 10th in my first Permatex 300.

We never had any great results down there, but we did all right. We could hang around the top 10 against guys who knew that game a lot better than we did.

For a guy who only messed with the superspeedways for a couple of weeks a year, Boehler always had the car running well. And as a driver, I felt like I did my job, too. Once I got the hang of those heavy cars, and once I understood that you really could haul around Daytona wide open, I never felt like I was out of my element.

I always climbed into the car knowing—inside, where a driver has to know it—that I could handle that kind of racing.

Once you get that feeling, I guess it's hard to shake. I guess that's the best way to explain why, even after I turned down Ralph Moody's offer, I ended up taking a shot at Winston Cup racing anyway in 1970.

It started when somebody put Lenny Boehler and me in touch with a guy from Daytona named Richard Brown, who wanted to be a big-time car owner. I went down there to see him, and it was obvious that he had some money; he was in the rest-home business in that area, and he lived in a big house on the water. He was kind of a flashy dude: alligator boots, fancy suits, the whole nine yards.

I can't tell you for sure why he zeroed in on me, other than the fact that those three modified championships had given me a pretty good national name. I guess if you wanted to look past the drivers who were already in Winston Cup, and bring in a guy from the outside, I was as good as any of them.

In February of 1970, he had me come to Daytona to drive a late-model sportsman for him in the Permatex 300 at Daytona. I was a little bit surprised when the ride turned out to be an old Cotton Owens dirt car. I'm not talking about a brand-new dirt car that had been adapted for pavement; you could still get away with that, barely, in that era. I'm talking about a car that had actually raced on dirt. They'd done a little bit of patchwork to slick it up for Daytona, but it was what it was: a dirt car.

When I rolled it off pit road for the first practice session and got it up to speed, the inside of the car was a cloud of dust from the last time it had run on some clay track. I had dust in my eyes, dust on the windshield, dust everywhere. I thought, What the hell have I gotten myself into?

Needless to say, we didn't impress anybody that whole week at Daytona.

But Richard Brown wanted to go Winston Cup racing, and he

The first time I drove for Richard Brown, we entered this Plymouth in the 1970 Permatex 300. Cotton Owens had actually run it in some Winston Cup dirt-track shows in previous years, and it sure wasn't the hot ticket at Daytona.
(Courtesy of Speedway Illustrated)

talked a great game. I don't mean that to sound the wrong way, because he was a nice enough guy, and his intentions were good. I'm just not sure he knew how big a bite he was taking by trying to go racing at that level. Even as new to all that stuff as I was, I thought he was way over his head.

But Brown figured he was solid. He thought he had a big sponsor lined up—he was chasing Coca-Cola, as I recall—and he had bought a Plymouth Superbird from Bill Ellis; it was actually the same car Richard Brickhouse had won with at Talladega in 1969. We were going to run a limited schedule, and see how things developed from there.

Brown's plan was that Ellis would supply the crew for our first race together, the World 600 at Charlotte in May, and then Boehler would come in to run the show. It sounded like a dream to a couple of Yankees like us. I mean, Lenny and I had high, high hopes.

Anyway, off I went to Charlotte in May. I was obviously a little bit of a new guy, but I did know quite a few guys on the Winston Cup circuit. Pete Hamilton was an old friend, and he had really become big down there, because he had just won the Daytona 500. I knew both Bobby and Donnie Allison a little bit from the modified racing we had done together, and I had passing acquaintances with guys like Cale Yarborough and Buddy Baker and Richard Petty. The modifieds raced in conjunction with the Winston Cup cars quite a bit back then, especially at Martinsville, so those guys had seen me around.

"Yankee," they all called me.

Except the ones who really knew me. Those guys called me "Crazy Yankee."

We had a pretty decent car at Charlotte, in terms of speed—we qualified 17th—but it was a bear to drive. It had no power steering and a big ole' 426-cubic-inch hemi engine, but none of that stuff bothered me; I was used to wrestling cars with more horsepower than that. What I had a hard time getting used to was the handling. Ellis had put a ton of castor split into the front end, and what that does is make the car pull to the left. That's an old oval-track trick that's supposed to make a car easier to drive, but he had gone way overboard. It took two hands tugging hard to the right at all times just to keep that thing halfway straight.

Ralph Moody was a Ford guy, and I was running a Plymouth, so he wasn't in a position to help me. But I remember him telling me that with the setup I was running, my guys must have been trying to kill me.

And during the World 600, they almost succeeded.

You want to know what hell feels like? It feels like four and a half hours in a bad Winston Cup car on a hot Sunday afternoon, with the cockpit temperature up around 120 degrees and no cool-suits or air blowers to keep the air moving. It's a good thing I worked out every day; if I hadn't been in such good shape, that damn car probably would have finished me off.

Before the race, one of those guys—I think it was Cale—was teasing me about how tough the World 600 was. He grinned and said, "Yankee, you may make 500 miles, but you'll never make 600. All of us have a hard time with that extra 100." And he was right. Donnie Allison, who was the official winner, actually got out of his car and let LeeRoy Yarbrough drive it the last 70 miles or so, and Tiny Lund, who finished fourth, was relieved by Dick Brooks. If I'd had any sense, I'd have probably bailed out, too, but I was too stubborn, too proud, to quit.

The muscles in both my forearms went into spasm about halfway through the race, and then tightened up—I mean, just shrunk to nothing—with 50 laps to go. Then, with 10 to go, the muscles around my right elbow short-circuited and went dead. I'd driven a thousand races by then, and never had anything like that ever happened. I still think it was because I was having to do so many weird things just to keep the car straight.

I drove those last 10 laps using my left arm to literally punch my right, pounding the hell out of it all the way around the track, just trying to shock those muscles back to life. At the same time, I was trying to keep that beast between the grass on the left and the concrete wall on the right. I wasn't going to give up.

We finished sixth, but it wasn't a brilliant sixth. Lots of cars broke down in those days; you didn't see 15 cars on the lead lap like you do today. Donnie beat Cale by two laps to win the thing, and I was eight laps down. Pete Hamilton finished eighth, and he was 12 laps down. The funny thing was, Pete was fast, but he'd had some mechanical problems, so he was in and out of the pits a lot. Later on, the two of us joked that he'd passed me seven or eight times, and I'd beaten him anyway.

I don't think I was ever as happy to see a checkered flag as I was that day at Charlotte. When I pulled back into the garage area, I sat in that car for a good five minutes, drinking from a big cup of water, trying to get a little bit of my strength back. When I thought I had recovered enough to at least walk over to the workbench, I climbed out the window, put my feet on the pavement, and, bam, I fell right to the ground. I had no legs under me, nothing at all. The lower half of my body was asleep, completely numb.

It was one hell of a first day on the job.

I had no doubt that I'd be a better Winston Cup driver by the time we ran our next race, and I had no doubt that Lenny Boehler would get my car driving better. What I did start to doubt before too long, though, was the rest of our operation.

Lenny and I ended up living in Florida off and on for a couple of months, working without any sophisticated equipment in what was basically a two-car garage. None of Richard Brown's big sponsor dreams had panned out, and he was struggling to fund the whole thing out of his own wallet. Honestly, I'd seen a lot of modified and late-model sportsman teams that had more stuff to work with, and more manpower, than we had at that little shop in Daytona.

We got the car ready for our next race, which wasn't until August at Atlanta, and we were at a point where there wasn't anything left for Lenny and I to do. So the two of us came home, me to look after the salvage yard and Lenny to get caught up with his modifieds. Brown had lined up some volunteer pit crewmen for the race, and they were going to haul the thing to Atlanta, where we'd meet them.

Well, Lenny and I showed up on time, but the car did not. When it finally materialized a day or two later, I met my new crew, which was basically a group of Brown's friends who didn't know much about racing. I described that gang in a magazine story one time as a bunch of "old men and preachers and teachers and bankers," and I'll stick with that. They were good guys, but they sure weren't a race team.

Boehler worked a little bit of his magic on that car, and I managed to qualify 16th. But not even Lenny Boehler could make chicken salad out of chicken shit, which was about all we had to work with. We went 24 laps on race day before the engine blew itself all to pieces.

All things considered, it was a mercy killing.

We went to Darlington in September for the Southern 500, and things hadn't gotten any better. Because that race was such a big deal, they used to let you practice for the better part of a week. Well, again our car showed up a couple days late. The first thing every driver talks about when he mentions Darlington is how tough it is to learn, and here we were, a rookie team, spotting everybody all that practice time.

In 1970 I drove this winged Superbird in three Winston Cup races, but it wasn't a competitive situation. In the end, I went back to what I knew, which was the modifieds. (Berghman Family Collection)

We qualified 25th, but I'm sure we'd have been higher if Lenny and I had more time to figure that place out.

The race itself was a disaster. At the start, my tires were so out of balance that the car was trying to shake itself to pieces. That's the sort of thing that just doesn't happen to good race teams. But when you've only got one solid guy looking after the car itself and you leave the rest of the show up to volunteers, these are the kinds of problems you get. The vibration was so violent that I honestly could not read the gauges on the dashboard; my vision was too blurred. And it's amazing that I didn't bite my tongue off, the way my teeth were chattering. I'm not trying to pat myself on the back, but you wouldn't believe a guy could drive a race car that was so bad.

Of course, I only drove it for 42 laps, until another engine exploded on us.

I remember standing in the Darlington garage area and realizing that I was wasting my time. Even back then, there was an enormous gap between the haves and the have-nots at the Winston Cup level. I'd look at what Lenny and I had at our disposal, and it was hard not to drool when I glanced over at the Petty Enterprises outfit, or at the Wood Brothers, or the Holman-Moody team.

I still had hopes. I still had dreams. But I was smart enough to know that you couldn't win at that level without a lot of money we didn't have.

And when you're used to winning, hopes and dreams aren't enough.

So Boehler and I left Darlington, and we never went back. We came home and focused on what we knew, which was modified racing. The big story that year was that Freddy DeSarro won the NASCAR modified championship driving for Sonny Koszela, but Boehler and I won a bunch of races and had ourselves a lot of fun.

I never once viewed that move—jumping back to the modifieds—as a failure or a demotion. It wasn't until the second half of the seventies, when Winston Cup really started coming on strong, that we started looking up to those guys a little bit. Even then, it probably took several more years before a lot of us realized they were any bigger than we were. We still thought we had the ultimate form of racing. We were modified racers, man. That was *it*.

Everybody always asks if I regret the way things worked out for me, as far as the Winston Cup stuff goes. Well, my quick answer is usually no, because I'm happy with the racing and the winning I've done. But, sure, there's a touch of regret there, just because I wonder sometimes what might have been.

Over the years, a lot of other drivers to͟ ͟ ͟ ͟ody up on offers like the one he made me. Ca͟l͟ ͟ ͟ ͟of them. Cale was a hungry young guy sweep͟ ͟ ͟ ͟loody, and when Fred Lorenzen retired from ͟ ͟ ͟ ͟to the seat. The record books tell us Cale ͟ ͟

I'll say this: I never once felt like W͟ thing I couldn't do. If I'd had the right co͟ backing, good people—it would have worke͟ er or later. I *know* that.

There's no question in my mind that I could hav͟ there. No question at all.

Bill Slater on Bugsy

Bill Slater, legendary modified driver and official: "There's a million Bugsy stories. Where do you start? What about the time Firestone was testing tires at Stafford when I worked there? Bobby Summers, who handles Hoosier tires today, was working for Firestone back then. Bugsy was the big Firestone driver, so he did the test. Well, after they were done, we're all standing around. Naturally, one thing leads to another, and before you know it, there's a party going on. A tire test turns into a six-hour party! But that's how it was. If the races ended at 10:30 at night, you could check the parking lot at 5:00 in the morning and he'd still be there, him and all his friends.

"Bugsy was voted the most popular modified driver in NASCAR [in 1971 and '72]. Well, his fan club people held a party for him in Pawtucket, Rhode Island, to celebrate that award. I didn't want to go, because we had a big race at Stafford the next day, but I was basically forced to go; his fan club made a big deal out of me being there. So I go, and we have dinner, and we present Bugsy with this plaque or this trophy or whatever it was, and now it's getting late. It's turning into a wild affair. The whole time, all I keep thinking is, I've got to be up at 6:00 in the morning to get ready for this race at Stafford. So I finally managed to leave, but what I remember is that Bugsy was still going strong. He was the life of the party. That's what made Bugsy such a big deal: He won a lot of races, and he was always ready to party.

"A lot of race drivers used to be hell-raisers. It's not that way today, but it was true when Bugsy was racing. Now, not all of us were like that; I drove race cars for years, and I was never that way. I never raised hell. Chase women, yes, but raise hell, no. I never drank, and none of my crew did either. And there were other guys later on who were the same way: Fred DeSarro, Eddie Flemke, those guys didn't party. But there were guys like Bugsy and Richie Evans who definitely knew how to party.

"The thing about Bugsy was, he always had people around him that were as crazy as he was. Let's face it, you can't party by yourself. He had a few different people who ran his fan club over the years, and some of those guys were wacky. So when Bugsy got done racing for the night, he'd just get together with those guys, and they were already partying. And he always drove for people who liked to party: Lenny Boehler was like that, and later on Sonny Koszela.

"At some of the bigger races, every night was a party. At Martinsville in the spring, everybody stayed up all night partying together because some of them hadn't seen each other since October. One night at the Dutch Inn, a bunch of people were up on the second floor, drinking beer all night. Well, what do you do with all the empty beer cans? You throw them down, that's what. Charlie Jarzombek had his ramp truck backed up to the motel, just

Fast Times

From the left: Richie Evans, Ron Bouchard, Bugs Stevens, and Bill Slater, New Smyrna Speedway, 1978. (Courtesy of Speedway Scene)

below the balcony, and all those empty cans went right into the back window of his race car. At Langhorne and Trenton, you'd be down there for four or five days, and it always got wild. They'd burn down the outhouses at the race track, they'd party in the parking lots, they'd party in the hotels. Bugsy was usually in the middle of all that.

"The thing about those big races was, everybody came in from different areas. You had the New York people, the Long Island people, the New Jersey people, the New England people. Back then, you only saw all those people together two or three times a year, usually at Martinsville and the Race of Champions, so it would be like a big reunion.

"The Thompson 300, when it first got started, had that same atmosphere. See, I worked at Thompson then, and we had qualifying races at all these different tracks around the Northeast, where the winner was a guaranteed starter in the 300. I used to go to Danbury, to Claremont, to Monadnock, everywhere, passing out flyers and giving out the trophies at those qualifying races. Well, when the 300 came around, all the people from those little tracks came to see how their guy did in the big race, and while they were there they partied all weekend.

"That sort of feeling is gone. NASCAR doesn't let you run qualifying races, so now you don't have a bunch of people coming just because they know their hero is going to be in the race. So the party is gone, too.

"Bugsy definitely came along at the right time. I'm not sure a guy like him would fit in today. He was a Jekyll-and-Hyde kind of person. You know, he was a serious racer. He wouldn't have won all the races he won if he wasn't a serious racer. But I think that's the only time Bugsy was serious. After that, it was party time."

Fast Times

Fast Times

(Rene Dugas Photo)

EVEN TODAY, all these years after I was in my heyday, the one thing everybody always wants to talk about is the hell-raising. Wherever I go, I get that; we'll talk about the racing for a while, but before long somebody's asking me if things were really as crazy in the sixties and seventies as all the old stories claim.

Well, it's like this: a lot of those old stories are absolutely true, but some of them are way out of whack, totally over-exaggerated.

For example, there was one silly story that got around about a night at the Dutch Inn, where a bunch of us used to stay when we raced at Martinsville. Supposedly, there was this bunch of crazy Canadian guys and girls partying in a room near mine, drinking day and night, and somebody ended up betting me that I wouldn't walk into the hotel's fancy dining room escorting one of those drunken Canadian girls. And, supposedly, we actually did stroll in together, at the height of the dinner hour.

With her on my shoulders.

Absolutely nude.

Okay, so that one story was true.

(Berghman Family Collection)

I guess there's no way to reflect on my career without looking back at the fun times. It all figures into the big picture.

No matter what I was doing in life, I did it hard. Work hard, play hard, party hard. I've always been that way, clear back to my days in high school and college sports. If we were playing football, I wanted to run right over you. If I was pitching a baseball game, I wanted to throw three fastballs right past you. I'd battle you right to the end, with everything I had. But win or lose, I'd shake your hand, and then I'd want to sit back and talk about the game and have a laugh. Later, I carried that same attitude right into my racing.

I was always big on camaraderie. That's something that we've lost over the years, I think, that sense of genuine camaraderie. What we had was truly special. Three, four, five nights a week, a bunch of us would go out and race each other as hard as we could, and when the feature ended it felt like the night was only half over. Most of the driv-

To me, the camaraderie was an important aspect of racing. Even waiting for a feature to start, it was natural for guys like Ronnie Bouchard and Leo Cleary and me to shoot the breeze.
(Courtesy of Speedway Scene)

ers, owners, mechanics and crew guys would hang out, bullshit about the race, and talk about the *next* race. It was natural, casual thing. It was just part of racing.

At Seekonk in my earliest days, we'd all end up in the parking lot, eating steamed clams and drinking beer. It was a big social scene every Saturday night. When I moved up to Norwood Arena and NASCAR, it was the same scene with different people. Hell, Norwood had a full-fledged bar right there on the property, and after the races the drivers and mechanics would pile in there and mix with the fans. It was a great atmosphere, and I loved it.

And wherever I went after that—from Oxford Plains up in Maine all the way down to Daytona Beach—things were pretty much the same. If there was a party going on, I wanted to be in on it. A lot of times, I was the party.

Twenty-five years ago, somebody said to me, "If we're looking for you, all we've got to do is find for a crowd of people." And that was true. I always had a gang around me. I'm not sure why that was; some people just naturally become the leaders of their own bands, I guess.

We weren't exactly *wild*. It's not like we went around doing stupid things, the kind of stuff that would hurt somebody. We just liked to have fun, and get a little crazy. I was never aware of anybody being officially tested, but I guess we had a few folks around who were pretty close to being certifiably insane. Me included sometimes.

I never apologized for living that way, and I'm not sorry about any of it now.

Look, when it was time to race, I *raced*. I think I accomplished enough in my career to prove that I had my priorities in order. But to me, there was more to life than just winning the next 100-lapper. Sure,

You've got to enjoy life. Here's a bunch of us studying a pro football handbook. If you think the girl on the cover was a knockout, you should have seen the rest of the squad!
(Burton E. Gould, Jr. Photo/ Courtesy of Speedway Scene)

I wanted to win it if I could, but it wasn't the single most important thing in the world. I've said this forever: Life is short. You might as well enjoy it. And I did.

Each track had its own little party routine. At one place, we might hang around all night right there in the pits. At another one, we might all load up our cars and meet out in the parking lot. Someplace else, we might go to the same gin mill every week.

When we used to run up at Catamount, after the races a bunch of us would head down to a steak house owned by Ken Squier and Tom Curley. I drank a lot of beer there, had a lot of laughs. There was always a good mix of guys in that place: Vermont racers, New York racers, Canadian racers, and a handful of us from down in Massachusetts and Connecticut.

Not far from Thompson Speedway, on the shores of Lake Webster, there used to be a saloon called Waterfront Mary's. The woman who ran that joint, Mary, was a tough old gal. She had been a dancing girl in her younger years, and even when she was 60 years old she'd walk around in these skimpy little outfits. But, let me tell you, she ran one hell of a barroom. If you got me and Fats Caruso and our pals in there after the races, stand back, because there was going to be some fun.

Waterfront Mary's had a dock out back, and one night I did a running belly flop off the thing, clothes and all. Well, a week or two later, Billy Schultz decided he wanted to jump into the lake, too. There were two problems there: Billy had had way too much to drink, and he executed a nice dive instead of a belly flop. He went straight down into thaqt shallow water, and the poor guy broke his neck. Luckily, Freddy made a full recovery. We marked him down as one of our rare casualties.

Generally speaking, nobody ever got *too* far out of control. Once in a while, somebody might get a little stupid and start a fight, and every now and then one group would forget to nominate a designated driver and pay the price for that. I remember one modified team hauling out of Martinsville, heading back to New England, and they never even made it out of the county before they flipped the whole rig. There might have been a few beers involved in that adventure. But for the most part, we all got home in one piece every week.

Luckily, I always seemed to stop just short of getting into any real trouble. Whenever the party appeared to start getting out of hand, I'd be the one guy who slipped away just before the cops showed up. What saved me there, I guess, was the same sixth sense that used to help me avoid crashes on the race track. Because, when I look back at it, everybody we ran around with got carted off in handcuffs at least once.

But not me. I never woke up in jail.

I did, however, wake up a time or two with absolutely no idea where I was.

What's life without a few practical jokes?
(Tim Christopher Photo/ Courtesy of Speedway Scene)

For years, the bigger the race was, the bigger the party was. One reason for that was, for most of us the major races—Martinsville, Trenton, Daytona—were pretty far from home. And whenever you're out of your neighborhood, you tend to stick together, eat together, party together. Boys will be boys.

And another reason was that for a lot of diehard modified fans, those journeys to Martinsville or to the Race of Champions were their only extended road trips of the year, their only chances to really let their hair down. Don't forget, these were regular average working people. All year long, they did their nine-to-five jobs every day, and then they'd go watch us at Stafford or Albany-Saratoga, but they didn't get many opportunities to hang out with our hardcore racing crowd. So when they went to these big shows, they'd hit the ground running wide open, and then they'd hook up with a few of us who were *always* wide open.

Most of the time, when you heard about a motel room getting turned upside down or something like that, it wasn't done by the guys who were in town to compete in the event. It was all those crazy cusses who ran around with us, looking to raise hell.

At Martinsville, Jerry Capozzoli, a friend of ours who drove modifieds and mini-stocks back home but used to come to the bigger races strictly for the good times, was terrorizing one of the hotels with his mini-bike. He was zooming around the parking lot and up and down the hallways. At one point, when the cops were looking for him, he shut off the engine, snuck the mini-bike into the restaurant, and hid it under his table as he sat pretending to wait for his meal. I think he finally rode the damn thing into the pool.

Another year in Martinsville, I was sitting quietly in the dining room at the Dutch Inn, enjoying my dinner with the rest of the innocent people, and I was surprised, completely *shocked*, to learn that some folks had dug a bunch of shrubs out of the hotel's landscaping and relocated them all to Lenny Boehler's room. He found bushes placed around the bed, on the TV set, everywhere. A few fingers got pointed in my direction, as if I was the mastermind behind the whole thing, but I had absolutely nothing to do with it.

That's my story, and I'm sticking to it.

All this stuff was just harmless fun, as long as you understood that there were certain limits. Some of us went through enough of this nonsense that we were basically trained professionals. It was the amateurs who kept getting themselves into trouble.

Over the years, three or four of my friends ended up in divorce court from trying to keep up with me. These were intelligent, white-collar guys with solid lives, but they'd spend a couple weekends following me around, and pretty soon that's all they wanted to do. They just couldn't stand to be sitting home with the little lady, I guess, while the rest of us were out having such a great time.

I had a bunch of different running buddies in those hell-raising days. Honestly, who I hung around with kind of depended on the year, and even on who I was driving for, because generally I'd get the crew involved. It was kind of a revolving pack; a couple new guys dropped out of sight, and a couple new guys came along to fill those shoes.

As far as the other drivers, Bobby Santos raised a lot of hell in those days. That damn Frito Bandito—that's what we called Bobby, because he always had a long moustache like the Fritos guy—was always right in the thick of things. Around the race track, he was a little bit more quiet than some of us, so he never got a real partying reputation. But, I'm telling you, Santos was a cuckoo clock. He and I had an awful lot of laughs up and down the East Coast.

And, of course, everybody knows Richie Evans was nuts. Richie was a lot like me: he'd party win or lose. Sure, he'd be happier when he won, but losing wasn't going to stop him from enjoying the rest of the night.

A lot of people thought Bobby Santos was a pretty quiet guy, but that was an act. The Frito Bandito was as crazy as any of us.
(Burton E. Gould Photo/ Courtesy of Speedway Scene)

Most times, we ran with our own separate crowds; Richie had his New York bunch, and I had my New England gang. But we definitely did our share of hanging around together. Sometimes it was just a quiet beer and a long talk after a race, and sometimes it was something a little bit louder.

In Daytona, there was a barber pole on the side of Route 92, the main drag from the beach out to the Speedway. Every day for years, we all drove past that pole. It was just part of the scenery.

Well, at two o'clock in the morning, my phone rings. It's Richie.

"We got that barber pole," he says. "Took it right off the sidewalk. It's in the back of our truck. You've got to come out and see this."

Sure enough, they had stolen that barber pole. Took it right out of the ground, wires and all. None of them had a damn clue what they were going to do with it, or *why* they'd stolen it, except that it seemed like a fun thing to do.

The best part of the story was, the next morning the pole was gone. Somebody else spotted that thing in the back of Richie's pickup truck, and grabbed it up. And that was probably just as well, because by then the theft of this landmark barber pole was big news. The cops were looking everywhere for that thing.

Richie was crazier than I was, believe me. He and his guys had a contraption that was basically a tennis-ball cannon. They'd pack some kind of stuff down into a long cylinder – gunpowder, I guess – and drop in a few tennis balls. Then they'd light a fuse down underneath the thing, and, *boom*, those damn balls would fly all over hell.

His crowd loved to blow things up. One night in Daytona they got their hands on a giant inner tube, pumped the thing full of acetylene gas, threw it into a dumpster, and started tying together a long fuse made out of shop rags soaked in gasoline. I had to be someplace else, so I left while they were putting this whole operation together, and I'm actually kind of sorry I did. They told me later that the explosion blew out windows in a couple of neighboring hotels, and I guess a whole pack of fire engines came rolling right down Atlantic Avenue to investigate. That would have been something to see.

Everybody knows the famous story about Richie driving a rental car into the ocean on a bet. I wasn't there, but I wish I was. I can still picture that crazy bastard revving up that engine and running straight into the waves, laughing all the way.

A couple of times, he and I both happened to fly into Greensboro at the same time, on our way to the modified races at Martinsville. The two of us rented Lincolns, and between the airport and the hotel we'd run into each other a dozen times. Richie would sneak up behind me . . . *Bang!* I'd get behind him . . . *Boom!*

Those Lincolns have awfully tough bumpers.

*When I look back, I spent an awful lot of time with Richie Evans. That's the two of us with Brian Ross after Brian beat us in a big show at Stafford.
(Howard Hodge photo/ Courtesy of* Speedway Scene)

Yeah, Richie was a real beauty. I had a lot of fun with that guy, and I sure miss having him around.

I might be the only national champion in the history of NASCAR who ever traveled to the races with his own limousine.

His own *chauffeured* limousine.

Actually, there were two different limos, and for a while I also rode around in an honest-to-God hearse. But the one everybody remembers most was my stretch job, a big 'ole gray 1966 Cadillac. You could fit eight people in the back, 10 if they were good friends. It even had the formal slide-up divider window between the passenger compartment and the front seat.

Nine times out of 10, the guy at the wheel was my buddy PeePee Miguel. His real name was George, but every last person in the pits knew him as PeePee, because he'd had the nickname forever. PeePee was as loyal a friend as you could ever find in this world. He ran all over the countryside with me in my busiest traveling years.

The limo nonsense all started back in my point-chasing days. All that running up and down the road was getting to be too much: race all evening, party all night, and then rush home before dawn to open up the salvage yard. Forget burning the candle at both ends, I was burning it in the middle, too. I was living on fumes.

So I came up with the bright idea of getting my hands on a limousine. I bought that used Caddy, and PeePee slid behind the wheel. From that day on, he was the chauffeur. He even called me Boss.

With that limo, I could sleep on the way to the races, and sleep on the way home. With all that room, I'd stretch out and get some real rest for a change. But it made for some funny moments: PeePee would roll up to the pit gate, and to wake me up he'd just slam on the brakes and let me flop right onto the floor. Then that divider window would slide down, and he'd holler, "We're here, Boss."

I'd pick myself up, light my cigar, climb out the door and stroll right over to the sign-in window. I've got to admit, we had a way of making an entrance.

That limousine went everywhere. It made regular trips to upstate New York, it went to Long Island, it went to Martinsville. You know how everyone says Martinsville was such a party place? Hell, some of the best parties in the history of that track occurred right in the back of that limousine. One day I won a race there, and somebody handed me a jar of peach moonshine just as we were all climbing into the limo for the ride home. By the time we got to Roanoke, I was on another planet.

Sometimes I used to think that limo kept me alive, because it meant I had my own designated driver. But, looking back, it's amazing that PeePee didn't get me killed. He was always so afraid he was missing out on the party in the back seat that he'd spend about a third of the time looking out the windshield, a third of the time glancing at

In my craziest traveling years, George "PeePee" Miguel was my sidekick and chauffeur, and sometimes my babysitter.
(Mike Adaskaveg Photo)

the rearview mirror, and a third of the time with his head cocked around, grinning at us.

I'd just point at him and say, "There he is, folks. That's our driver."

He was a reliable chauffeur, all right, but he was crazy.

One Sunday night—late, late, late—we were coming home from Utica-Rome, just PeePee and me. I woke up from a deep sleep, and I poked my head up to try to figure out where we were. By then, I'd been up and down the New York Thruway and the Massachusetts Turnpike so many times that I could recognize every tree, every speed limit sign. Well, this time all I saw out the side window was solid white. I thought, God, I know I've been drinking, but can I really be *blind*?

I pushed the button to lower the divider, and I hollered, "PeePee, I can't see a damn thing."

He hollered back, "Me neither, Boss."

I looked straight out the windshield, and it was so foggy that it was impossible to see 10 feet past the end of the hood. Then I checked the speedometer: we were going 90 miles per hour.

PeePee said, "I think we're somewhere near Springfield."

I was sitting there, thinking, Well, PeePee knows this highway as well as I do, and the visibility is so bad that he's got no idea where we are, and yet we're doing 90 in a limousine. Just another night at the office.

I had an even crazier trip home from Utica-Rome in 1973. It was on the same day they had the big scoring controversy at Pocono after the Coke 250, when they initially awarded the win to Richie and then later gave it to me. I was driving for Sonny Koszela and he stayed at Pocono to plead our case, but I had to scoot out of there because Dick Waterman, the promoter at Utica-Rome, was paying me to show up that night.

That was nothing new. I'd been making hurry-up trips to Utica-Rome since the sixties, when a bunch of us would run at Thompson in the afternoon and then haul ass to Utica—four hours by truck—to get there just in time for the consi. Some of us were luckier; as time went on, we hooked up with people who owned their own private planes, and they'd fly us up to Utica-Rome. We'd land right on the drag strip next to the oval track.

On this trip, a buddy of mine from Boston named Bob Riley—Rip, we called him—met me at a small airport someplace near Pocono. He was a computer guru, a real intelligent guy, but almost as wacky as I was. He had a nice little four-seat Piper Commanche that would zip along at about 180 miles per hour, and he was always willing to fly me from Point A to Point B.

It was foggy in those Pennsylvania mountains, and Rip said the weather was bad all over. I told him it was his call if he didn't want to fly, but he said we'd be okay. We got out of there all right, and flew through pea soup all the way up into New York. We could barely find Utica-Rome; it was only after circling lower and lower that we saw a cluster of lights forming an oval in the middle of the darkness. We buzzed the race track, and they switched on the lights to the drag strip.

Now, that was a tricky place to land even in the daytime. You had to clear some trees, then drop down pretty quick to get beneath some wires that ran over the strip. Taking off, it was even scarier; you had to stay low enough to get under those wires, then climb super-steep to jump up over the trees. I flew out of there pretty often, and I never got comfortable with that departure. Even today, I can still picture those green trees getting closer and closer, just praying we'd pull up in time.

Anyway, we ran the race at Utica-Rome, stuck around for a couple of beers, and then Rip and I set sail for Taunton Airport, not far from Rehoboth. Naturally, because we had landed at the drag strip we weren't able to fuel up, so almost as soon as we got airborne Rip was looking for a place to get some aviation gas.

I said, "Are you insane? It's a foggy, rainy night, past midnight. Every little mom-and-pop airport is closed."

Well, Riley got on the radio, calling around for anybody who could hear us, and finally this lady answered. She ran a private strip which had closed for the night, but since we were pretty close to running dry she agreed to flip on her lights and sell us some fuel. We made a quick stop, then we were back in the air, right back in that soup.

That's when things *really* got rough. We hadn't even reached Albany when we found ourselves smack in the middle of a thunderstorm. The lightning flashes would just about blind us, and that plane blew around like a piece of paper in the wind.

That might be the only time in my life—even with all the crashes I've been through, and all the crazy stunts I've pulled—when I just *knew* I was going to die. The worst thing was, I had absolutely no control. To be honest, for a while even Riley had no control. Mother Nature was in charge that night, and we were just a toy she could play with.

Eventually the storm faded, but we still had all that fog to deal with. We flew along by compass, running from navigational beacon to navigational beacon through Massachusetts and Connecticut and into Rhode Island. We started our descent, still blind as a couple of bats.

"Start looking for something you recognize," Riley said.

I told him, "I recognize this fog. I've been looking at it all damn night."

We started to see clusters of lights not far below us. It was the city of Providence. All I knew about Providence was that there was one huge tower, the Industrial National Building, sticking right up in the middle of everything. I was thinking, First the fog, then the thunderstorms, now that skyscraper. There's no way I'm going to live through this night.

I'll tell you how bad the visibility was. As we circled around, I recognized the floodlights from a Cadillac dealer I knew in East Providence. I told Riley, "See that road? That's Route 44. Let's follow it up to Taunton." Imagine that? We've got compasses and radios and all this navigational gear, and we end up following the street lights home.

When we climbed out of that airplane in Taunton, I literally got down and kissed the ground.

Looking back, we should have stayed in Utica, but I was determined to get home to open up the salvage yard in the morning. A lot of pilots and passengers get killed taking those kinds of chances in bad weather, and we were a couple of fools who got lucky.

For most of my career, I always had a couple of planes available to me, and there were times when they came in handy by helping me squeeze in an extra race when the limousine couldn't possibly get us there in time. But some of those pilots were as crazy in the air as PeePee was on the highway; they'd make moves that probably didn't conform to FAA regulations. Let's say we were flying down to Virginia, and we wanted to get there as quick as possible. Rather than following all the right clearances and routes, we'd just get out over the water in Rhode Island and fly low over Long Island, then trace the shoreline past Atlantic City and Philadelphia and down over Delaware.

One time, my old friend Leo Walsh flew back from a race down South with one of these guys. I wasn't along for that ride, so I'm guessing I probably stayed down there for another race or something. I talked to Leo a few days later, and he said, "That crazy pilot wasn't twenty feet off the water when we crossed Long Island Sound. We came up on some guys in a fishing boat, and they actually dove overboard! They thought we were going to dive-bomb 'em!"

I had a pretty good support network. It's one thing to have solid car owners and great mechanics on your side; all the good drivers manage to do that. It's a whole different deal to have the army I had over the

Clowns to the left of me, jokers to the right: Me, PeePee and Seymour the Clown, aka John Farone, at Stafford Speedway.
(Mike Adaskaveg Photo)

years. I had Dominic Ferri, a perfectly normal pharmacist during the week, doubling as my babysitter and bodyguard on the weekends. I had Doc Torman, my chiropractor, keeping my body reasonably straight. I had guys driving me around and flying me home in the dead of night.

I always had good people around me. I mentioned how loyal PeePee was—that guy would have killed for me—and a bunch of these other guys were every bit as faithful.

The funny thing is, all this stuff seemed so normal at the time. When I think about it now, I can't imagine a short-track racer zooming up to the pit gate in a limousine. I mean, if you had Mike Stefanik pull into Stafford for the Spring Sizzler in a stretch Cadillac, it would be one hell of a big deal. I guess it probably looked like a big deal even when *I* did it, but I never gave that much thought. It was the same with landing on the Utica-Rome drag strip, hopping out of some little airplane, and then jumping into somebody's modified. That was just part of the game.

Today, though, I can see how strange it all was. The average race driver, even then, sure wasn't living like I was living.

And the average nine-to-five guy from Rehoboth, Massachusetts, lived a life that was completely foreign from mine.

Did all the good times ever take a toll on me? Hell, yes.

I ran a few races hung over, or at least with the last little bit of a hangover. Don't get me wrong, in 99 percent of the races I ran, I was in absolute peak shape, mentally and physically. Even if I'd had a few beers the night before, I'd be up early, exercising and getting lots of fluids into my body. But there were a few mornings when I showed up at the race track feeling just terrible. It's not something I'm proud of, but why lie about it?

There was probably only one time when all of the partying bit me hard, and that was in the late sixties. Lenny Boehler and I had hauled all the way down to Louisiana for a race at Baton Rouge. That track awarded NASCAR modified points, but the cars they ran were more like open-competition late models. Our coupe didn't fit their rules, so we took our big ol' Ford, the Daytona car. We knew we weren't going to be anywhere close to competitive, but we were so wrapped up in chasing those points that we felt like we had to go.

Anyway, we raced in Baton Rouge on a Saturday night. I booked a commercial flight out early on Sunday morning so I could make it back to Thompson, where some of Lenny's guys would have the coupe waiting for me. It was a good plan, but my execution *wasn't* so good.

I got tangled up with some of those Louisiana boys after the races. They hauled me down to this tavern, and we had ourselves a hell of a time. At 3)) a.m. in the morning, I crawled out of that place skunk-drunk. One of those guys drove me back to my motel, but then I couldn't find my room key, and the front office was closed. I ended up sleeping in the car.

As soon as it got light, somebody woke me up and took me to the airport. At 6:30 Sunday morning, still wobbly, I was on an airliner headed to New York City. We landed at LaGuardia, where a friend of mine picked me up in a small plane. We landed that thing in a cornfield just down the road from Thompson, and a few minutes later I was walking through the pit gate like a big hero.

Some hero. Later that afternoon, I was halfway down the back straightaway when everything went dark. All I can figure is that I must have passed out from the hangover and the lack of sleep. That coupe hit the third turn sandbank running wide open, flew over some trees, and nosed into a swamp.

Was that stupid? Of course it was. That crash could have killed me, and it all went back to that barroom in Baton Rouge. I've got no real excuse for it. All I can say is that those were different times.

People always tell me I was lucky to come along when I did, because this sort of crazy behavior is frowned upon these days.

(Mike Adaskaveg Photo)

"If you came along today," they all say, "you'd have had to tone things down, play the game, be more professional."

Well, let me tell you something: If I came along today, I'd probably be doing most of the same damn things I did in 1965 and 1975. I'd be raising just as much hell. Because, see, that stuff wasn't an act. I was just being myself, and a leopard can't change his spots.

Besides, I think a lot of these kids get mixed up when they talk about professionalism. It's something that gets drilled into their heads, but they don't know what it means. Just because they *say* they're acting professionally, do they think they take racing more seriously than I did? That they take it more seriously than Richie Evans did?

Come on. The two of us were as professional as any race drivers who ever lived. We just laughed more than most of 'em.

Val LeSieur on Bugsy

Val LeSieur and Bugs Stevens, Stafford Speedway, 1983.
(Courtesy of Speedway Scene)

Val LeSieur, publisher, Speedway Scene: "Our paper came along at a time when you had so many top drivers—Bugsy and Freddy DeSarro and the Bouchards and Eddie Flemke, and later on Geoff Bodine—and some really great racing. At Stafford and Thompson in those days, it was unbelievable racing. So you didn't have to go too far to look for good stories, because there was so much going on right here close to home.

"From the newspaper side of things, Bugsy was a guy we keyed on. You *had* to key on Bugsy; he had already been the national modified champion, plus he had such a great personality. You couldn't help but be attracted to him, and everybody was.

"He was such a character. He pull out a snake—a real one or a rubber one—or he'd have a water pistol. Or he'd have some kind of little gadget that shocked you or pinched you. Every time you saw him, there was some new kind of mischief he was up to. He'd keep everybody laughing.

"Don't forget, those were different days. Everything wasn't one hundred percent serious, like it is today. You didn't have big sponsors to worry about, or anything like that. Bugsy was serious once he climbed into that car, and he always did a hell of a job. But off the track, he was this free-wheeling guy, full of fun. He was never a guy who worried about his image. He was who he was. In fact, I think his image helped him.

"Bugsy had what I feel was probably the only true fan club for a race driver. They had parties, they had activities, they had deals to travel to different tracks, they had a newsletter. And in that newsletter, they had a comic strip, which we even ran in the paper at times. Think about that: This was almost 30 years ago, and here was a short-track driver who had a comic strip about him.

"But the thing about Bugsy was, he wasn't just a character; he was a big winner, too. There's not many guys who are both. He helped our paper, no question, just by being the kind of guy he was. People were interested in him.

"I've actually known Bugsy for years and years, because we played football against each other in high school. He played for Dighton, and I played for Oliver Ames High in Easton, Massachusetts. He scored two touchdowns, and I still tell him I don't think he carried the ball 10 yards in the whole damn game. But he was one hell of a football player. He was a hell of an athlete, period.

"In his racing days I ran around with him quite a bit, and we had some good times. Once a week or so, he used to go to this used car auction a few miles from my house, and on his way there he'd stop at my house with baskets of tomatoes and potatoes and corn. I finally told him we couldn't eat all that food, and I didn't have a permit for a farm stand, so maybe he should slow down the deliveries a little bit.

"I don't see him as much as I used to, but he'll call sometimes, and it's always fun to run into him. He's still crazy, but that's Bugsy. He's just a great human being."

The Seventies

The Seventies

I DROVE MY FIRST RACE in the fifties, won all three of my NASCAR national championships in the sixties, and retired in the eighties. But if I had to pick the decade that best represents my career—the decade that was *me*—there'd be no question. It was the seventies.

For reasons I've never completely figured out, that was my era, my time. I guess it's mostly because that was a time when the media was just starting to really get into covering the sport, and I happened to be the guy on top at the time, at least in New England. I was already established, already *somebody.* And so every time my name appeared in a news story, every time it showed up in an ad, every time it was announced on a public-address system, I was, "Bugs Stevens, three-time NASCAR national modified champion …"

I'll tell you one thing about being Bugs Stevens in the seventies: There was never a dull moment.

Lenny Boehler and I got almost as much attention for breaking up as we'd gotten for all the races and championships we'd won. Looking back, I guess it's understandable; we'd done so much winning together between 1964 and the time we split, at the start of '71, that it was bound to be a pretty big shock to people.

To this day, I think that whole episode is a little bit misunderstood. People seem to think that Lenny and I went our separate ways because of some big blow-up, some problem between us that we couldn't solve. It wasn't anything like that.

It all went back to Lenny's wife passing away. That's such a huge event in a person's life, and it definitely affected his attitude. I can remember Lenny telling me that there were times when he wasn't sure he wanted to race anymore; if you knew Len Boehler, knew how much this sport meant to him, then maybe you can understand how strange it was for me to hear him talk like that. I hoped that it was a passing thing, so it didn't exactly send me out looking for another ride. At the same time, it made me aware that I ought to at least keep my eyes open for anything else out there, any other quality ride that might be available.

From left, that's Dave Tourigny, Sonny Koszela, Fred DeSarro and Zip Zeller in 1970, the year Freddy won the NASCAR modified championship in Sonny's car. (John Grady Photo)

While all this was going on, Sonny Koszela and Fred DeSarro were having problems of their own. They had just won the 1970 NASCAR modified championship together, but they got bickering about this or that, and pretty soon there were rumblings that they were getting ready to dissolve the team. Before long, sure enough, Pop Koszela called and offered me the ride.

Now, I'd driven for the Koszelas before; I'd won that Stafford championship with Pop way back in 1966, on the dirt. By 1971, their asphalt car was as good as anybody's, so this seemed like a great situ-

When Freddy and Sonny split, it was kind of natural for me to just slide right in. I'd driven for the Koszelas before, so it was a good fit. (John Grady Photo)

109

ation for me. At the same time, Freddy DeSarro and I were pretty good buddies, and I didn't want to be the guy who came along and stole his ride. But Pop Koszela told me not to worry about that; Sonny and Freddy were broken up, done, period. At the same time, Pop offered me an excellent deal, financially.

At that point, I had a situation to fall back on if I needed one, but no matter which way things went it was going to be tricky. Remember, not only were Boehler and I teammates, we were also partners in the salvage yard. So I asked Lenny flat out if he thought he was going to race, and he said he still wasn't sure. At that point, I pretty much knew I'd be on my own.

I told Pop I'd drive for him and Sonny, and I started figuring out a way to smooth out the other side of my relationship with Lenny. To make a long story short, I ended up buying his end of the business, and we parted company.

That's the whole story, in a nutshell. I needed to have a direction in my life and in my racing, and Lenny was pretty much direction-free at that moment. So we split.

Life was a little bit awkward between Lenny and I for a while after that. It probably couldn't be anything *but* awkward when you're with a guy that long, when you've done so many things together, and then you go your separate ways. What probably saved our friendship was the fact that things ended up going so well for both of us. I had some of the best seasons of my career with Koszela; meanwhile, Lenny stuck Freddy in his car, and he kept right on winning for years, too.

Somebody called that switch—me going from Boehler to Koszela, Freddy going from Koszela to Boehler—modified racing's version of "the shot heard around the world." No matter how you looked at it, it was big. Like I said, I was in the middle of a bunch of big stuff in those days.

Sonny wasn't too interested in chasing points by the time I got with him. He had already won the NASCAR championship with DeSarro, and I'm sure he was probably feeling like Boehler and I had felt after our 1969 title: Mission accomplished, and that's that.

Still, we did our share of traveling, especially in our first few years together. If there was a big modified show just about anywhere between 1971 and, say, 1974, chances are pretty good that we were there. And wherever we went, we were solid. In 1972 alone, I won twice at Martinsville in Sonny's number 15 coupe, the Woodchopper Special; we won the 250-lapper there in the spring, and a 100-lapper the day before the Winston Cup race in April.

When Freddy DeSarro jumped into Boehler's 3 and I took over the Koszela 15, it was big news in modified racing.
(Balser and Son Photo)

Closer to home, we still ran at least two or three times a week, even without chasing points. Stafford had been purchased by Jack Arute, who had been around modified racing for years as a car owner, and he had moved its race night to Saturday nights; once Norwood Arena closed, that just made sense. Under Jack and his family, Stafford kind of became the center of the universe for New England modified racing. Sonny put a lot of emphasis on Stafford, and we won the track championship there in 1971 and again in '74. But we'd still haul out to Albany-Saratoga, and Utica-Rome, and Islip Speedway down on Long Island, and any other track that was putting up decent money. Sonny was still into racing his modifieds—first the coupe, and later a Vega that I had a ton of success in—on a fairly regular basis.

Although, I have to say, that didn't always mean Sonny was a hands-on participant. If he had business commitments—the Koszela family ran a lumber yard, and aside from that Sonny built a hell of a speed-shop business—we just went racing without him. It'd be me and Dave Tourigny, who built Sonny's cars and was our chief mechanic, or me and Zip Zeller, who was another one of the real cogs in that operation. And if those guys couldn't get away for some reason, sometimes it'd just be me. There were nights when I took that truck by myself to Albany-Saratoga or Utica-Rome.

Sonny and I were as good an instant fit as Boehler and I had been back in 1964. I won 26 races in 1971 with that Woodchopper coupe, so we got off to a pretty good start. And from '71 through '75, we were probably the dominant combination at Stafford; Freddy DeSarro and Ronnie Bouchard were the champions there in '72 and '73, but we were always right there in the picture, either winning or running somewhere in the top three or four spots. And in 1974, when we were really hot with that Vega, I won the Stafford championship, the 200-lapper there on Labor Day, and the Spring Sizzler, which was not only Stafford's biggest race at the time, but probably the most prestigious race in New England.

The early seventies were a neat period. In the autumn of 1971, Bob Judkins rolled out his famous 2X Pinto, the first of the new subcompact bodies used in a NASCAR modified. People had played with late model-type bodies on the modifieds before; from about 1968 through 1970 or so, a bunch of guys ran Corvair bodies and chopped-up Camaros and Mustangs. But most of those things were big and bulky and ugly as hell. Bobby's Pinto was really a sleek-looking piece for its time.

And it was fast, too. Gene Bergin ran it the first time out, and he blew the rest of us right out of the water in the Stafford 200.

That was a big, big deal in the sport. The "Pinto Revolution,"

In the early 1970s, lots of modified owners were playing with late-model body styles. This is Sonny Koszela's Corvair at Trenton.
(Mike Adaskaveg Photo)

everybody called it, and that's what it was. It opened the gates for the rest of us to start building Pintos and Vegas and Gremlins, and within a year or two the old coupes and sedans had almost disappeared.

A lot of people, the real hard-core traditionalists, hated the new bodies. But I think that whole Pinto Revolution thing was good for modified racing. Don't get me wrong, I still love the look of those old coupes, especially the way they'd evolved by the beginning of the seventies; there's something really special about those cars. But you've got to go with the flow, in racing just like in the rest of life. It's the only way you'll keep up with the outside world.

The end result of the Pinto Revolution, in my opinion, was that we ended up with better-looking cars everywhere we went. A lot of those Vegas and Gremlins and Pintos in the mid-seventies were beautiful cars. In fact, they still look great in pictures today.

There are people out there who'll tell you that the modifieds should still have coupe bodies. Well, I guess my answer to them is, Are you still watching a nine-inch black-and-white TV at home?

After the Pinto Revolution set off by Bobby Judkins, the whole look of modified racing changed. Sonny came out with this mean-looking Vega, and that thing won me a ton of races between 1973 and '76 or so.
(Dick Berggren Photo)

It wasn't just the look of the cars that was changing in the early seventies. A lot of exciting stuff was happening right around that time. Some of the track owners were starting to get sharper about the way they promoted the sport. Instead of just opening up the gates and expecting people to come, they really began to market the big-name

113

I was usually game for any publicity gimmicks the promoters and PR people wanted me to take part in. I can't recall exactly what this photo was all about, but I do remember that Leo Cleary ended up smashing that slice of pizza in my face! (Lloyd Burnham Photo/Courtesy of Koszela Family Collection)

drivers. In a way, they *had* to. Since there wasn't an organized tour at the time, a NASCAR modified driver could hop around and race wherever he wanted to, so the smart promoter would wheel and deal to make sure the top guys were at his track.

I remember taking part in a four-way telephone conference call with Larry Mendelsohn from the Islip Speedway. He had Richie Evans, Jerry Cook, and me on the line, trying to talk us all into coming to Islip for some big show he was putting on. I remember Mendelsohn saying, "Come on. I'll give you guys $500 apiece." But none of us would budge; we kept working his price higher and higher. I think we had him up to $800 each before we had ourselves a deal.

Now, this was probably somewhere around 1974, and $800 was a lot of money back then, especially if you had to pay that much to three different guys. But Mendelsohn was no dummy; I'd won three national championships, Cookie had won two in 1971 and '72, and Richie was the 1973 NASCAR modified champ. With the three of us locked in, Islip had itself a heck of a field, and to Mendelsohn that meant a heck of a crowd would come, too.

In exchange for any show-up money we got, we'd help the tracks with whatever publicity they needed. A lot of times, I'd roll into town a day or two early to do newspaper and radio interviews or whatever the promoter had lined up.

Hell, there were a hundred times in my career when I did that stuff even without getting paid. I'm not trying to pat myself on the back, but whenever I was asked to promote a certain race or a certain track or even NASCAR modified racing in general, I usually went out of my way to do it.

Sometimes that meant going the extra mile to send the fans home happy. For example, there were nights at places like Stafford when I could have won the feature by a full straightaway, but I'd backpedal a bit instead and keep the second-place guy just out of reach, four or five car-lengths back. That was something a lot of us would do, and I think that philosophy all went back to Ed Flemke. When I first got out of Seekonk and into NASCAR, I'd hear Eddie preaching, "Don't ever run away with a race. As long as you know you're going to win anyway, why not put on a show for the fans?"

Ninety-nine times out of a hundred, nobody had a car dominant enough to stink up the race, so the racing was real, particularly in the features when the money was on the line. But a bunch of us made a habit of playing to the crowds in the heat races, where your finishing position didn't mean a damn thing as long as you made the qualifying cut.

One night at Stafford—I don't remember the year—Ronnie and Kenny Bouchard and I happened to be in the same heat race on a night

Putting on a show, that's what we thought heat races were for. That's me on the inside, Ron Bouchard in the middle, and Kenny Bouchard outside at Stafford in 1977. We ran this way for about five laps and I guess we thrilled everybody there, including NASCAR's Bill France Jr. (Mike Adaskaveg Photo)

when the big guest of honor was Bill France Jr., the NASCAR president. Well, the three of us talked things over in the pits, and we decided we'd really give Billy a performance. We all started toward the back, as usual, but as soon as one of us got the lead we fell into formation, three wide. We ran that way for about five laps. It was absolutely, completely staged, but aside from a few people in the pits, nobody had any idea that we were playing, France included.

The crowd loved it. France loved it. And I know Jack Arute loved it. I mean, look at it from Jack's perspective: Bill France Jr. shows up at his track, and even before the heat races are done he's seen a three-wide battle for the win with the fans going crazy.

I mentioned Eddie Flemke a minute ago, and it's amazing how much of my viewpoint on promoters goes right back to that guy. In the early 1970s, when both of us were still doing a lot of traveling and working our various deals with promoters, Flemke said, "You know, Bugs, we've got to work with these guys, no matter what we might think of them. This game is our bread and butter. We've got to put people in the grandstands. Let's help those guys promote the races, because that will promote *us*."

That sort of thinking made stars out of a lot of us.

If you were a modified star in the seventies, there was no telling what that might lead to. One day in 1972, I got a call asking if I'd be interested in running an SCCA Trans-Am race on the road course at Lime Rock, Connecticut. The promoter up there, a nice guy named Jim Haynes, thought having me in the show might be a good way to attract some oval-track fans. I'd never done a bit of road-racing in my life, but, hell, it sounded like fun.

I ended up driving a Mustang as part of a two-car team with Tony DeLorenzo, one of the veteran guys in that series. My car was one the team had bought from Bud Moore, who was Ford's main man in the Trans-Am at that time; Parnelli Jones had driven it in 1971. It was a good car, and the team was a nice enough bunch of guys, so in general the weekend was a lot of fun. On the track, though, things couldn't have gone much worse. We blew up two engines in practice, slapped another one together out of some spare parts, and qualified 10th in a 30-car field, which wasn't bad. But on race day, we only made it about a half-dozen laps before the damn thing blew up again.

I ended watching the race from the hillside in the Lime Rock infield, drinking a beer with a bunch of modified people who'd shown up, so at least the whole thing worked from a promotional point of view.

Pete Zanardi, a Connecticut sportswriter who had become a friend of mine because of all the modified races he'd covered, was at Lime Rock working for the *Hartford Times*. He asked me what it had felt like to play in the big leagues for a day, and I told him, "Peter, let me tell you something. There's the Formula One and Indy cars on top. Then comes the modifieds. Everything else is a step down."

Zanardi used that line for years when he was making me famous.

Two more wins at Stafford. On the left, that's Mike Joy interviewing Bill France Jr., and on the right I'm getting ready to answer a question from Bill Welch. (Mike Adaskaveg Photos)

Pete Zanardi, by the way, was an invaluable part of the whole modified scene in those days. I really believe that. He was the kind of guy who covered racing the way other sportswriters covered the stick-and-ball sports; what I mean is, he wrote about the *people* in the sport instead of just reporting the results. And just by doing his job that way, he ended up promoting modified racing. He was primarily a daily newspaper guy, but you'd also see his stuff in the national magazines, and he helped expose a lot of us to a wider audience than we'd have gotten otherwise.

Peter was always a great writer, and a smart guy. He'd get inside your head and really pick your brain about an issue, and when you saw the story later you could tell that the guy had been paying attention to you. That sounds simple, but it's not. So many other writers would interview you, and when you read the thing later on you noticed that they took whatever you said and bent it to fit whatever *they* wanted you to say. I can pull out a dozen different major profiles that have been done on me in the magazines and newspapers, and there are always a few things in there that are just slightly wrong. All that shows me is that those writers listened to half of what I was telling them, and ignored the other half.

Zanardi was different. His stories helped the modified division, they helped New England short-track racing in general, and they definitely helped me.

Don't forget, there weren't too many racing writers around back then. These days, it seems like there are a few dozen at every race, and I don't know half of 'em. In the early seventies, there was only a handful, and I knew 'em all.

All those guys used to talk about how I was "a good interview." Well, to this day I don't know the difference between a guy who's a good interview and another who's a bad interview. I just liked to talk to people—*good* people—and I especially enjoyed talking about racing. It was just a natural thing to me. So I'm not sure I was a good interview, but I was probably an *easy* interview, and that worked in my favor.

Something else happened, media-wise, that boosted my career in the early seventies. The weekly trade papers were starting to really catch on in New England, especially Val LeSieur's new paper, *Speedway Scene*. Until Val showed up, most of the racing papers were based somewhere else; there was *Area Auto Racing News* out of New Jersey, the old *Illustrated Speedway News* from Long Island, *Gater Racing News* from upstate New York, and Chris Economaki's paper, *National Speed Sport News*. They all covered the bigger modified events, but they kind of missed the boat on all the weekly stuff happening in New England, which was really a booming area. Well, when Speedway Scene came along, that took care of that. Every week I was in the headlines, and a lot of times I had my picture on the front page.

Val and I were friends, but that certainly wasn't the reason he played me up so big. Let's face it, if you own a racing paper, the hottest driver around is the guy who's going to get the ink, because you want to sell papers.

And, man, I was hot right then.

The seventies were a great period to be on top, because the fans were just so heavily into their modified racing. Everybody wore jackets with their favorite driver's name and number on 'em. You could spot a guy across the pits, or notice a family sitting up in the grandstands, and know instantly whether they were pulling for Ronnie Bouchard or Richie Evans or Eddie Flemke.

Or me. Back then, especially in New England but in a lot of other places, too, I always felt like I had as many fans as the next guy. That was a good feeling. Hell, it's a good feeling even today.

Fan clubs used to be a very big thing in short-track racing; all the short-track hot dogs seemed to have them. I had a bunch of dedicated people involved in mine—Art Rivet, Tony Ward, Carroll Thatcher, Tammy Shaw, just a whole bunch of different hardcore fans over the years—and I'd say it had to be as big as anybody's in the Northeast. They'd hold picnics, have gatherings at race tracks, send out newsletters, the whole nine yards. Thatcher used to draw up this ongoing comic strip—"The Adventures of Da Bugman"—as part of the newsletter. Then Val LeSieur started running the strip in *Speedway Scene*, and the whole thing got even bigger.

I had the greatest fans in the world. They were terrific to me, and I always tried to be good to them in return.

Especially the kids.

I love kids. Always have, still do, always will. Even today, I can't get enough of the little squirts. The beautiful thing about kids is that they haven't got any evil thoughts in 'em yet. When they look at you, you are what they want you to be, not what somebody else has *told*

It seems crazy now, but my fan club used to keep up an ongoing comic strip based on our racing adventures, and for a while it also ran regularly in Speedway Scene.
(Berghman Family Collection)

119

The great thing about kids is, they just want to have fun and cheer for their heroes. This is Thompson Speedway, and I'm sneaking in a few last-minute autographs before the feature.
(Mike Adaskaveg Photo)

them you are. All they want to do is smile and laugh, and I love being a part of that.

At some of the tracks where the fans could get up close to the pit fence, you'd always have a pack of kids eager to just say hello, or maybe shake your finger through the pit fence. I spent a lot of time standing alongside those chain-link fences, just talking to kids, from toddlers to teenagers. I think they appreciated that, and I could always tell that their parents did.

Can't a guy enjoy his cigar in piece. Seymour the Clown was a regular fixture at Stafford for years, and here he's managed to sneak up on me and Billy Harmon.
(Courtesy of Speedway Scene)

120

Another crazy publicity shot. When Sonny Koszela and I were winning everything in sight at Stafford, somebody dreamed up the slogan "Only Raid can stop the Bugman," and got John Farone and I to pose for this picture. (Rene Dugas Photo/Courtesy of Speedway Scene)

    At Stafford, a guy named Butch Farone used to dress up every race night as Seymour the Clown. He'd put on a show during intermission: he'd climb the fence, do these ramp-to-ramp jumps in a little motorized car, all kinds of stuff. Then he'd fool around with the drivers as we got ready to run the feature. It was entertainment, a way to keep the crowd interested. And whenever things got dull, Butch knew he could count on a certain few of us—me, Flemke, Bouchard, Gene Bergin and more— to play along. If I was sitting in Koszela's modified, Butch would squirt me with a water pistol, and I'd fire up that car and chase him around the infield, just inches from his heels, with every little kid in the grandstands going nuts.

    I didn't realize at the time just how big an impact all this stuff had on my career; all the clowning around, all the time I spent with the kids. To me, it was just a way to have fun. Hell, I'm just a big kid, too. But as time went along, I started to sense that it meant an awful lot to some people. I *know* it did, because as the years rolled along, some of the kids I'd first met when they were young teenagers started showing up at those pit fences with their own kids. By the time I got out of the game, I'd met three generations of a whole lot of families.

    But all this stuff—the jackets in the grandstands, the big fan club, the kids at the pit fence—only worked because we were backing it up on the race track. If I was a fun-loving guy who finished fifteenth every week, it wouldn't have worked. I'd have been just another nice-guy race driver. But I was winning races, and that made a difference. That put me on Broadway.

While we were together, Sonny Koszela's car was always my primary ride, and we had some incredible success in the middle seventies. We had put the old coupe out to pasture, but the Vega, with a big-block Chevy under the hood, was a rocket. We won at Martinsville again in the spring of 1975, and won a ton of races at Stafford. Then, in '77, when the Vega was getting outdated by all the hot tube-framed small-block cars that were coming in, Sonny rolled out another toy, a Pinto with a great Ford engine built by Tommy Turner down at the Holman-Moody shop. We won eight races at Stafford that year, including five in a row.

That was a tremendous season for me, because in '76 Geoff Bodine had won a bunch of races in New England and made the rest of us look pretty bad. I heard stuff here and there suggesting that maybe I was over the hill, so it was nice to come out in '77, particularly at a place as competitive as Stafford, and shut all those people up.

We closed out the 1977 season by absolutely annihilating the field at Martinsville in October. I mean, nobody came close to touching us that day.

Man, that Pinto was a weapon.

Sonny had really trimmed down his schedule by then, but I wasn't ready to slow down just yet. So I'd run for Koszela at Stafford and in the bigger spring and fall shows, but if there was an open-competition race someplace else that interested me, I'd just find another car to drive. I don't know what Sonny thought of all that, because we never really talked much about it. I just figured, Hell, if Sonny's not going to show up at some little bullring with his car, I'll just jump in something else.

In the late '70s, I did some serious ride-hopping, running Joe Brady's 41 in a ton of open-competition shows. This is at Westboro, and that's Kenny Bouchard in the 04 and Pete Schwarz in the 4X.
(Mike Adaskaveg Photo)

A lot of us did that back then. Leo Cleary was in and out of a bunch of different cars, and Kenny Bouchard had two or three rides he'd jump between, depending on the night and the track.

Bobby Santos and I ran a lot of races as teammates for Joe Brady in the mid-seventies. We'd go to Westboro on Friday nights, and to Monadnock or Thompson on Sunday afternoons. Joe had two white homebuilt Pintos, we ran one as the 41 and the other as the 41M. Then I ran a race or two for John Stygar out of Connecticut, who'd won a bunch of races with Flemke, and did the occasional Seekonk race with Steve May, a car builder and mechanic I've known for years. And when Bob Judkins was between steady drivers, he and I teamed up for some races.

Over the years, a lot of that stuff has become kind of foggy to me; I guess I did so much jumping around that, unless I ran with a guy for a long time, it all just blends in. But I know this: whatever I ran in those days, we were always competitive.

Judkins told me not long ago that he and I won three out of the five races we ran together, or something like that. He's got a better memory than I do. But I know we won a couple of races in the old Wednesday-night Yankee All-Star League, one at Star Speedway and one at the Waterford Speedbowl. Bobby says I passed Ronnie Bouchard on the last lap at Waterford, and if that's how he remembers it, that's good enough for me.

"I thought we were going to have to scrape you off the wall," Bobby always says.

Those open shows were a lot of fun, because they put you into battle with a lot of drivers who didn't run the bigger tracks very much. Up at Monadnock, you had to deal with Punky Caron and Pete

Sandy Gustafson was the Seekonk trophy queen for years, and she handed me a lot of hardware.
(Johnny Mercury Photo/ Courtesy of Speedway Scene)

Every track had its hot dogs. One of Monadnock Speedway's best runners was Punky Caron, and we had some good battles. On this particular day, I ended up passing him for the win. (Mike Adaskaveg Photo)

123

I had a heck of a year in 1977 with a little Vega that Fred Fusco and I put together. We won the Seekonk Speedway championship, which was a pretty neat thrill for me.
(Courtesy of Speedway Scene)

Fiandaca; at Star, there were guys like Ollie Silva and Mike Murphy; Waterford had Dick Dunn and Bob Potter and Moose Hewitt; at Westboro, you'd have to fight off a veteran like Fats Caruso or George Savary one week, or a hot new kid like Jeff Fuller the next week. At those smaller tracks, a guy didn't need a big-buck car with all kinds of horsepower to run up front, so that just added to the mix.

I even had a little bit of success driving a car of my own. In 1977, I won the track championship at Seekonk Speedway with the Freetown Auto Parts Special, a little white Vega. When Steve May first built it, that car was actually going to be a late-model, but Fred

Anthony Venditti built and ran Seekonk Speedway, and he was one of New England racing's real characters. This is from awards banquet after my championship in 1977. (Johnny Mercury Photo/Courtesy of Speedway Scene)

Fusco got his hands on it and turned it into a modified. Stafford had switched to Friday nights that year, and that left my Saturdays open for Seekonk, which was like going home. It was fun, because I had friends like the Chiavettone brothers, Nat and Jerry, working with me. But I'll tell you, that was a tough period at Seekonk; on a typical Saturday you'd have Fred DeSarro, the Bouchards, Geoff Bodine, Eddie Flemke, George Summers, and all the locals, too. That was some of the best racing I've ever been involved in.

It had been twelve years since I'd left Seekonk as a regular, so it was an awful lot of fun to go back there and be a champion again.

That ride-hopping stretch was a fun time, a hectic time. And, looking back, I guess it shows just how badly I still wanted to race. I didn't have to keep going, that's for sure. When Sonny scaled back his schedule, I could have done the same thing. A lot of those extra races I ran didn't pay much, and, you know, it's not like I needed more trophies to fill up the shelves. I just still had the desire to drive race cars.

If there was one downside to the seventies, it was that modified racing was starting to get ridiculously expensive. Dick Armstrong had kicked that off in the early part of the decade by buying the Tant-Mitchell operation, and he definitely upped the ante when he started buying engines from Jack Tant. In 1976, when Geoff Bodine was driving for him, the rumor was that they'd bought a couple of small-block engines for $7500 apiece. Today that seems like pocket change to a car owner, but in the mid-seventies that was just unheard of.

Armstrong had made a lot of money in the jewelry business, and he liked to go racing in a flashy way. He loved fancy paint jobs and chrome wheels—hell, chrome *everything*—and he'd always spent a bundle making his cars look good. That never bothered any of us, although it amused the low-dollar guys like Lenny Boehler. But when Dick started buying those monster engines, that definitely got our attention, because the only way to beat horsepower is with more horsepower. And horsepower costs money.

The price of poker had gone up.

It went up again when the store-bought chassis craze came in. Maynard Troyer was probably the best-known builder; he'd already been a big winner as a driver, and once he went into producing cars for sale he had the hot design for a long time. But there were other builders, too: you had Chassis Dynamics and Rollie Lindblad, and even drivers like Eddie Flemke and Richie Evans were in the chassis business to some extent. A small number of guys were still building their own cars, but very few were sharp enough to compete against the kind of technology you could buy from those chassis builders. The problem was, technology is never cheap.

That was a pivotal time in NASCAR modified racing, I think. The crowds in the late seventies were still very solid at most of the weekly tracks, but, generally speaking, the purses didn't keep up. That never made sense to me; if a promoter is struggling, I'll cut him some slack, but if he's making money—and some of those guys had owned tracks for years and were in no hurry to sell 'em, so you can't tell me they were *losing* money—I think it's only fair to expect that the payoff ought to increase right along with the cost of competition.

That might have been modified racing's last chance to really get on top of that whole economic situation, either by trying to keep the costs down or by raising the purses. But neither one happened. And, little by little, the backyard racer got phased out. The only guys left in the game—at least the only guys with a prayer of winning—were the wealthy businessmen who were involved racing as a hobby. They either owned the top cars or they sponsored them, and, naturally, they had the top drivers locked up. If you weren't with one of those guys, you were in a pretty deep hole.

Bodine had Armstrong; Ronnie Bouchard had Billy Hood, a salvage yard operator out of Bellingham, Massachusetts, and then Marvin

Just as we were getting to the mid-1970s, I thought the modified division was in great shape. Everywhere we went, there were lots of cars and lots of fans. But just after that, the cost of racing began to shoot out of sight.
(Mike Adaskaveg Photo)

126

Rifchin from the M&H Tire Company; Flemke had Bill Thornton from Manchester Sand & Gravel; Richie Evans had Gene DeWitt, who ran a big trucking outfit in upstate New York.

When I had Sonny Koszela, I could hold my own with any of those guys, whether we were at Stafford or Trenton or Martinsville. But I'd go to Thompson on Sunday nights with Joe Brady, and no matter how hard Brady worked or how well I drove, we weren't going to beat Geoffrey and Ronnie and those big-dollar cars. That was an awfully frustrating time for me as a race driver.

I think about all this today, and it's like the whole game turned around in maybe a five-year period, between about 1974 and '79. In '74, as long as you had your act together, you could go to a place like Stafford with a car you built yourself and a relatively cheap big block Chevy engine and be competitive. By 1979, those days were long gone, brother. You needed a store-bought chassis and the best small block money could buy, or you were just wasting your time.

Maybe we should have all been more worried about that at the time. The problem was, most of us never looked at the big picture; we were too busy trying to do better in the next race. In my case, I was too busy thinking like a race driver. Economics, hell, I just wanted to win.

That desire to win was what led to me getting out of Koszela's car in 1978. That caused almost as big a fuss as I'd caused by first climbing into Sonny's coupe back in '71.

It happened one night at Stafford, on a night when for some reason—a rainout the previous week, I guess—there were twin features. This was in a period when every one of the fast guys was rolling out with a new set of tires in every feature. It was just the way the sport had changed. Bodine was doing it, Bouchard was doing it, and unless you wanted them to dust you off, you did it, too.

We ran the first feature on used tires. That was Sonny's idea. Well, we got blown into the weeds. Now we were getting ready for the second feature, and I didn't see any new rubber laying around. I told Sonny, "Look, if we don't put new tires on this thing, I'm not driving it. I'll quit."

I don't think anybody figured I was serious, but I wasn't kidding around. There was absolutely no way we were going to run with Geoff or Ronnie or any other decent car on old tires, and that was obvious. Sonny was asking me to run a foot race without any soles on my shoes.

He told me he didn't want to put new rubber on, and I knew right

Here's a little bit of history. When I left the Koszela car in 1978, Kenny Bouchard finished out the season with Sonny, and I showed up at Stafford once or twice with my own car, a Plymouth Arrow-bodied number 0. This was taken on the very first night we went head-to-head.
(Harry Moore Photo/Courtesy of Speedway Scene)

then that the game was over. I quit that car on the spot. I didn't make a big deal over it; I just put my helmet into my uniform bag, threw that thing over my shoulder, and walked right out of the pits before they ever got around to running the second feature.

To me, it was a matter of principle, a pride thing. I'd have looked like a bum, and I wasn't going to let that happen. I could understand Sonny wanting to save some money, but I had a lot at stake, too. In this sport, the people in the grandstands see one driver winning and the other drivers losing; I'd been through that in '76, when we got behind a little bit and I watched Bodine win every other week. In the pits, the racers and the mechanics understand that a lot of things go into who wins and who doesn't – including things like new tires – but all those fans know is where their guy finished.

I didn't want that race car to make a jackass out of me, and I told Sonny that. People expected me to win back then, or at least to *challenge* for the win. If I couldn't do that, I wasn't interested in racing.

That's the reason I left that team. That's the gospel.

If you look at the numbers alone—all those wins and championships at Stafford, all our Martinsville success, all our victories *everywhere*—I had a great run with the Koszela team. And if you look past the numbers, it was even better.

Because, see, the numbers leave out some of the great days when we *didn't* win, but everybody in the place knew we were there.

In the Stafford 200 in 1973, I was leading the race, just kind of cruising, when Leo Cleary started reeling me in. Leo had struggled a

128

little bit early in the race, and in the course of that long race I guess we all lost track of him. Everybody in the place figured Leo was a lap down, including me, so when he came after me late in the race I didn't put up much of a fight. I thought he was just unlapping himself, and the officials thought the same way. I got the checkered flag, but there was all kinds of confusion on the frontstretch after the race because Leo and his car owner, Joe Brady, insisted they had won the thing. After a short delay, I was called up onto the victory podium and we took all the photos, and it looked like just another great day at Stafford. Then they rechecked the scoring, and an hour or two later they declared that Leo had won. Well, Sonny raised hell. He appealed the decision all the way to NASCAR headquarters in Daytona Beach, which kept the results in limbo, but it did him no good. After three weeks, they named Leo the official winner.

Maybe I'd have held off Cleary if I'd known it was a straight fight, and maybe he'd have beaten me anyway. Either way, it would have been better than losing the thing by some appeals process.

Those "what-if" losses are always the worst.

In 1977, I was leading the Thompson 300 just a little bit past halfway. We were running Sonny's Pinto, the Ford-powered car, and we were really humming. Well, a caution flag waved; I can't remember if it was because it was drizzling, or if the caution waved and *then* it started spitting rain. At any rate, Sonny called me into the pits for gas and tires. It was a good call if the rain stopped, a bad call if it kept falling. Naturally, the rain kept falling, and the race was called early.

This was going to be a great finish: Richie Evans and I played cat-and-mouse for the last third of the Dogleg 200 at Trenton in 1978 before I ran out of gas with two laps to go. (R.N. Masser, Jr. Photo/Courtesy of Speedway Illustrated*)*

The end of the trail. Dave Tourigny is pushing me out of the pits to finish that Dogleg 200, but it was like the wind had gone out of our sails. We should have won that race, and instead I have absolutely no idea where we finished.
(Mike Adaskaveg Photo)

Eddie Flemke was on a different pit cycle than we were, so he'd stayed on the track under that yellow. He ended up with the win, but, no disrespect to Eddie, I'd had him covered all day long.

In April of 1978, again with that Pinto, Richie Evans and I were having a hell of a see-saw battle for the lead in a Trenton race called the Dogleg 200. It was down to the two of us—nobody else was in our league—and to this day I'm sure I was going to win. But with two laps to go, my gas tank ran dry and Richie's didn't. He won, and nobody, including me, even remembers where I finished. Like I said: What if?

Probably the toughest loss Sonny and I had came in the 1974 Race of Champions at Trenton. There's only a couple of major modified

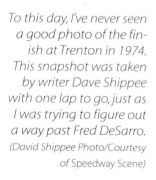

To this day, I've never seen a good photo of the finish at Trenton in 1974. This snapshot was taken by writer Dave Shippee with one lap to go, just as I was trying to figure out a way past Fred DeSarro.
(David Shippee Photo/Courtesy of Speedway Scene)

After Freddy beat me in the Race of Champions, there's no way I wasn't going to go to Victory Lane to congratulate him. That's Joe Gerber, the ROC promoter, next to me at the far left.
(Courtesy of Speedway Scene*)*

races I never managed to win, and the ROC was one of them. Without a doubt, that '74 race was my best shot.

I was in Koszela's Vega. Freddy DeSarro was leading the thing with Boehler's car, and in the final ten laps I had run him down. But my car had a serious problem: Trenton was one of the few places where the modified guys played with aerodynamics, and we had tried to get cute by taking some of our front spoiler away and adding more downforce to the back. It didn't work. At speed, the front end was just way too light, especially when I got close behind Freddy. I could turn the wheel from left to right halfway down that straightaway, and sometimes the car wouldn't even twitch. Trust me, that's not a good feeling; at 160 miles per hour, you want that thing to go where you're aiming it.

Still, I was betting that I could slingshot my way past him on the last lap. The start-finish line at Trenton was way down at the end of the frontstretch, almost in turn one, so it made it tricky to know exactly where to pull out of a guy's draft. We came flying out of turn four, me closing right in on his tail, and when I thought I had built up enough steam I pulled the wheel to the left. It hesitated a bit because of that lack of grip in the front end, but I steered out of Freddy's draft and drove right up alongside him. We flashed across the line side by side, and I actually beat him into turn one.

I thought I'd won. I was almost sure of it. But the officials decided I didn't actually get past Freddy until after we'd crossed the line. I

Sonny Koszela and I won a bunch of big races, including the 1974 Spring Sizzler, where Jackie Arute blasted us with champagne. But I still think we were a better team than our record shows. Wherever we went, we were tough. (Dugas and Glaude Photo/Courtesy of Speedway Scene)

trusted their judgement completely, but even now I'd like to look at a good photo of that finish. I've never seen one, and I'd love to know exactly how much I lost by.

It was a hard loss, because it was another what-if thing. It made me ask myself a lot of questions. Like, on that final run down the straightaway, did I have to work the wheel more than normal, because the front end wasn't sticking? Did that slow me down? Or did I just time my move wrong, and pull out of Freddy's draft just a tick too late?

People kept slapping me on the back, saying, "Geez, Bugs, in another lap you'd have had him." But the truth is, we didn't *get* another lap. The race was over, and DeSarro beat me.

The next year, I thought I might get a little bit of payback in the Race of Champions. I was battling with Ray Hendrick in the Armstrong Pinto and Merv Treichler, who was driving some swoopy-looking thing with a Monza body. I didn't have those guys covered, but I didn't think they had me covered, either. Then my right rear tire blistered and chunked, and I had to either back off or risk blowing the thing. I watched Ray and Merv drive off into the sunset, in that order, and I finished third.

Right there, we're looking at two Race of Champions victories, plus a Thompson 300, a Stafford 200, and a Dogleg 200 which, with just the tiniest change in circumstances, could have very easily belonged to Sonny and I. Man, wouldn't our record together have been something special then?

But like I've said a million times, I'm not a stat person, so it's not so much the big wins and the big losses I recall from that period. I remember that Sonny and I and the rest of that team ran together for just shy of eight years, and almost everywhere we went, we were competitive. I'm proud of that.

When we were at the top of our game, we were as tough as any NASCAR modified team in the world.

The seventies, to me, consisted of two great eras. The first was from 1971–74, when the cars were changing and the media was starting to expand the sport and the promoters were really having to work overtime. The second lasted from 1977–79, after the Stafford switch to Friday nights, just because that brought back the era of racing modifieds three nights a week in New England. We'd all run Stafford on Fridays, then split up and go to Seekonk or Riverside Park or wherever on Saturdays, and on Sundays we'd all be back together at Thompson.

Both those periods drew good crowds and good fields, and everybody seems to look back on both of them really fondly. I've even heard each of those times referred to as a Golden Age of modified racing.

What I'm happiest about is, I got plenty of punches in each time.

Ron Bouchard on Bugsy

Ron Bouchard and Bugs Stevens, Monadnock Speedway, 1979.
(Burton E. Gould, Jr. Photo/Courtesy of Speedway Scene)

Ron Bouchard, modified legend and 1981 Winston Cup Rookie of the Year: "I really got to know Bugsy in 1971 and '72, when I first went to Stafford. When I got there, the people on top were him and Freddy DeSarro and Eddie Flemke, guys like that. And the thing I noticed right away about Bugsy was that if he was fast enough to pass you, he'd pass you; he wouldn't just rub his way by, ever.

"I always looked at it like, however a guy treated me, that's how I'd treat him right back, so I raced Bugsy as clean as he raced me. We had nights where we'd run 50 laps side-by-side and nose-to-tail, and barely ever touch. And if we did touch, it was an accident, and both of us knew it.

"It wasn't that way with everybody, believe me. You knew the guys you could jump alongside and be sure that they weren't going to run you up against the wall, or down into the infield. Other guys, you weren't so sure; with those guys, you always wanted to be up in there far enough.

"You got used to how people drove in certain situations. Geoff Bodine was a guy who could get you riled up; he would drive down into the corner, and if he slid up into you, well, he just used you as a cushion. Freddy DeSarro used to do the same thing sometimes at Thompson: just drive 'er down in there, bounce off your car, and take off. When those guys would do that to me, I'd get super mad, because I knew it could have been avoided. But if it was somebody like Bugsy who ran into me, I never thought twice about it. I *knew* it wasn't intentional. If he hit me, it was because he slipped.

"The other thing was, if one of us did get into the other guy, we'd never take unfair advantage of it. What I mean is, if Bugsy knocked me sideways in the heat of battle, he'd get out of the gas, let me straighten out my car, and we'd get back at it again. I'd do the same thing if I ran into him.

"Now, don't get me wrong; even though Bugsy was a pretty polite race car driver, if you turned his butt around you had to deal with one angry character. But if you raced him clean, he'd race you clean. Those were the kinds of ethics we had, and that stuff was more important to us than just winning a race any way we could.

"I always wanted to win, but I was also the kind of guy who figured that if the best I could run was second, that wasn't too bad; if the best I could run was third, that wasn't too bad. Bugsy was the same way. If he and I finished first, second, third, wherever, as long as we'd done everything we could, we were happy. And the better the battle was between us, the more fun we had. It was really exciting to us in the cars, and I know it was to the people in the grandstands, too, because at some of these places you could actually see 'em jumping up and down.

"I think that's what people come to the track to see: good, hard, clean racing. And most of the guys we raced with—Bugsy, Eddie, Richie Evans— were the kinds of drivers who could put on that kind of a show. You could *depend* on those guys. You knew that if you got outside of them, they were going to leave you a lane.

"I watched a modified race at Thompson not too long ago, and it seemed like rather than trying to pass somebody, they'd just run into each other. That always irritated me when I raced. If we couldn't get under somebody, we tried to go around him. But you don't see that now; if they can't get inside a guy, they just knock him out of the way. It's like, 'I couldn't pass you clean, so I'll just run over you.' I have a hard time looking at some of the things they do out there and thinking it's all right.

"When we raced, that stuff was a crime. You just didn't do that. Hell, you didn't *want* to do it. Because, see, when that race was over, we were going to go out in the parking lot and relax. It was nothing to see five or six haulers sitting there, and a bunch of people enjoying themselves. Somebody was going to cook some clams and lobsters, and we were going to drink some beer, and Bugsy was going to smoke his cigar, and we were all going to laugh."

Etiquette

Etiquette

I MENTIONED IN THE LAST CHAPTER that there have been a few different Golden Ages of modified racing, periods when the sport was really booming. It's probably impossible to say which one was *the* Golden Age; you can debate that subject all day and night.

But I will say this: If you want to judge a division by the level of the competition, I don't think modified racing has ever been any better than it was in the sixties and seventies. And when I talk about the competition, I don't mean the difference in the lap times between the fast guys and the slow guys; I mean, the *quality* of the racing.

I don't want to sound like an old fart, but there was a higher level of driving back then. I'm positive about that.

Now, I'm not saying we were better drivers than these guys today. But I do think we were better *racers*. And I think that's true right from the top of the sport down to the local level.

In the past 10 years or so, I've seen a real lack of discipline start to creep into the sport. It gets worse with every new crop of young drivers. Honestly, I think it's brought on by what they see on TV; they watch those big-league drivers get away with all kinds of bumping and slamming, so they figure it's all right to do the same thing.

Well, it's not all right with me.

In my day, we were taught to out-*drive* the other guy, not out-*bang* him. We were taught that you passed another driver fair and square, or you didn't pass him at all.

Obviously, a lot of drivers today don't have that same attitude. Look how many times over the past few years we've seen Winston Cup and Busch Series races on television where one guy just knocked the other guy out of the groove to pass him. Look how many times we've seen the leader get nudged out of the way in the last couple of laps, or get spun out altogether. Then the winner stands there in victory lane and says, "Well, I did what I had to do."

Well, that's not true. He didn't do what he *had* to do, he did what he *wanted* to do. He wanted to win that race at any cost, damn the other guy.

That sort of thing has gotten so common that whenever it happens, people say, "Hey, that's racing." But it's not racing to me. It's stupidity.

You're supposed to pass the other car, not knock it out of the way. These are races, not demolition derbies. And these are race cars, not dodge-'em cars at the carnival.

I raced modifieds for 25 years, and I can't remember a half-dozen races in all that time when one driver took out another—I mean, blatantly moved him out of the way—to win the race. It just didn't happen. Sure, in the early stages of a race or in the middle laps, there were times when you might get a bit physical if a guy was blocking you, really running you around. But if it came down to the last couple of laps and none of your best moves was good enough to get past the leader, you settled for second and told yourself you'd get him tomorrow night. You might not have been *happy* finishing second, but at least you were satisfied in knowing that you had taken your best shot. For us, that was good enough.

You know what it all comes down to? We had a higher degree of respect than these kids today. I mean, respect for our equipment, respect for one another, and especially respect for the ethics of driving. We *cared* more about that stuff. There's no question about that.

One night at Seekonk, late in my career, I was in a tight battle on the last lap of the feature; I was running second, but I was all over the leader. Well, the guy left me a hole on the inside, and I jumped right in there. Sure enough, as soon as I got the nose of my car in there so far that I couldn't back out, he came down, and we touched. Not *hard*, but we definitely touched. He probably didn't mean to chop me—maybe he just figured I wasn't down there—and I sure didn't mean to run into him. But when we bumped, the contact shoved him up the track. I won the race, and he ran second.

I didn't feel the least bit guilty about what had happened, and I still don't. I was in that hole, no doubt about it, and he made a mistake. My conscious was clear. But you know something? I didn't enjoy winning that night like I normally would have. It wasn't the same excitement I always felt after a clear-cut win.

Today, when a driver wins a race that way, he's jumping around and high-fiving the guys on his team. And they're all saying, "That's racing."

I think that sucks.

For years and years, race drivers lived by a set of unwritten rules. The best drivers, I think, still follow them.

They're pretty simple, really.

If you're faster than the guy ahead of you and you're trying to take his position, you've got to have your front wheel beside his cockpit,

In my day, most of us raced according to the same set of unwritten rules. That's Eddie Flemke and me running hard but clean at Albany-Saratoga in 1973. (Mike Adaskaveg Photo)

where you *know* he can see you. If you're not up that far, he owns the groove; he's got the right of way. But once you do get up to his cockpit, you expect that guy to realize that you're there, and it's up to him to give way. You've got the line. It's a give-and-take thing.

You apply that same basic theory when you're in his position, with a faster car behind you. You're the boss when you're in front, and you've got a right to defend your turf. But once that faster car gets a wheel on you, you've got to surrender the line. That doesn't mean you have to surrender the *spot*; you can still fight as hard as you want to in whatever lane you've got left. But the groove now belongs to the other guy. He earned it.

Nobody knows for sure where these rules got started, but I'm sure they originated in open-wheel racing because at one time that's all there was. Around the Northeast, most guys my age watched a lot of midget races in the 1950s, and that's the way those drivers behaved. And, of course, it makes sense to drive with a little bit of courtesy in an open-wheel car; if you get too stubborn and you hook wheels, you might get the worst end of the crash.

But regardless of where they started, those same general rules applied wherever you raced, and whatever you raced. In the modifieds, they were the law, at least in my eyes. If a guy got a wheel under me, I surrendered the line. If I had a wheel on him, I expected the same treatment. It made for great racing, *fair* racing.

I don't know what happened to that philosophy. You watch a Winston Cup race, and those guys talk like it's okay to beat and bang one another. And it's not just the Cup guys; even the weekly racers are rougher than ever.

Don't get me wrong, I've been in my share of tough races. I ran a hundred races at Seekonk and Westboro where it seemed like all night long we'd be clanging into each other, but it was all just accidental stuff, the kind of thing you get on tight tracks: One guy lifts, the next guy doesn't, and you have a little chain-reaction bumping. But it sure wasn't intentional. It sure wasn't expected. And it sure wasn't *accepted*.

When I think about the best racing I've ever done, I don't necessarily think about winning. I think about the nights I ran side-by-side, lap after lap, with guys who felt the same way about fairness that I did. And there were an awful lot of drivers like that.

Ronnie Bouchard and I have gone wheel-to-wheel around Stafford so many times that we've both lost count, and we never even came close to touching unless one guy made an honest mistake. Freddy DeSarro and I did the same thing on Sundays for years at Thompson. George Summers and I ran many, many Seekonk features door-to-door. At other tracks it was me and Eddie Flemke, or me and Richie Evans. I enjoyed all those races, even the ones I lost, because of the way we treated each other.

For the most part, none of the modified guys drove dirty. Nobody who did much winning, anyway.

Sure, some guys were sloppy. Sometimes you'd have a driver who was a bull in a china shop, who just didn't have the patience or finesse

It doesn't get much closer than this. Ronnie Bouchard and I ran a thousand laps like this at Stafford. (Mike Adaskaveg Photo)

it took to run wheel-to-wheel without running into the side of you. But those guys weren't dirty, they were just undisciplined. You keep a close eye on a driver like that, because that kind of guy can screw things up without even meaning to. In that situation, I'd watch his front wheels, watch his hands on the steering wheel, and be ready for any sign of a bobble. That's just experience. Once a guy gets in trouble enough times, you learn to watch him.

But even those guys knew the code: As long as you raced fairly, you got raced fairly in return.

Of course, if you broke the code, there were probably going to be consequences. There's an old saying: If you live by the sword, you die by the sword. Our version was, If you want to race in a way that isn't fair, well, we can do that, too.

I never liked to drive dirty, never liked to play rough. But if I had to, I could. Sooner or later, most of the guys who crossed the line with me ended up paying for it. I didn't wreck 'em, because that wasn't my style. But one way or another, I got even.

I spun Jerry Cook two or three times at Albany-Saratoga, and every time it was in response to something he had done to me. Looking back on it, Cookie probably wasn't any tougher on me than he was on anybody else; he was just a hard-nosed racer. If you tried to pass him on the low side, he'd run you into the infield. If you looked to the outside, he'd squeeze you right up to the wall. If you gave him a tap, he might give you a brake job in return. And things weren't any easier when he was following you. If Jerry could get to your rear bumper, he was going to use it up. I'm not saying he was dirty, but

Jerry Cook and I played our share of bumper tag. This time, he turned me around in the first turn at Stafford ...

… and I wasn't in much of a mood to listen to his explanation later on. But we put it behind us, and down the road we went.
(Mike Adaskaveg Photos)

Cook definitely had a different style, a *rougher* style, than I did. All I did was race him the way he raced me, and that didn't always work out too well for him.

I dumped Eddie Flemke one night up at Catamount, in a national championship race. I have to say, Eddie was one of the cleanest drivers I knew, and he was a friend of mine, too. But on this particular night, I was ahead of him, and he was trying to get past me. He had a faster car at that point in the race, but I was in the groove; I wasn't *blocking*, I was just running my line, following those unwritten rules. Well, Eddie kept banging me: *wham, wham, wham*. He turned my car sideways three or four times, and the last time I damn near spun out. That was enough. Catamount didn't have an outside wall on the backstretch, but if you got a wheel off the track and into the dirt you were in for the slide of your life. I let Eddie get alongside me through the first and second turns, and as we came out of two I drifted up and ran him right off the race track.

Now, I didn't *crash* Eddie, but I did send him out into the boondocks. I didn't enjoy doing it, but the way I saw it, I had taken enough. I could put up with a shot in the bumper as good as the next guy if I thought it was just incidental contact, but, man, don't get me crossed up again and again. That's what Eddie had done, and it got me pissed off.

I don't remember where I finished that night, but it was better than Flemke finished. As soon as I climbed out of my car, I walked

This was a pretty big night. In 1975, Geoff Bodine pinched me into the fence at Stafford out of turn four, and I ended up crashing down the whole front straightaway. (Eugene Frankio Photo/Courtesy of Speedway Scene*)*

right over to find him. He was furious, just ripping mad, but I stayed calm.

I said, "Eddie, you *know* what that was for."

We talked for a minute, and he was still mad when I left, but I'm sure we both let go of it before we ever got to the next track. Eddie was a pro about things like that, and so was I. We raced together for 20 years, and, looking back, that might have been the only problem we had.

One of the best examples of payback I've ever been involved in happened while I wasn't even on the race track. In 1975 at Stafford, Geoff Bodine and I were battling for the lead toward the end of a 30-lap feature. That was Geoff's first year driving for Dick Armstrong, which made it his first year racing on a regular basis in New England. He probably felt like the new kid on the block, and I think he was trying to prove himself. Anyway, I had my car outside his as we ran through turns three and four, and Geoff *knew* I was out there. But I guess he figured that if he crowded me toward the wall coming out of four, I was going to lift.

Well, he guessed wrong, because I didn't lift. I stayed right in the throttle, and we came out of turn four together.

At that point, Geoff was supposed to stop crowding me. He was supposed to leave me a lane. But instead he kept on coming, and stuck me right into the fence. I kept my foot in it, hoping that I'd just bounce off the guardrail, but my right-side tires climbed the fence and I had a hell of a wreck. Frankie Sgambato, who was the Stafford starter for years, told me later, "I was sure you were coming up into that flagstand with me." I ended up crashing all the way down to turn one, trailing a big shower of sparks behind me.

Everybody in the place knew that Bodine's move had crossed the line between what was fair and what wasn't. I knew it. Geoff *had* to know it. And Bobby Santos sure knew it. Santos had been running third in Joe Brady's car, so he had a pretty good view of the whole thing. Now, Bobby was a hard racer, but he'd run you clean, run you fair. He was like the rest of us: he had strong views about that sort of thing.

And as soon as they got the race restarted, Santos put *Geoff* in the wall. Took him right out of the race. The way Bobby saw it, that was the right thing to do.

Like I said: Live by the sword ...

But, again, that stuff was pretty rare. I didn't have to pay many guys back, and neither did most of the top drivers, because our crowd raced pretty cleanly. We drove in ways that didn't get us in trouble very often. I know I keep using this word, but we instinctively treated the other guy with respect. We left him a lane instead of rubbing nerf bars with him.

Now, this wasn't necessarily because we were looking out for each other. I mean, I'm sure all those guys wanted to beat me, and I damn sure wanted to beat them. Believe me, I didn't spend much time worrying about the other guy. But the fact that we followed those unwritten rules in just about every situation kept us clean even when that seemed impossible.

In the seventies, Thompson used to run small-block modified races every Sunday evening, and those shows attracted cars from all over New England. Like most places, Thompson handicapped the line-up according to the money you'd won recently, and it was always

Me, John Rosati and Ron Bouchard ran a lot of laps together in the 1970s and early '80s. (Harry Moore Photo/Courtesy of Speedway Scene*)*

143

Some of the best racing I've ever done was at Thompson in the 1970s. That's Freddy DeSarro in Boehler's Vega and me in Koszela's Pinto in the summer of '77.
(Mike Adaskaveg Photo)

the same group of fast guys in the back: me, Freddy, Eddie, Ronnie and Kenny Bouchard, Geoff Bodine once he moved out here, John Rosati, and one or two more. There was a huge difference between the good cars and the bad cars, and that *really* showed up at a big, fast track like Thompson. We were constantly in traffic, fighting our way through the slower cars, knowing that whoever got to the front first had the best shot at winning. Things happen fast at Thompson even when you're out there alone, but when you've got five or six fast guys closing in on all these slower cars, it's a real adventure. It was a job just to make it through that mess without getting yourself into trouble, and yet most times we managed to keep *each other* out of trouble, too.

If we had been a bunch of hardheads, we could have had a major crash every damn Sunday. But very seldom was there ever a problem.

I'll tell you how much things have changed. There was a time when the writers would refer to me as an "aggressive" driver, because I always charged to the front. They said the same thing about Bouchard, Freddy, Richie, a lot of us. Well, when anybody today uses that term —aggressive—what they really mean is that the guy makes a lot of contact.

Think about it: Every time the TV people talked about Dale Earnhardt being aggressive, they didn't show him passing cars; they showed him running into somebody. That's a shame. Earnhardt had an amazing amount of talent, but he's remembered for roughing people up. In a way, that helped make all this seem okay to younger drivers. They saw Earnhardt and other guys get away with it for years, so they figure it's acceptable. In my mind, excess contact is not acceptable. Even the worst driver can run into another car.

As much as I holler about all this, I'm not sure it's a problem that can be solved. Now that's it's gotten this far out of hand, it'd be awfully tough to get racing back to the way it was.

Maybe it all comes down to basic training. If every young kid learned by driving quarter-midgets instead of by watching those Winston Cup guys run into each other on television, they'd be better drivers in the long run. *Cleaner* drivers. I think that's why you seldom see guys like Ken Schrader, Tony Stewart and Dave Blaney make crazy moves. In open-wheel cars, you learn that there are consequences to sloppy driving. You learn that if you don't race with the proper respect, you're liable to take a bad ride.

Then again, maybe the reasons for all this rough stuff go beyond racing. I mean, society in general is different than it used to be. My generation was brought up to respect so many different things: our parents, other people's property, money, you name it. What do these kids respect today?

I know what a lot of them *don't* respect, when it comes to racing: all those old unwritten rules. That shows up every weekend, whether you're watching a Winston Cup race or sitting in the grandstands at some short track. They'll chop the guy on the inside, they'll spin the other guy out as soon as they can get to his bumper, they'll knock the leader out of the way if that's what it takes. And they won't feel the least bit sorry about it.

I'm telling you, I'd be in a lot of trouble if I raced against some of these guys. I'd wake up every Monday morning with sore knuckles.

In the old days, I was called an aggressive driver, but that word meant something entirely different back then.
(Mike Adaskaveg Photo)

Geoff Bodine on Bugsy

Geoff Bodine, modified legend and 1986 Daytona 500 winner: "In one of my very first races in New England with Dick Armstrong's car, we had a little incident at Stafford. I ran into Bugsy coming out of turn four, and he wrecked, and I think that set the stage for our future.

"The majority of fans at those tracks at that time were Bugsy Stevens fans, and when you tangled with Bugsy, you knew you were going to have to deal with all of those people. So after that incident, I got booed pretty much everywhere out there: Stafford, Thompson, Seekonk, Westboro, wherever we went. That was my introduction to modified racing in New England. I definitely didn't get off on the right foot. Bumping into Bugsy Stevens was the wrong thing to do.

"To this day, when somebody mentions Bugsy's name, the first thing I think of is that incident at Stafford. It still comes back. That was just so big a thing at the time.

"Looking back on it, our rivalry definitely helped establish me with the race fans in New England. It made me an item in that area. Some people liked me, and some people booed me. But you know something? Whenever you have a rivalry going, it means you get people coming out to see which guy is going to win on that particular night. If you didn't have that sort of thing going on, they wouldn't care as much.

"So I think you need to have rivalries. They keep things interesting. Otherwise, things get stagnant after a while. You get used to the same guys battling it out every week. It's good to get some new blood in there sometimes, somebody who comes in and goes up against the local guy. And I think that in Bugsy's case, I filled that position.

"But I never had any bad feelings toward him. I mean, we were fierce competitors; Bugsy wanted to win just as badly as I did. When you went to the race track, you knew he was a guy you'd have to beat.

"The best thing about Bugsy was, he'd race you clean. That's how I remember him, as a clean driver. A hard driver, sure, but a clean one. There were plenty of guys around who didn't race you quite as cleanly as he did.

"Without Bugsy—actually, without a lot of the drivers I raced against back then—I might not have made it to Winston Cup. Because those guys weren't just good drivers, they were great drivers. And that's how you learn, by racing against the *great* drivers.

Rivals

Geoff Bodine and Bugs Stevens, Thompson Speedway, 1978. (Mike Adaskaveg Photo)

"If you always race against average drivers, you end up being average yourself. So I was very lucky to race against guys like Bugsy Stevens who were way, way above average. They were right at the top. They were the best."

Rivals

147

Rivals

I WAS NEVER VERY BIG on ranking the guys I raced against. At the same time, that's one of the things people want you to do once you have any success. Right from the time I had enough of a name for reporters to interview, they'd always ask, "Who's the toughest guy you've ever run against?"

Usually, I just dodged the question. The way I looked at it, that sort of thing could only get me into trouble. For one thing, it's a very hard call. I raced against hundreds of guys, maybe thousands. In that group, there were a bunch of very race drivers, and the ones who were good usually had different qualities that *made* them good. If one guy is excellent at the big tracks and another guy is fantastic on the bullrings, which one of them am I supposed to believe is actually better?

And, don't forget, I raced against guys from a few different eras: the coupe days, the Pinto and Vega days, and even a handful of guys who are still racing today. Every one of those periods had drivers who stood out, and it's awfully tough to take a guy who was a big star in the eighties and compare him to a guy who was a big star in the sixties. Unless you can see how guys match up head-to-head over a certain span of time, it's hard to put one above the other.

It's a pretty big subject, a deep subject, and I always figured it was easiest to just leave it alone.

But I guess if I'm ever going to address it, this might be the right place.

One thing that comes to mind when I look back at some of the great modified drivers is how many of them were supposed to be big enemies of mine.

Years ago, before everybody in racing was a goody-two-shoes, the promoters used to manufacture these big rivalries. For example, they'd hype up the fact that two guys had each won three races at this particular track, and this Saturday night was going to be the big rubber match. At the same time, they'd make it sound like those two guys really didn't like each other very much. Or they'd make a big deal out of the fact that an outsider was coming into town for some major race, and they'd play him off against the track champion, the local hero.

Nothing sells tickets like a rivalry.

Well, I guess I must have been a promoter's delight, because for twenty years they built up these rivalries between me and whoever else was winning at the time. At different times it was me and Eddie Flemke, me and Ray Hendrick, me and Jerry Cook, me and Freddy DeSarro, me and Ronnie Bouchard, me and Geoff Bodine. I've been the new guy, the veteran, the local hero, the good guy, maybe even the bad guy sometimes.

However they wanted to use me, that was all right. If it brought people out to the race track, it was okay by me. I thought it was part of my job, so I always played right along with it.

It did get a little bit funny sometimes, because most of us were pretty good friends. I mean, I'd be standing in the pits shooting the breeze with Freddy or Ronnie, and in the background we'd hear the announcer getting the crowd fired up about these big feuds between us.

But, you know, those crowds were pretty big, so it was working.

When I first left Seekonk and started racing at Norwood and Thompson, Eddie Flemke was one of the hottest guys in New England. Hell, Eddie was a hot guy *everywhere*, because he was just coming out of his Eastern Bandit phase, when he traveled down South every weekend and beat those guys up pretty badly. Eddie wasn't much older than me, but he had definitely been *around* more; even in the mid-sixties, he was seen as one of the veterans in the modifieds.

Eddie Flemke was half race driver and half psychologist, a guy who really knew how to get into your head. He taught lessons to a lot of race drivers, me included. (Mike Adaskaveg Photos)

149

Jerry Cook and I were never big rivals in my mind, but sometimes the promoters played it up that way. (Mike Adaskaveg Photo)

Because of that, and because of the fact that I was pretty hot with Lenny Boehler's car, it made sense to pit me and Eddie as rivals. At the same time, though, we always got along. Right from the start, I felt like we respected each other.

Flemke was a smart, smart guy, a *thinker*. And I'm not just talking about his chassis knowledge, because everybody knows Eddie was a great setup man. What I mean is, Eddie was a real psychologist. He played all kinds of head games with you, on and off the race track, and most of them worked. But he was also an excellent teacher; people talk about the way he helped guys like Pete Hamilton and Denny Zimmerman, but he was one of *my* professors, too. Many times, Eddie took me aside and talked to me, and not just in my early days; that

This was a rivalry of drivers and cars: me in the Boehler 3 against Ray Hendrick and the Tant-Mitchell 11. (Balser and Son Photo)

went on right up into the eighties. I think Eddie enjoyed that side of racing, and that paid off for a lot of guys, me included.

Flemke was a terrific driver, a guy you could trust, and he won just about everyplace he went. The only thing you could ever put down as a mark against him is that he never had a great deal of success on the bigger tracks, places like Trenton or Langhorne. But, you know, that never hurt him much, because the short tracks were his bread and butter. And for a long time, Eddie Flemke was *the* guy to beat on a lot of nights.

Once Jerry Cook started chasing NASCAR points in the late sixties, it seemed like some people played up the idea of him and me being rivals. But I never really saw us that way; it was something the promoters and the writers dreamed up, I think, because now you had one guy who had won three championships and another guy who was out to win the title himself.

Cookie and I had different styles. I always raced to win, and I think he was more concerned with making money and chasing those points. And that's not a knock against him, by any means; Jerry knew the system, and he sure knew how to make it work for him, because the guy won six NASCAR modified championships. I didn't always agree with the blocking and the banging he'd do, but there's no doubt that Cookie was a good race driver.

There was a stretch in the late sixties and early seventies when the New England promoters used to bring up Ray Hendrick and then make a big deal out of the two of us going at it. They'd throw a few dollars to Ray and his car owners whenever there was a special show at Thompson or Stafford. For some reason, people always acted like I

Ray Hendrick and I were always pretty good buddies, even when we were supposed to be the fiercest rivals in modified racing. (Dick Berggren Photo)

Freddy DeSarro and I were both smart enough not to let our big ride swap in 1971 come between us. Some of the most fun races of my life came against that man. (Courtesy of Speedway Scene)

ought to be mad about that, but I never was. I had enough confidence in myself to believe that if my car was right, I shouldn't have to worry about anybody they brought in. Plus, I had seen the other side of that coin in the late sixties, when I spent a lot of time on Ray's turf. Boehler and I would show up at some of those tracks in Virginia and North Carolina and, man, we were a *big* deal. I'd get all these big write-ups in the local paper: the Yankee hot dog was coming in to steal the money from the local guys, that's how they played it. So I understood the promotional value of bringing Ray to our neck of the woods. It made sense.

Hendrick was a hard charger, a guy who only had one speed: flat out. But he also had a ton of ability. Sure, he had superior equipment, the best of its time—I mean, that Tant-Mitchell 11 was a fast sonofabitch—but you can't underestimate what Ray brought to that package. He was a fierce competitor who didn't take any prisoners, and if you saw that number 11 in the pits, you knew you were in for a race.

Even in the middle of that big North/South thing, Ray and I were friends. We used to joke around quite a bit when raced together, and even more so when I'd see him someplace like Martinsville after he retired. He's definitely one of the all-time greats, in my book.

Fred DeSarro was another great racer. He was aggressive, but he used his head, too, and you can see that by all the races he won. Freddy was a factor just about everywhere he went, but it seemed like he was tougher at Thompson than anywhere else. Part of that, I'm sure, is because he drove so long for Lenny Boehler, and Lenny always had that track figured out better than anybody.

We got pretty close, Freddy and I. Once a month or so, he'd stop by my salvage yard with a case of Heineken and the two of us would put a pretty good dent in that box of beer. It's funny to look back on that, because this was all in a period when he and I were supposed to be the two biggest rivals in New England; it wasn't much earlier that we'd done that big Boehler/Koszela ride swap. But there was never any bad blood between us, ever. In fact, when Freddy beat me at Trenton in '74, I was genuinely happy for him. I mean, he was a friend of mine, a *good* friend, and he had won the Race of Champions. That was quite an accomplishment.

We had an awful lot of battles together, because it seemed like we usually ran the same circuit every weekend: first Stafford, Norwood, and Thompson; then Albany-Saratoga, Stafford and Thompson; then Stafford, Seekonk and Thompson. Wherever you saw one of us, you usually saw the other one. Some of the best racing I've ever done, I did alongside Freddy DeSarro. He was as solid as they came.

Ronnie Bouchard was one of the better drivers I ever ran against. People forget this, but Ronnie came from a racing background. His father, Bob, had owned coupes and cutdowns for years up around Westboro and the old Pines Speedway, and Pete Salvatore had won a lot of races driving those cars. So Ronnie *understood* the game better than a lot of other young guys did, and he was competitive right from the time he showed up at Seekonk in the mid-sixties. He won four or five track championships there before he started running the NASCAR modifieds, and that was when he really began to shine.

He was such a steady guy; you could bet your life on Ronnie not trying anything stupid. Looking back, I think he felt that way about

Ronnie Bouchard came along a few years after I did, but we became friends and we stayed friends, even though we raced like the devil three nights a week. (Courtesy of Speedway Scene)

me. He *must* have, because the two of us had some great fights. For a while there in the early seventies, when he was driving for Bob Johnson and I was with Sonny Koszela, Ronnie and I took turns being the king of the hill at Stafford; he was the track champion in 1973, and I won the title in '74, and in both of those seasons we dominated that place. Later on, after Stafford switched back to Friday nights, Ronnie and I had some really fun battles at Seekonk.

On top of that, we were friends. I liked Ronnie as soon as I met him, and we stayed friends through his whole modified career and his whole Winston Cup career, too. Hell, we're *still* friends. I see him occasionally, even now that neither one of us has raced in years. Ronnie is like me, in the sense that he saw a life outside racing. He's got a half-dozen automobile dealerships, and he's done really well for himself. I'm proud of him.

Probably the one rivalry in my career that ever got a little bit out of hand—that ever *felt* like a rivalry—was the one between me and Geoff Bodine. It started almost right from the time he moved from New York to Massachusetts to work and drive for Dick Armstrong.

I had raced with Geoff a bunch of times when he had his own cars, and he was fast from the beginning. He won Trenton in '72 with a Valiant-bodied modified he had built, and it had a bunch of different ideas on it. You could tell right away that Geoffrey had his shit together. I'd also see him at Martinsville and some of the bigger races in New England, or when Koszela and I would tow out to New York. But in that period, I never really knew him; he was just a kid who was becoming one of the guys to beat.

Once he hooked up with Armstrong, Geoff went from being *one of* the guys to being *the* guy to beat. Dick always had great equipment, and when he hired Geoff—who was a super chassis man, very clever—and let him run the show, they were a dynamite combination.

Bodine and I kind of swapped good seasons at Stafford. He was the champion there in 1975, but I won more races that year, so I was all

That's Geoff Bodine in his old Valiant, leading me on the three-quarter-miler at Pocono in 1972. Right from the time he got started, Geoff was awfully fast. (Courtesy of Speedway Illustrated)

This is Geoff Bodine in the Armstrong number 1. Geoff and I on got really close on the race track a hundred times, but never off it. We were just different people, I guess.
(R.N. Masser, Jr. Photo/Courtesy of Speedway Illustrated)

right with that. The next year, Geoffrey had the most wins, but I had him and everybody else covered in '77, the year Sonny and I had that Ford-powered Pinto. Then Bodine had a killer year in '78, not just at Stafford but *everywhere*; he won something like 54 races that year.

As much as we raced together, I never did get close to Geoff. He didn't associate with the rest of us, and I don't believe he ever wanted to. And, looking back on it, maybe we didn't want to associate with him, either. I'm sure there was some jealousy on our parts, because here you had a kid who had all this great equipment at his disposal, kicking our asses. Geoff was smart, he was a very good race driver, but the only thing a lot of people saw was Dick Armstrong's money. Everybody resents the idea that they might be getting bullied by a big-dollar team, so it was a natural thing for a lot of people to look at Bodine as the bad guy.

Of course, there were a few nights when Geoff really *was* the bad guy. He crashed me that one time at Stafford, the night when Bobby Santos stuck him in the fence, and we had another controversial wreck at Seekonk. Sometimes he was overaggressive, and that frustrated me, because when you've got equipment like Geoff had and talent like he had, there's no need to bulldoze your way to the front.

Some people made a lot out of the fact that Geoff was an outsider coming into New England to race, as if that was the reason he wasn't accepted, but that's not it. Sure, for a long time every area had its own little cliques, but that stuff had pretty much passed by the time Geoff came over from New York. I mean, we accepted Richie Evans. We accepted Maynard Troyer. And whenever I went to New York to race, I *always* felt accepted. I think it all comes back to personalities.

You know what it was? Geoff went to the track for one thing, and

There's one thing about Geoff Bodine: He wasn't in racing to make friends. When he got booed after we crashed at Thompson in 1978, he gave the grandstands a double thumbs-up, which fired them up even more. (Mike Adaskaveg Photo)

one thing only: to race. He wasn't there to make friends. He was trying to build his career, and you can't deny that he accomplished his mission. He won all the big modified races, and when he moved on he won all the big NASCAR late model sportsman races, and later on he won *the* biggest Winston Cup race, the Daytona 500. And you've got to admire him for that.

If Geoff is happy with the way his career went, hell, I'm happy for him. It just so happened that I lived and raced a different way. And, you know, maybe that's what made our rivalry so interesting to people.

There were so many good guys over the years that I almost have to break them down into groups, according to when I first saw them.

I raced against George Summers for about as long as I raced against anybody. He was already one of the hot dogs at Seekonk when I got started there in 1961, and when he retired more than twenty years later he was still a hot dog. He won the last race he ever ran, at Thompson in 1983, and just can't imagine going out any better than that. I've always felt that George was one of the most underrated guys in modified racing. Not underrated by his fellow drivers; we all knew how good he was. But a lot of the winning he did, especially in the seventies, was at Seekonk and Westboro at a time when those places didn't get the publicity some of the bigger tracks got. Summers might win at both of those places one week, but on the front page of the next week's *Speedway Scene* you'd see me or Ronnie or whoever won at Stafford. But late in his career, when he joined up with Art Barry and started running Stafford and Thompson on a regular basis, George proved that he was as tough at the bigger tracks as he was at the bullrings. He was incredibly talented and he was smart, and it was always fun to run with him.

When I first got out of Seekonk and started running NASCAR, Bill Slater was the top guy at Norwood. If you beat Slater and his car—that famous black V8—it was like you had punched out King Kong. Well, I got going well enough in Lenny Boehler's coupe that I beat Bill a few times in our first season up there, and I believe that created a little bit of friction between us. Not from my side, ever, but I think from Bill's; I mean, here I was, a Seekonk guy stepping up to the big-time and knocking him off his perch. I might be wrong, but back then I felt like Bill resented me for intruding on his territory. I tried to be friendly, and I *was* pretty friendly with his mechanics; I'd stop by the V8 in the pits, and we'd all talk. But Bill and I didn't click until later on, after he retired from driving and became an official at Stafford and then Thompson. We became good friends, and we still are.

In the Norwood days, it seemed like whenever Slater didn't win, Leo Cleary did. Leo would drive the balls off anything he sat in, and at Norwood that aggressive style won him a lot of features. But he was tough wherever he went: Thompson, Stafford, Westboro, Seekonk, you name it. Cleary understood the mechanical end of racing, and on top of that he had a lot of ability behind the wheel. But the biggest thing he had going for him was his determination. I mean, he was the single most determined race driver I've ever seen. Today's fans know about Dale Earnhardt being so determined, but Leo Cleary was Earnhardt *before* Earnhardt.

Three guys on the way up: From left to right, that's Leo Cleary, me, and Fred DeSarro. (Balser and Son Photo)

When he was in the right car, Gene Bergin was as tough as anybody. That's 'ole Gene with Monadnock promoter Bill Brown and me at Monadnock in the late 1970s. (Burton E. Gould, Jr., Photo/Courtesy of Speedway Scene*)*

In 1966, when Boehler and I really started traveling, Ernie Gahan was the NASCAR modified champion, so he was somebody I looked up to. His big strength, I think, was his versatility; he was as good on dirt as he was on pavement, and in those days that really paid off. Before Stafford was paved, Ernie was one of the kings of that place, and he was also really tough out at Fonda, against some of the best dirt racers in the Northeast. But he was no pushover on pavement; I still remember some of the battles we had at Norwood Arena.

Fats Caruso was another guy who was on top when I came up, but it seemed like once I got to that level, Fats's career went kind of hot and cold. I think one of the things that plagued Fats as the years went along was that sometimes he was in top equipment, and sometimes he wasn't. There were times when he got stuck without the right mechanics, and I think it showed in the results. But if he was there, you knew he was going to run hard. He was somebody you'd have to deal with.

Gene Bergin was a great natural talent, a charger who drove hard from the green flag to the checkered flag. That wasn't always easy in those old coupes, but Bergin could hang it out there as good as any of 'em. Unfortunately, you can say the same thing about Gene that I said about Fats: late in his career he sometimes he ended up in cars that weren't the greatest, and he suffered because of that. But whenever he drove for guys like Bobby Judkins, or when he was in Beebe Zalenski's M6, Gene was awfully tough.

But it's like I keep saying: There were so *many* good drivers.

As the years rolled on, some of those guys stuck around, and some of them didn't. The ones that left got replaced by the next group of guys who came along. That's how it goes; there's always somebody who'll come along and fill up an empty seat.

At the time, I didn't sense that the tide was changing. My life was so hectic back then that I just showed up and raced whoever was there. I never said, "Okay, this guy is gone, but now I've got to handle that guy over there." It just happened. The faces changed, and I never really noticed it.

But, looking back, I can see it pretty clearly, the way every few years a whole new bunch of drivers came along.

Kenny Bouchard—ol' Zeke, as I always called him—was a very good race driver. He did better at some places than others, but, again, that might have been an equipment thing. I know one thing: you sure can't say anything bad about Kenny from a driving standpoint. Just like his older brother Ronnie, you could trust him all night long, lap after lap after lap. If there was any problem with Kenny, I think it's that maybe he was too complacent. He was a happy-go-lucky guy, and I think he was content where he was for a long time. Later on, he tried chasing that Winston Cup deal, and in 1988 he was the Rookie of the Year down there, so he had the ability to do bigger things. But I don't believe he pushed himself soon enough, or hard enough.

When I think of Maynard Troyer, I think of the way he paid attention to the mechanical end of things. Don't get me wrong, Maynard could definitely get the job done behind the wheel, but it was his engineering ability that really kept him up front. His cars were always on the cutting edge of the latest modified technology; I think he had that in common with Geoff Bodine. Maybe it was a New York thing, I don't know. Both Maynard and Geoff spent a lot of time around the

Maynard Troyer was a tough guy to beat, because he'd show up with some pretty trick cars and then drive the wheels off them. That's Maynard and me at Stafford in 1977. (Mike Adaskaveg Photo)

Charlie Jarzombek was best known for being the king of the Long Island bullrings, but I chased him at a lot of places, including Trenton, where this shot was taken. (Mike Adaskaveg Photo)

supermodified guys at Oswego, and I'm sure that showed them a different way of looking at things. You can always get a few ideas for one division by studying another division, and Maynard had lots of tricks.

There were a bunch of really good drivers to come out of Long Island—Fred Harbach, Ted Wesnofske, and a few more—but you'd have to put Charlie Jarzombek right at the top of the list. They didn't call that man Chargin' Charlie for nothing; I mean, he had balls like a brass mule. He was one of the few guys I'd put in the Leo Cleary category when it came to being determined.

Charlie was the kind of guy you raced according to how he raced you. What I mean is, he'd dish it out, but he could take it. Charlie would bang me, and I'd bang him right back, but we both knew where

Just as my modified career was starting to wind down, a whole new bunch of talented guys came along, including Reggie Ruggiero. On this day in 1981, I won at Oxford Plains and Reggie ran second. (Courtesy of Speedway Scene)

to draw the line. He was never a dirty driver, but you'd definitely have to say that Charlie's style was *physical*.

You know, people talk about those Long Island guys being so rough, but when you really look at it, you couldn't *help* but be rough at the places where they learned to race. In the sixties I ran at Islip Speedway with a fuel-injected big-block and brakes that were primitive compared to what's out there today. You want to know what that felt like on that tiny little track? Go bolt a 327 Chevy into your lawnmower, and try to do U-turns in your driveway.

Honestly, it's amazing that those guys on the Island didn't crash *more*.

The thing that sets Charlie apart in my eyes is that he was one of the few Long Island guys who was pretty successful on the bigger tracks, too. He won races at Martinsville, won a championship at Stafford, and was always in the picture at Trenton and Pocono.

Toward the end of my career in the modifieds, there was a whole new group to deal with: Reggie Ruggiero, Greg Sacks, Brett Bodine, Mike Stefanik, Jimmy Spencer, Mike McLaughlin. By then, it was like all the guys from my old group were gone. Again, it made no real impression at the time; I showed up and raced whoever was there, same as always. But there were some real good drivers in that bunch, that's for sure.

By that point, though, I was kind of winding things down. When I look back on that period, I can see where I started taking things for granted, which you should never do in racing. I mentioned earlier how I used to study the competition in warm-ups every chance I got, but by the end of my career I had stopped doing that. That was stupid, because in this game you can't give up anything to anybody, whether it's Ray Hendrick or Mike Stefanik. If you do, they're going to beat you.

Maybe what happens is, once you've done something long enough and successfully enough, you think it's all automatic. But it's not. I don't care what level you're competing at, you've got to pay attention if you want to do well.

There are plenty of other drivers who come to mind, guys I only raced with occasionally. Look at Dutch Hoag. That guy was the king of Langhorne—he won there on both dirt and asphalt—and he was one of the very best guys in upstate New York. He didn't come out to New England much, so we never squared off all that often, but there's no doubt that Dutch was a great driver.

Of the Southern boys, I remember Perk Brown as being a good

racer. Max Berrier was tough. Jimmy Hensley and Billy Hensley, two cousins from just outside Martinsville, were strong, particularly at Martinsville. Sonny Hutchins was a wildman, a hard driver on the race track and a crazy bastard off it; we had a lot of laughs together. Paul Radford could drive the hell out of anything he climbed into. Satch Worley was a few years younger than those guys, but he won a bunch of races.

And, even though most people don't think of him as a modified guy, I had some good races in the sixties with Bobby Allison. Which reminds me: when I won the Trenton 200 in 1967, the guy I passed for the lead was Bobby's brother Donnie.

The one thing about the Southern drivers, though, is that very few of them had much success when they traveled up our way. Hendrick was tough anywhere, of course, and Satch Worley had some good runs; he won a 150-lapper at Stafford back in 1975. But for some reason, most of those guys struggled once you got them off their own turf.

When I dabbled in dirt racing in the sixties, running Stafford and those open-competition shows at Lebanon Valley, I went up against some guys who were obviously excellent drivers. Don Rounds, from Rhode Island, was awfully tough, but he was kind of backing up by the time I got going good. It was clear to me that some of those New York

Sometimes Jimmy Hensley and I fought for Victory Lane, and sometimes we shared it. This time, he won the late model sportsman half of a Martinsville doubleheader, and I won the modified half. (Courtesy of Speedway Scene)

Rene Charland drove hard, and partied harder. It's probably a good thing we didn't hang around together any more than we did! (John Grady Photo)

guys were really talented: Bill Wimble, Pete Corey, Kenny Shoemaker, guys like that. Maynard Forrette and Rene Charland were good racers, but even better hell-raisers. Don Wayman was a strong competitor at Fonda.

I raced against a lot of those dirt guys when they ran the pavement events in the old All Star League. Will Cagle impressed me as a guy who always had his act together. Buzzie Reutimann was a dirt specialist, but he knew how to drive an asphalt track, too. Andy Romano, who came from a big New York racing family, was tough on both surfaces. And Lou Lazzaro won an awful lot of races on pavement; he's remembered as a dirt racer, but he probably would have been just as successful if he had concentrated on pavement. Louie was just a good, good driver. You could say the same thing about Gil Hearne, who is thought of mostly as a pavement driver but was very strong on dirt in the sixties and early seventies.

I think about all these names today, and it dawns on me that I raced with a pretty incredible cast of characters. And there are more guys, maybe dozens of good drivers, I'm leaving out. I apologize for that, but I hope you'll cut me some slack. Hell, I'm getting old.

But I guess we ought to get back to the original question: Who was the toughest guy I ever raced against?

Year in and year out, no matter what the track was, I'd say Richie Evans was the toughest guy I ever faced. We ran an awful lot of laps together, including this one at Stafford in 1977. (Mike Adaskaveg Photo)

Well, if I have to pin it down to just one, I'd have to say that Richie Evans was probably *the* guy. It's not a hands-down thing, and I'm not saying that Richie was necessarily the best modified driver ever. It's just that in my mind, he was the toughest opponent.

Richie had everything you need: he had balls, he had brains, and he had talent. It didn't matter if you were at Islip, or Trenton, or anywhere in between, Richie was going to be in contention. You go back through all the years they've been running modifieds, and you don't see that kind of range in very many drivers.

Even in the coupe days, when he was young and struggling, you could see that the guy had a lot of raw ability. He did a lot of winning at Albany-Saratoga and Utica-Rome against some very tough competition, and it was obvious that he didn't have any money behind him. Later on, once he got some solid backing from Gene DeWitt, the whole world found out how good Richie was. Having good equipment allowed his talent to shine. He won his first NASCAR modified championship in 1973, and then won every one from 1978 through '85, when he was killed in a practice crash at Martinsville.

Richie did his own thing. He built his own cars for just about his entire career, and in the early days he built his own engines. Even later, when he could afford to buy good engines and he was getting tire deals from Firestone and Goodyear and parts deals from everybody, Richie was the guy who put everything together. He ran the show; when you saw that orange 61 out there, Richie was part of the product. When you added that mechanical and organizational knowledge to the driving talent Richie had, you got a pretty tough package. He was a hell of a race driver, and a good friend of mine, too.

Looking back on it, Richie really hit his stride five or six years after I'd hit mine, so it's like each of us had his own time at the top. I was going strong when he was just getting started, and he was still going strong when I started cutting back. But there was a period in there, right in the middle of the seventies, when things sort of overlapped, and we were both winning lots of races. And in that time, whenever I beat Richie I was very happy. I knew what I had done. I'm pretty sure he felt the same way.

I know how tough it was to beat any of these guys, because I beat them all at one time or another. I don't say that to brag; I say it just to point out that I know what I did, and I'm proud of it.

It's something that's hard to talk about without sounding like a loudmouth, but, yeah, I take a lot of pride in what I've accomplished. Every time I raced, I wanted to be the best. A lot of times, I *was* the best, and we won.

And when I lost, it took the best to beat me.

Sonny Koszela on Bugsy

Sonny Koszela, longtime NASCAR modified owner: "My father and I got started with Bugsy on the dirt at Stafford [in 1966]. Bugsy was looking for something else to do, I guess, so he ran one of our cars over there. And, don't you know it, he goes out and wins the championship!

"There are a few things I remember about that season. The first is that we won the title even though we didn't win a race. We had some good finishes, but he never did win a feature. And I remember that in that last race, Bugsy got stuffed into a telephone pole by another car, and the front end was toed-out by about a foot. Well, Bugsy really wanted to win that championship. The pits at Stafford were outside the backstretch then, and he stopped there. Naturally, we didn't have radios in those days, so he was yelling to me from inside the car: 'Hey, Sonny, if I bang into the fence a few times, do you think I can straighten it out?' I had to tell him, 'No, no, don't run it into the fence. You don't *fix* a car that way.' That was Bugsy. He wasn't very mechanical.

"In fact, that reminds me of something else. We should have won one race that year, because he with two or three laps to go he was leading by a straightaway. Well, the driveshaft fell out. And who do you suppose originally put the driveshaft in? Bugsy.

"We liked him a lot, so when things didn't work out between us and Freddy DeSarro—we just didn't gel right, even though we'd won the (1970 NASCAR national modified) championship—it just made sense to try to get together with Bugsy. He was the guy we wanted.

"Early on, we traveled a lot together. We raced all over New York, on Long Island, down South. We even went up to Canada, up around Montreal and somewhere near Quebec City. We'd run Malta on Friday night, come all the way home [to Rhode Island], go to Stafford Saturday night, come home again, then take off and go all the way up to Utica-Rome on Sunday. These guys today, they run once a week and they're tired!

"But the thing about Bugsy was, no matter where you took him, he ran good. It didn't make one bit of difference which track you were at. Whether the car was right or wrong, he'd get the most out of it. God, he loved to race.

"I guess my favorite period would have been when we were winning all those races with that small-block Ford [in 1977-78]. I can't imagine how much money Dick Armstrong spent trying to beat that thing. He had Jack Tant with him every week, trying to figure out how to outrun that little Ford. They had been winning all the races for a couple of years, Armstrong and Geoff Bodine, but now we were killing them.

"At Martinsville [in October of 1977], Geoff led the race at the start, but Bugsy was all over him for about 50 laps. Finally they came up on a lapped car, and Geoff followed that car into the corner. Well, Bugsy just drove right past him

Just a Jockey

Sonny Koszela and Bugs Stevens, Stafford Motor Speedway, 1977. (Courtesy of Speedway Scene*)*

on the outside. It was such a surprise that Geoff drove right into the back of that lapped car. Within five laps we were about a straightaway ahead, and Bugsy was gone. We won by almost three laps.

"The next year we had that race at Trenton, when we ended up running out of gas and Richie Evans won. Later on, Richie said, 'Man, you had us beat.' Then we talked a while, and Richie was laughing about how deep he and Bugsy were driving into that first turn. I mean, it was like they were never going to back off. Richie said, 'Tell me the truth, Sonny: Were you afraid?' I said, 'Nah, not with you two guys out there.' And Richie said, 'Well, you should have been. We're lucky we didn't end up out in the parking lot!'

"We had so much fun with Bugsy. I mean, fun at the track, fun away from the track, fun just chasing each other down the road. We'd get out of Stafford and come back here to my house and start swimming and partying all night, and sometimes all morning. He was crazy. Crazy.

"Sure, he'd drive you nuts sometimes. Like, we were at Pocono; we had qualified there on Saturday afternoon, then Bugsy went back to Stafford and won up there that night. Anyway, they had a warm-up session the morning of the Pocono race. We were trying some crazy thing with the tires, running a different compound on every corner, and we really needed that morning practice time to see if it worked. Well, we can't find Bugsy. Nobody knows where he is. He'd been up late raising hell, I figured. When he finally showed up, I took the biggest wrench I could find, and I shook it at him. I said, 'All right, you bastard, now you're going to have to race this car the way it is, whether it's good or bad.'

"But you know something? He drove his ass off, and he won the race."

Just a Jockey

Just A Jockey

I'VE SAID THIS right from the time I started racing, and to this day I sincerely believe it: The mechanics are the real stars of this game. As a driver, you're only as good as the guy who turns those wrenches. For you to perform, *he* has to perform. You are the end result of what he knows.

It comes down to this: If your mechanic can build a car that goes around a corner fast, you'll be able to go around a corner fast. If he can't, you're going nowhere. It's that simple.

It's not like there was one single moment when all this dawned on me. It just kind of grew in my head over time. What happened was, there were enough nights when I got beat by guys I knew I had outdriven, but they were driving cars that handled better, or went down the straightaway better, or both. I finally came to the conclusion that, when you get right down to it, we're just the jockeys. We're only as good as what you give us to ride.

Sure, some jockeys are better than others. There's no getting around that. But there hasn't ever been a jockey in the world who could win with a lame horse.

Everybody sees the drivers as the big stars in racing, but to me it always more about the equipment and the mechanics.
(Mike Adaskaveg Photo)

One of the greatest questions in racing—maybe *the* great question of all time— is the one about the relationship between the driver and the car. Which one is more important? What percentage does each one play? Figuring out the actual numbers is impossible, but it's still something people love to talk about.

In the coupe days, the driver was more important. That's a fact, and everybody knows it. I'm not knocking today's drivers, because the cars I drove at the end of my modified career weren't much different than they are now, and it's not like just *anybody* can drive one and win. The guys who win are good drivers, no matter what era you're talking about.

But if you go back to, say, the middle sixties, there was much more left to the driver because the cars just didn't have many adjustments to make them handle. You had straight-axle front ends, and all you really did was play with the inclination of the kingpins up front, maybe cock the rear end a bit to favor one side or the other, and mess around with the tire stagger. That was pretty much the range of your chassis tuning.

Back then we ran big-block engines with a ton of horsepower, so you could get all the speed you wanted. But once you got to the end of the straightaway, you had to have a guy in the seat who could wrestle that thing around the corner.

Again, to put an actual number on it is difficult, but if you said it was 70 percent driver and 30 percent car, I wouldn't argue. The equation started to change a bit in the late sixties. First the tire companies

In the 1960s, when the cars were straight-axle coupes with huge engines, it was a handful to wrestle a modified around almost any race track. The driver was more important back then, no question about it. (Dick Berggren Photo)

began to build wider tires, and those things stuck so well that it allowed every good mechanic to play around with his chassis configuration. In that period, the cars themselves improved a lot in a very short time. The sharp guys were all experimenting, trying different things. Most of them didn't pan out, but a few did, and whenever that happened it made everybody play catch-up.

For example, Clayton Mitchell, who co-owned Ray Hendrick's cars with Jack Tant, came up with a torsion-bar front end that worked better than probably all the straight-axle cars the rest of us were running. I was driving for Boehler then, and the two of us got pretty tired of chasing Ray and that Tant-Mitchell car. Lenny studied that thing and studied it some more, and eventually he built a torsion front end for our car, too. But even as sharp as Lenny was, it took him almost a year to get all the kinks out, and get that new setup just right. Oh, we were able to win some races —in fact, that car won its first night out, in a 1969 All Star League race at Norwood Arena—but we weren't anywhere close to perfect for a long time. And we were coming to a point when you *had* to get a car just about perfect.

From that point on, I saw the horse—meaning, of course, the car—get more and more important. It has never, ever gone the other way. Throughout the seventies, engines only got better, suspensions only got better, tires only got better. And that old driver/car equation kept changing.

By the time I ran my last modified race in 1987, the percentage had turned almost completely around from what it had been when I started, and I'd say it's about the same today: 70 percent car, 30 percent driver, in that range.

Sometimes, a car comes along that makes everybody play catch-up. Jack Tant and Clayton Mitchell gave Ray Hendrick a car like that in the late 1960s. They called it the Flying 11, and it flew, all right.
(Dick Berggren Photo)

Like I said before, the guys who are winning today are obviously good drivers, because they've still got to know how to get to the front, know how to pass, know how to work traffic. But it's easier for a guy who's a marginal talent to go fast today than it has ever been. As long as he's got the money to buy good equipment and to hire people who know how to dial in the chassis, he'll be quick. Because, compared to the way those old coupes drove, today's cars pretty much go where you point 'em.

There's one thing that has never changed: It helps a great deal if the driver understands his race car. That's another advantage today's driver has, because he can go to the chassis builder if he's got a problem, or if he wants to look into this stuff himself there's a ton of reading material out there. Even a guy who is a dummy, mechanically, can gain a lot of knowledge just by paying attention.

Twenty or 30 years ago, most of the drivers we considered to be chassis guys were self-taught. Eddie Flemke had a lot of us covered that way in the sixties, and Leo Cleary was smart with a race car, too. In the next group to come along, you had guys like Maynard Troyer, Richie Evans, and Geoff Bodine. The fact that all those guys really understood how a chassis worked was a big part of whatever success they had. They were all terrific drivers, sure, but they made sure they had great cars to drive by looking after that stuff themselves.

See, when a driver and a mechanic have to communicate about a handling problem, there's always the possibility that something is going to get lost in the translation. Maybe the driver won't do a good enough job of explaining the problem, or maybe the mechanic will just plain misunderstand him. And then there are the times when the mechanic and the driver agree on what the problem is, but *disagree* on how to fix it.

There were many nights when I'd say to Lenny, "Here's what the car is doing. Why don't you put a turn of wedge into the right front?" Well, instead, Lenny would go to the left rear, the opposite corner, and take a turn *out*. It's two slightly different ways of attacking the same problem, and you're always open to having those differences of opinion when the decision involves more than one person.

With Flemke or Bodine, there was no need to work through a mechanic. They diagnosed the problem, they made the changes they wanted to make, and that was that.

I was never one of those guys who had a deep understanding of the car. Oh, I had things pretty well handled at the hobby level, when I got started down in Texas, but it wasn't because of any great knowledge

I was always the kind of driver who was better leaving the mechanical end to other people. That's me with Fred Fusco, and you'll notice that I'm doing all the listening. (Mike Adaskaveg Photo)

on my part. It was more like, whatever I did, I happened to do right. I'm the first to admit, I'm not the best mechanic in the world; if my guys saw me grab a wrench, they'd take it away from me. My biggest problem is, I just don't pay attention to things as deeply as a good mechanic has to. The best mechanics are on top of everything, all the time, and I guess I didn't have the attention span for that. So as I moved along, I left the mechanical end to other people, and because the cars weren't so complicated back then it was easier to do that.

I do think I was always able to *help* my mechanics. I knew what I wanted, and like any good racer I was always searching for something better than I had. I'm sure there were a lot of days when my mechanics thought I was a pain in the ass, wanting some little last-minute adjustment, but I always wanted to get going better, faster.

As a race driver, I was at my mechanic's mercy. If he was on top of his game, I could be on top of mine. We could *win*.

The relationship between a driver and a mechanic is just like a marriage: It's a 50/50 arrangement that requires two people to trust one another, and, more than anything, to believe in one another. If the mechanic doesn't believe in the driver, the team isn't going to amount to anything. Same thing if the driver doesn't have faith in the mechan-

ic. They might luck into a little bit of success, but they aren't going to be very good over the long haul.

There's another thing you need, too: Patience. See, drivers and mechanics are both human; they make mistakes sometimes, and you've got to accept that. Even the best driver in the world is going to mess up once in a while, and the mechanic has to understand that. By the same token, even the smartest mechanic in the pits isn't always going to hit the hot setup. He'll have nights where he takes an educated guess at something just before the feature, and it won't work out. It happens.

Hell, if this stuff was easy, everybody would be a champion.

The important thing is to maintain that faith in the other guy. In fact, it's probably more important to believe in one another than it is to get along well. For years, I watched Bob Johnson scream at Ron Bouchard. The crazy thing was, he *loved* Ronnie, but Bob was just a high-strung guy. You'd watch those two fight, and you'd listen to all that hollering, and you'd think there was no way in the world they could ever win a damn thing together. But they *believed* in each other. Ronnie knew Bob would give him a good car, and Bob knew Ronnie would drive the wheels off it. And, man, there were a lot of nights when I ran second to Ronnie Bouchard and that Johnson car.

Still, I'm glad I was never in that kind of a relationship with a car owner or a mechanic. If I'd ever had a guy scream at me like I watched Bob scream at Ronnie, the relationship would have been over right there. Goodbye.

Here's three great owner-driver combos on the podium after a 100-lapper at Stafford. From the left: Bob Johnson and Ronnie Bouchard, me and Sonny Koszela (with race sponsor Frank Ferrara between us), and Fred DeSarro and Lenny Boehler. (Courtesy of Speedway Scene)

I've won races with a lot of mechanics, but it would be fair to say that I had most of my success with two guys turning the wrenches: Lenny Boehler and Dave Tourigny.

There are a few other guys who stand out in my memory. You've got to take your hat off to Bobby Judkins, because he won with just about every driver he had: Flemke, Gene Bergin, both Bouchard brothers, you name it. Then there was ol' Joe Gerrior—Injun Joe, everybody called him—who worked for years with Joe Brady and was one of the most underrated guys around. Hop Harrington was a great chassis man; when I drove Dick Armstrong's car in 1981, Hop turned the wrenches, and we were fast everywhere we went. And Freddy Fusco, who built the car I drove to the '77 Seekonk championship, was a wizard with both midgets and stock cars. Fusco was a real student of Indy car racing, and he based a lot of his short-track theories around Indy car designs; I ran a few races in a rear-engined midget he built by scaling down Al Unser's old Johnny Lightning Special Indy car.

But Lenny and Dave were special in my career. They had a few things in common. They were both pretty quiet, they were both a little bit eccentric, and they were both good people.

And, of course, they were very, very talented mechanics.

Lenny had a natural-born knack for anything mechanical. He wasn't a brilliant, book-sharp engineer, and never pretended to be. But if you gave him the time, that man could figure out things as thoroughly as any engineer could.

Not all the great mechanics get to be famous. Two of the most underrated guys I ever worked with were Injun Joe Gerrior (left) and Tiny Levesque. (Courtesy of Speedway Scene)

174

I had a blast driving this rear-engined midget for Fred Fusco. Freddy was a guy who could build anything. (Bob Miour Racing Photos/Courtesy of Speedway Scene)

    If you go back and check out any old pictures of those Boehler cars, you'll see that they always looked a little bit different than whatever the next guy was running. Maybe the rollcage was different, maybe the frame was different, maybe it was the way the body sat. Lenny had his own ideas, his own theories. I guess that's why in the late seventies and early eighties, when everybody else figured it was easier to buy cars from one of the chassis builders, Lenny kept on building his own stuff, and did that right up until the day he died in 2001. He simply wasn't satisfied to just go with the flow. It challenged him more to do his own thing.

    But don't kid yourself: Lenny Boehler might have minded his own business, but he paid attention to everybody else's business, too, when it came to race cars. A good racing mechanic, even one as independent as Lenny, is always interested in any car that goes faster than his own. It's the mechanic's nature to want to know *why* that car is faster. And Lenny, wise ol' owl that he was, would notice things.

    Take that torsion-bar coupe Clayton Mitchell rolled out in the late sixties. If we were at a race and Ray Hendrick was there with that car, Lenny would take a stroll past their pit stall and give that thing a good look on his way by. It may have taken him a while to figure it out, but the point is, he *did* figure it out, and eventually we were winning races with our own torsion-bar car.

    You didn't keep Lenny down for long, that's for sure. I mean, for more than 35 years—from the days of the big coupes with their skinny tires, through the Pinto and Vega era, right up through the offset cars you see today—Boehler's stuff won. We're talking about a guy

Lenny Boehler was the last of the backyard geniuses. If the guys he beat ever got a look at how little Lenny had to work with, they'd never have believed it.
(Dick Berggren Photo)

who won three NASCAR championships with me in the sixties, and three more in the nineties.

And you can never forget this: Whatever Lenny Boehler did, he did with no money. *None.* If some of the big-dollar guys he was beating ever saw Lenny's operation, they'd probably have quit racing on the spot. I was down at his shop a while back, probably in the 2000 season, and there was Lenny, welding on a chassis that was sitting on the cement floor. It could have been 1968 all over again.

Lenny Boehler was a piece of work, one of a kind.

Dave Tourigny was another smart guy, and one of the finest mechanics I've ever been around. In fact, I'd put him up against anybody, and I've raced for and against some pretty respectable mechanics.

I've never believed Dave got the recognition he deserved for all the success we had with that Koszela car. Looking back, it's not hard to figure out why; in those years, there was always a lot of hoopla surrounding me, and Sonny got a lot of the limelight too because, after all, it was his car, and this was a period when car owners were starting to get a little bit of attention. But Dave Tourigny was there all along, in the background, making us both look good.

The guys in the pits, the other mechanics and drivers, *they* knew how smart Dave was, but outside of that small circle he was an unsung hero. And, you know, I'm sure that was fine with Dave. He didn't go for a lot of flash; he was just a quiet guy who stood off to the

Check out Boehler in the suit and tie, and the beard! When Massachusetts Governor Frank Sargent honored me after my third NASCAR championship, Lenny was part of the ceremony. (Dick Berggren Photo)

side, minding his own business. We'd win a race at Stafford or someplace, and while Sonny and I were on the podium accepting the trophies and having our pictures taken, Dave would be walking around that car, checking the tires, looking everything over.

He had pretty much that same demeanor back at the shop. The Koszela cars were kept in a building right next to Sonny's house. It was nothing fancy, but it had all the essential stuff, all the tools a winning team needed. I remember there being a homebuilt wood stove on

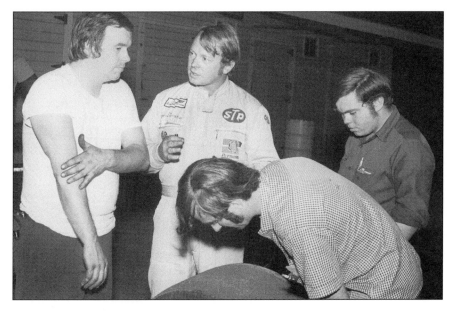

Dave Tourigny and I had a great relationship. That's Dave listening to me while Sonny Koszela checks out a tire. The three of us did a lot of winning together. (Courtesy of Speedway Scene)

one end to keep the place warm. Anyway, there were a bunch of local racing people who would drift into Sonny's shop at night, some helping out and some just hanging around, but no matter who showed up or what was going on, Dave kept plugging away, getting that race car ready.

Like so many short-track people, Dave was never a full-time race car guy. His father ran a company that made plastic utensils and things like that for hospitals, and Dave looked after the machinery end of the family business. Racing was basically a hobby to him, something to play around with, and yet he turned out to be brilliant at it. All those winning Koszela cars —the coupe, the Vega, the Ford-powered Pinto that went so fast in the late '70s—were Dave's babies. He designed them in his head, and then he built 'em all from the ground up.

Stop and think about all the races those cars won, whether it was me driving or Freddy DeSarro, and you begin to understand what a talented guy Dave Tourigny was. He had the mechanical end handled, had the fabricating handled, had *everything* handled.

Dave did have one advantage over Lenny, I suppose: Lenny was spending his own money, and in Dave's case we had a little bit more of a budget with the Koszela car. But, to be fair about that, Sonny's team wasn't extravagant by any means. Whatever Dave needed, he got, but it wasn't necessarily anything more expensive than the other top teams had.

This was taken during some kind of photo shoot for Stafford, I remember that. Sonny Koszela and I just about owned that place for a big chunk of the 1970s.
(Mike Adaskaveg Photo)

Bob Garbarino and I were good friends when we raced together, and we're still good friends. We won several races together, but for some reason we never really hit our stride like I hoped we would. (Courtesy of Speedway Scene)

Still, at that period you couldn't overlook how important money was becoming in modified racing. And once that happened, you had to start factoring the car owner into the old horse/jockey equation, because without a decent amount of backing even the best mechanics and drivers were going to struggle.

Racing is like everything else, I guess, because money spoiled a lot of the fun in this sport just like it spoiled some of the fun in *every* sport. Let's say you're a baseball player; you'll probably never have more fun in your life than when you're young and you've got a cheap bat and an old ball and you're playing just for fun. Once the big dollars came into the modifieds, a lot of the laughs went out of the game, and I don't think that was necessarily a change for the better.

I guess I've driven for guys all along the economic scale. Boehler and Judkins and Brady were low-buck owners, and some of the other people I was with were anything *but* low-buck, like Armstrong and Bob Garbarino. But, you know, it never made any difference to me how big a guy's bankroll was. I was more impressed by what the guy was made of. You are what you are. I mean, you're either a racer, or you're not a racer, and guys like Armstrong and Garbarino took racing as seriously as the backyard guys did.

I know one thing: I never changed my approach to a race based on the team owner's pocketbook. Like I've said, I always drove to *finish* a race, because you couldn't win if you didn't finish. I thought that way when I drove Boehler's coupe, and I thought that way when I drove Armstrong's Pinto. It didn't matter.

The funny thing is, I had as much success or more in homebuilt

When I raced with Joe Brady, we never had a ton of resources but we sure won a lot of races, including this one at Stafford.
(Courtesy of Speedway Scene)

stuff—whether it was with Boehler or Dave Tourigny or Judkins or whoever turning the wrenches—as I did in some of the big-dollar cars. People always say that money talks, and that's obviously true to some extent, but it doesn't always determine who wins. If it did, how could you explain Lenny Boehler's record? How could you explain what Joe Brady and I did? Joe didn't spend half as much as a lot of the guys we raced against, but we won races at Thompson, Westboro, Seekonk, Monadnock, Stafford, New Smyrna, *everywhere*. On the flip side of that, Bob Garbarino had great equipment, but even though we won a bunch of races together I don't think we ever did the kind of winning we could have.

It's *chemistry*. People use that word all the time these days, but in this case it fits. If you don't have every piece of the puzzle in place and every man on your race team on the same wavelength, some other outfit will, and that outfit will beat you.

Brady and I got into that rut a few times. I think what happened was, Joe had a lot of people around him, so he would end up listening to too many theories at once. When you do that, it's easy to get off track; that happens to teams at every level of the sport. But whenever we just stuck to the basics, Brady and I won plenty.

No matter how much money you've got, racing always comes down to chemistry and dedication and common sense. Just like life.

One thing I'm happy about is that none of my relationships with mechanics and car owners ever really ended on bad terms. Well, maybe it's more correct to say that they never *stayed* bad. I mean, when Lenny and I had the run we did, winning all those races and those three championships, I never believed we'd break up that team, so it wasn't an easy thing when it happened. And it wasn't easy to split with Sonny after all the success we'd had together, either. Those weren't pleasant times; I guess there are always hard feelings at first when something like that happens. But after a while, I got along with both those guys, and I think I could sit down today and have a beer with just about everybody I've ever gone racing with.

I think what it comes down to is this: I always gave my 100 percent, and my owners and mechanics knew that. At the same time, I was always fortunate enough—or maybe good enough, I don't know—to be with guys who gave me back *their* 100 percent.

I've had good people around me almost every step of the way. A lot of times, I had the *best* people. I might have been the guy standing in victory lane, and I might have been the guy whose picture showed up in the paper, but those people were the stars.

As a jockey, I sure got a lot of good horses to ride.

Oxford Plains, 1981, after a great win with Dick Armstrong's car. (Courtesy of Speedway Scene)

Richie Evans on Bugsy

The late Richie Evans, nine-time NASCAR national modified champion: "Bugsy and I were walking through the pits one night at Albany-Saratoga. This was in 1972, '73, somewhere in there. It was a big race, maybe a 150-lapper or a 200, and the two of us were going to be on the front row.

"So we're walking along, and I say to Bugsy, 'How do you want to play the start?' Because, see, I didn't know if he was going to go for it right away, or ride for a while, or what, and I didn't see any sense in fighting him too hard for the lead if it didn't really matter to him.

"Anyway, I asked him about the start—'What do you think you're going to do?'—and Bugsy didn't say anything for a minute.

"Finally, he said, 'Kid, it's like the story about the two bulls on the hill.'

"I asked him what he meant.

"Bugsy said, 'There's these two bulls standing at the top of a hill, looking down on a field full of cows. It's one old bull, and one young bull. The young bull says, 'Hey, I think I'm gonna run down this hill and fuck one of those cows.'

"And the old bull just sort of nods his head and says, 'You go right ahead. I'll *walk* down this hill and fuck 'em all.'

"You know, like, What's the hurry? It's a long race. He was telling me to do my own thing, because he was going to do his own thing.

"By now we were back at my car, so I stopped, but he just kept right on walking. Didn't even look back. Typical Bugsy.

"I never forgot that: 'I'll walk down this hill and fuck 'em all.' Pretty good strategy, huh?"

It's a Mental Thing

Richie Evans and Bugs Stevens, Pocono International Raceway, 1980.
(Courtesy of Speedway Scene)

It's a Mental Thing

It's a Mental Thing

WHAT SEPARATES THE GREAT DRIVERS from the good drivers? Hell, if I knew that for sure, I'd be rich. But I've definitely got some ideas about what a great race driver needs.

First of all, I always believed that racing was more a mental game than a physical game. Your brain controls everything you do, from winking at a pretty girl to pushing the gas pedal harder than the next guy.

Sure, there are certain physical requirements a race driver almost has to have. For instance, upper body strength is very important. You've got to have good arms—and if you didn't have good arms in my day, those old coupes would build 'em up for you—and it's important to have strong neck muscles to combat all the G-forces you go up against. A lot of drivers never ever exercised their necks, but I paid a lot of attention to that. I'd see some guys halfway through a long race with their heads laid over, and I just *knew* they were tired. Their cars were still fast, but they weren't, and I knew I had them beat.

There are other physical attributes that are critical. Obviously, you've got to have good eyesight, and some people are more gifted in that area than others. I think I was one of those lucky ones; I always had terrific depth perception and excellent peripheral vision, and I'm sure that helped me stay out of trouble more than I ever realized at the time.

That's me and Gene Bergin on either side of Leo Cleary. This was a Stafford PR photo dreamed up by Pete Zanardi to point out that the three of us had been football heroes in high school. In those days, you almost had to be a burly guy to be a race car driver.
(Mike Adaskaveg Photo)

Reflexes are another area where some people are just naturally gifted, and mine were great. But I'm a solid believer in the idea that reflexes can be improved. All through my career, I read anything I saw about ways to enhance your reflexes, and I took those suggestions to heart. I played all kinds of hand-eye coordination games; I juggled tennis balls, I played ping pong; I even played a lot of paddle ball with an old fellow I knew. Anything I thought might make my reflexes sharper, quicker, I tried.

But I'll stick with what I said a minute ago: racing is a mental sport. It has to be, because I've seen drivers who had all the physical ability it took to make their cars go fast, but they never seemed to win much. They had balls and they were aggressive and they could lead races, but they couldn't put the whole package together very often.

Put it this way: if you take two guys with identical physical skills and identical cars, the guy who's probably going to win the race is the one with more brains. He'll just out-think his opposition.

It's been my experience that almost every good race driver is an intelligent person. He might not necessarily be book smart—he might not have even gone very far in school—but if you really examine the guy you'll find that he's pretty sharp, fast on his feet, able to make decisions *right now*. Maybe that's why so many drivers are also good at coming up with a quick wisecrack; it's a sign that their minds are always working.

Writers have asked me how a driver processes everything that's going on during a race; you know, you've got a car in front of you, two cars behind you, another car bouncing off your inside nerf bar. Honestly, it's automatic. You deal with one situation, and, just like that, you're on to the next one.

It's an interesting topic, because, if you think about it, your mind must be working faster than the fastest computer out there. You're relying on your memory bank—this driver is a sucker for an inside move, that guy always overdrives a particular corner—and at the same time you're calculating what's going on right now and working out what might happen on the next lap. If you thought about all that consciously, step by step, you'd probably be so confused that you'd drive straight into the wall. That's why I say it's automatic. It's a quality that's simply built into the good drivers.

I look at Richard Petty's record—200 Winston Cup wins, seven championships—and it tells me that Richard had to be a brilliant guy. I don't care how good his equipment was, it took a lot of smarts to win that much. You'd have to say the same thing about A.J. Foyt, who won in everything he sat in. And look at the guys who won tons of modified races: Evans, Flemke, Bodine, Bouchard . . . all sharp guys.

I'd like to think I was in that group, too. I got outrun a few times

By the point, when I was strapped in and ready to race, I was always able to block out the outside world and concentrate on racing. My ability to focus was always very good. (Balser and Son Photo)

in my career, but there weren't many nights when I got outsmarted. I was always good at staying focused, even back in the days when I had all the kids chasing me around and I was the life of the party. I used to have a trick that a lot of people never caught onto: I'd take a little meditation break before the feature race. I'd just sneak off someplace where I could be alone—usually in the cab of the hauler—and just clear my mind.

For most of the night, all through the warm-ups and the heat races, I'd be standing by the car, either talking shop with my mechanics or just chatting with the rest of the folks. But during intermission, I'd get away by myself and clear my head of all the outside bullshit, all the conversations I'd had to that point. I'd lie back and think about where I was starting, who else was running good, how I could pass them, how much time I had.

It was a great way to get nice and calm before the battle. In fact, sometimes I got so calm that I'd almost fall asleep. People would joke, "That crazy Bugsy, he's so loose that he's taking a nap." Well, they weren't wrong, technically, because I really would conk out sometimes, but it was more meditating than napping. Because, see, when I woke up, I wasn't sleepy, the way you'd be just after a nap. When I climbed out of that truck, I was always ready to race.

The meditating did get to be kind of a ritual with me, but never to the extent that other guys had rituals, or superstitions. That was an area I never got into, but it's probably something you have to look at if you're talking about the mental side of racing.

I heard all the old racing superstitions over the years. Never drive a green car. Stay away from the number 13. Don't eat peanuts. I was around guys who really got wrapped up in that stuff; Lenny Boehler would shoo people away from his car if they were wearing, say, green socks, and it used to make Fred DeSarro crazy to see somebody eating peanuts in the pits. Imagine those two superstitious guys racing as a team all those years?

Which reminds me: Freddy was also scared to death of snakes. So, naturally, anytime I caught a little garden snake at home or at the salvage yard, I'd keep that thing until the weekend so I could use it to drive Freddy nuts. I'd chase him around with it, or, if I felt really brave, I'd hide it in his car. I never did it to mess around with his mind, or to take advantage of his phobia; actually, I wasn't smart enough to look at the psychological aspect of it. It was just a way to raise hell, and to get people laughing. Here was Fred DeSarro, probably as brave a race driver as there was, yet he'd run like hell to get away from a skinny little snake. We all used to get a kick out of that.

I was never big on good luck charms, although I did keep a little stone cross given to me by my friend Clay Earles, who owned the Martinsville Speedway. (Balser and Son Photo)

187

But as far as the superstition stuff went, I kind of shrugged it all off. I never thought anything was going to bring me bad luck, and, on the other side of that coin, I never worried about things that might bring me good luck, either.

Years and years ago, the late H. Clay Earles, who built and operated the Martinsville Speedway, gave me a little stone cross. As I recall, it was carved out of the rock from some cavern down there. Ol' Clay was always very nice to me—he used to say that all my success at his track made me an "honorary Rebel"—and we became good friends, so his gift really meant a lot to me. I carried that cross around in my wallet for a long time, but it wasn't because I thought it might bring me good luck, or anything like that. It was just a sign of how much I thought of Mr. Earles.

I've never believed in the idea that race drivers are supposed to be fearless. Nobody is completely fearless, unless he's ignorant. You've *got* to have fear, because I think fear and respect run together. You know what can happen in a given situation—that's the fear—and you act out of respect for that possibility.

It's not that you're *scared*. It's just that you understand the consequences that might result from something you do. For example, you show respect to your competitor because you understand that if you hit him, you might wreck him or wreck yourself. That's a consequence you don't want to deal with, so you learn to avoid it.

Early on in my career, I learned a hard lesson about fire. When I was racing in Texas, a buddy of mine crashed at San Antonio and ended up having horrible burns on his face; he had an open-face helmet with leather sides, and that thing did him no good at all. When I saw the damage to his nose and his ears, it gave me a very healthy respect for the fact that race cars could catch fire, and for the reality that I needed to be prepared for that.

It's funny: I never felt the least bit nervous about fire *outside* a car. I've handled gasoline all my life, especially at the salvage yard, and I've never once worried about smoking or tossing my cigar on the ground. For some reason, that never concerned me. But it scares the hell out of me to see a race car on fire.

And I've always had a great respect for high-speed race tracks. In a lot of ways they were the places I loved best, but there were definitely times when I tiptoed around until I learned a fast track I was seeing for the first time. Once I figured it out, I'd race balls-out, but I still carried a respect for it.

I never did worry much about getting hurt, even though I proved to myself several times that was possible to get injured. When I flipped Boehler's car in turn one at Stafford in the late sixties and fractured a cervical vertebra, I wasn't supposed to drive a race car for sixth months. I didn't even bother to sit out six *days*. That probably wasn't too smart, because who knows what damage I could have done to my neck in another bad wreck, but we were chasing points and I couldn't stand the idea of missing a race. And when I crashed Bob Garbarino's car in '82 and messed up my lower back—same track, same turn—I walked around like a mummy for a long time, taped up so tight I couldn't breathe.

I broke my sternum twice, both times at Seekonk. That's just a painful, painful injury; you tighten up those belts the next week, and you just want to scream. And I busted my ribs maybe a dozen different times. Take it from me, broken ribs are *terrible*. But they never stopped me from racing.

I'm sure the average guy wonders what makes an athlete do that. Why do racers drive with injuries? Why do football players tape themselves every week? Why do baseball players limp up to the plate when they probably ought to ride the bench for a few more games? Well, it's the love of competition, baby. Most times, you just can't *wait* to get back.

The good guys don't stay down. Oh, maybe they'll miss a game, or in our case miss a race. But then they're up again.

This is Lenny Boehler's coupe after I rolled it at Stafford and broke a vertebra in my neck. The amazing thing is, Lenny and I didn't miss a race. Hey, we were chasing points. (Balser and Son Photo)

After all, nobody ever won anything lying down.

Some of my friends have told me that after I got hurt in '82, they thought I drove more cautiously. To me, that would be a hard thing for them to know; maybe another good driver could convince me of that, or a mechanic who had been with me for years, but I'm not sure a guy who's basically a fan in the grandstands would be in a position to say that. They might see you on a night when you're getting passed left and right because your car isn't handling worth a damn, and decide that you're not trying hard enough. From ten or fifteen rows up, it's hard to know what a driver is going through.

Of course, racing is like a lot of sports: the smartest guy in the place is the guy closest to the beer stand. Just ask him.

Who knows? I don't think that wreck changed me, and I damn sure didn't feel that way at the time. But it's your subconscious mind that controls all that, and it's going to overrule your heart and your guts every time.

If the fear of getting myself hurt—or worse—was ever going to scare me out of racing, that probably would have happened early on.

Take the day Don MacTavish was killed in the 1969 Permatex 300 late model sportsman race at Daytona. Mac had just passed me on the high side of the banking in turns three and four. He cut down in front of me, so now he and I were single file, gaining fast on a big pack of cars ahead of us. He swung left to go under that pack, and I think he touched another car as he made that move. Donnie's car got sideways, and when he instinctively corrected, that car took a bite. It turned hard to the right, and shot into the outside wall.

Mac might have been all right if it had been just an ordinary wall crash, but he was unlucky enough to hit just at the point where the concrete wall is interrupted by the guardrail they use to cover the crossover gate. His car pushed that guardrail inward and then, when it hit the blunt concrete on the other side of the crossover opening, it got torn all to pieces.

I've never, ever seen another stock car come apart like that one did. The motor flew up in the air—I can still see it—and the entire front end ahead of the firewall was ripped away from the car. Poor Mac was sitting there, strapped in his seat, head down, with no protection whatsoever in front of him as that car spun around. All of us did what we could to avoid him—I steered so hard to the left that I ended up going down pit road—but Sam Sommers, a real good driver out of Georgia, couldn't miss him. He hit what was left of Mac's car head-on. It was as terrible a wreck as you could ever imagine.

Most of the time when something like that happens, you're not sure how badly hurt a guy is. You tell yourself that the cars are well-built, and that drivers walk away from some violent crashes. But that day at Daytona, there was no doubt in my mind that Don MacTavish was dead.

Two memories stand out from that whole thing.

The first is that a day or two earlier, Mac had just returned a uniform of mine he'd been wearing for most of the week. I can't remember exactly why he needed it—I guess maybe his own suit wasn't ready just yet—but it made sense that he came to me when he needed to borrow one. We had raced a lot of miles together in a pretty short time, going back to my earliest NASCAR races at Thompson and Norwood, and he was the guy I had beaten to win my first national modified championship in 1967. So it was good that in our last few days together, we were doing something friendly like exchanging uniforms.

The other thing I recall is that later in the race, it started raining hard over on the backstretch. Daytona is so big that it can be raining in one corner, but dry everywhere else. Well, we went roaring through turn one on a dry track, then we came out of turn two and it was pouring so hard that you couldn't see a damn thing through the windshield. I lifted, naturally, but we were still trucking along pretty good, and the only reference I had was what I could see out the side window.

I don't think I've ever felt more helpless in a race car; I'm suddenly flying blind at maybe 165 miles an hour, and just a little while ago I watched a friend of mine get killed. That's a tough, tough combination on your brain, buddy. That's a real mental test.

But you know something? Once the rain stopped and they restarted the race, I never had to think twice about standing on the gas again. I was a racer. That was what I was there to do.

I reacted the same way—exactly the same way—after the crash that cost Fred DeSarro his life. This was at Thompson Speedway, October 8, 1978.

Freddy and I were out running practice laps together. I was in Joe Brady's Pinto, the white 41, and he was in a new Vega that Lenny Boehler had put together. On any given day it's good to gauge yourself against the other fast guys wherever you're at, and Freddy was usually the fastest guy there was at Thompson.

I was right behind him as we got to the end of the backstretch, and then something went wrong. Freddy drove into turn three basically wide open, and his car flew up and over the sandbank. It looked a lot like my crash in Boehler's coupe must have looked 10 years earlier, when I flew over that same bank. The only difference was, I cleared the trees and landed in a swampy area, which probably cushioned my landing a bit; Freddy's car clipped the trees and he came straight down, which was about a 40-foot drop.

I was actually passing him as he went out of the place, but I spun my car to a stop, climbed out, and ran up and over the banking, down toward Freddy. It must have been just instinctive to me, because race drivers don't generally run to crashes. His car was sitting on its four wheels when I got to him. It was a bad, bad scene, an awful mess. Poor Freddy was bleeding like hell out of his mouth. It was clear that he was in desperate trouble.

Unless you've been through something like that, you just can't imagine how dramatic it is. It seemed like I was there by myself for half an hour. Obviously, it was probably just a minute or two until other people showed up; the Bouchards, Kenny and Ronnie, might have been the first ones, because I remember them running up, and then there were these other faces.

I was struggling to get Freddy's helmet unbuckled with one hand, trying to hold his head still with my other hand, and his blood is pouring out onto my uniform.

And I'm thinking, This is Fred DeSarro.

This is my friend. In my arms.

Maybe dying.

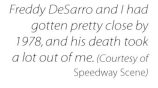

Freddy DeSarro and I had gotten pretty close by 1978, and his death took a lot out of me. (Courtesy of Speedway Scene)

192

Eventually we got him out of the car, and the medical people took him away. I walked back to the pits, Freddy's blood all over me. I remember being mad at the world, mad at God. For a long time, I got away from everybody, and just cursed the whole universe. But then, just the way it had gone at Daytona on the day MacTavish died, it was time to race again. I strapped into Brady's car, rolled out for my qualifying heat, and blew everybody's doors off.

Maybe it doesn't make sense unless you're a racer, but once I saw that green flag my instincts pushed everything else out of my mind.

Freddy hung on for three more weeks, fighting as hard in the hospital as he ever fought on a race track, but he passed away on November 1. That knocked the hell out of me. To be honest, it was something I had tried to prepare for—if you'd seen what I saw after his crash, you'd have prepared for it, too—but I still took it hard.

That guy had been such a big part of my life. We'd raced together since our Norwood Arena days, and in 1968 he ran second to me in the NASCAR modified standings. And, of course, it was his split with Sonny Koszela that opened the door for me to take that ride, and for Freddy to take my place in Boehler's car. We'd raced thousands of laps together.

Before he died, Thompson had already scheduled a special Fred DeSarro Day on November 5, and they went ahead with it. They ran the race as a tribute to his memory, and as a benefit to his family. I didn't feel like being there, just because it meant dealing with his death all over again, but at the same time there was no way I was going to miss it. Obviously, a lot of other people felt the same way. There was a standing-room-only crowd, and a huge field of modifieds showed up even though there was absolutely no purse; all the proceeds went to Fred's wife Linda and their kids.

I won the first heat race, and the feature line-up was basically a heads-up thing: the heat winners, followed by the runner-up finishers, then the third-place finishers, and so on. The only kink was that they wanted to leave the feature pole open in Freddy's honor, so I was going to start all alone on the front row.

That was eerie enough, rolling around in a row by myself, knowing that Fred was supposed to be right there beside me. But then, on one of the final parade laps, I'll be damned if things didn't get even weirder. Just as we rolled toward turn three—where DeSarro had crashed—a ball joint broke in the right front corner of my car.

That's something that doesn't ever happen on a slow lap. And, trust me, I'm speaking from experience. In all my years, it happened just that one time. But I knew that if it had happened at speed, I'd probably have had a hell of a wreck.

I remember mumbling to the guys from the track crew that it was

After Fred DeSarro died, his family established an annual sportsmanship award in his honor and presented it at the Pocono Race of Champions. I was the first recipient. That's Freddy's dad, Alfred "Pop" DeSarro, with the microphone, and to my right are Freddy's widow Linda and their two kids, Brian and Gary. In the background is ROC announcer Gary Montgomery. (Courtesy of Speedway Scene)

like Freddy was trying to tell me something. Since I was out of the race before it ever got going, somebody from the track management—probably Carl Merrill—asked me to serve as a last-minute honorary starter, and I did.

That ended up being quite an emotional day. Right after they took the white flag, with Geoff Bodine leading and Richie Evans running second, the entire field slowed down on the backstretch and then pulled into the infield. It was a symbolic thing, a way of saying that Freddy DeSarro had won one last race.

All the drivers got together on the frontstretch, and I basically got nominated to present the trophies to Freddy's two sons, Brian and Gary. In the pictures from that victory lane scene, I'm smiling, because I've got these two sweet little kids with me, and I wanted to do whatever I could to keep their spirits up. But it was a sad, sad moment, and it's still hard to think about.

I've already talked about how friendly Freddy and I were, but just gathering these thoughts really brought back a bunch of old memories. I think about all the times he invited me to go out sailing with him. Freddy had a nice boat, but I always declined. For one thing, I've never been a water person; for another, I remembered a day a few years earlier, when he was out on Long Island Sound and the fog boxed him in someplace. He actually ended up missing a race that night.

So I'd tell him, "No thanks, Freddy. You go ahead."

I wish I'd taken him up on that offer.

It's hard enough to go through something like that once, the stuff I experienced the day Freddy crashed. But seven years later, I went through it again.

I've been friendly with a lot of race drivers in my life, but it's probably fair to say that the guy I was closest to in 1978 was Fred DeSarro, and the guy I was closest to in 1985 was Richie Evans. I had known him right from the time he was struggling to get noticed at Albany-Saratoga and Utica-Rome. We were friends in my championship years, and all the way through his. By '85, we weren't racing together as much as we used to, but we still enjoyed getting together, especially at places where you could mix a little fun in with your racing. Like Martinsville.

The day Richie died—October 24—we had ridden to the track together. He told me he had been trying to find me the night before, looking to raise a little hell, but he never could. We joked that it was probably just as well, because we were a handful when you got us together.

This was a Thursday, and just before they opened the track for the morning practice session I wandered over to his pit stall. The two of us sat down for a coffee, and just shot the shit for a while. Finally, Richie said, "Come on, Bugs. Let's go run a little."

So we put down the coffee, climbed into our cars, and went out to practice.

We had run a few laps, me trailing Richie by maybe half a straightaway, when he had his crash. I'm flying down the backstretch, looking ahead at him just because you're always looking ahead, and I watched him go right into that third-turn wall. It was a hell of a hit, I knew that.

It's crazy, how much that crash was like Freddy's, as far as my involvement went. Again, I was right behind the guy. Again, I stopped my car as quickly as I could and ran over to see what I could do. In Richie's case, I wasn't the first guy on the scene; Tony Siscone, a nice guy and a really strong competitor from down in New Jersey, was already there. He had pulled down the window net, and I leaned in to get Richie's helmet unbuckled, and right away I knew he was gone. Again, it was just an awful thing, and the longer I stayed there the harder it hit me.

Finally, there was nothing to do but walk away. I was holding my own helmet in my hands, and I threw it at my car—Bob Garbarino's

On the day he died, Richie Evans and I sat down to shoot the breeze before the first practice session. That's when this picture was taken. Then we had a cup of coffee, climbed into our race cars, and he was gone. (Courtesy of Speedway Scene)

number 4—as hard as I could. And I yelled, "These fucking race cars are killing all my friends."

But just like with DeSarro, just like with MacTavish, losing Richie didn't slow me down any. We qualified for the Martinsville race that afternoon, and on Sunday I damn near won the race.

Actually, I should have won it. That was the first year they had cut the distance from 250 laps to 200, but nobody thought the strategy would be any different than it had been before, because 200 laps seemed like too far to go without a fuel stop. Well, Johnny Bryant, a Virginia driver who had done some winning down there but wasn't really a big threat that day, rolled the dice; he went the distance non-stop, and he won the race. I was on his bumper when the damn thing ended.

Of the guys who pitted—which meant every one of the big dogs—we ran first in class, but that wasn't good enough.

I would have loved to win that thing for Richie.

You don't think racing is a mental game? Try going through all of that: getting hurt, *driving* hurt, and literally watching your friends die. Try dealing with all the ironies I've to deal with. Then try blocking it all out, *completely* out, to the point where you can still process all that stuff I talked about earlier—the car ahead of you, the two behind you, the one bouncing off the side of you—better than the next guy can.

Good reflexes will win you a race now and then, but only a good brain will keep you at the top.

George Summers on Bugsy

George Summers and Bugs Stevens, George's retirement party, 1983. (Balser & Son Photo)

George Summers, legendary modified driver: "That decision to retire, it's tough for anybody. But it's different for everybody, I'm sure. I quit right at the end of 1983. I was 48, going on 49 years old, and what I had noticed as started to get a little older was, things started to bother me. I got tired, and I was hurting . . .

"The thing that really clinched it for me was the Thompson 300 that same year. I started near the front, and I ran in the top three, top five, for most of the day. I was in Art Barry's car, and that car was capable of winning. Well, about halfway through the race I was leading, but my back started hurting and my legs got a little numb. There actually came a point when I couldn't feel if I was stepping on the gas. Finally I said, 'What am I trying to do here? Do I want to end up hurting myself, or somebody else? I've been in this game for 30-odd years; I think it's time to give it up.' I actually had to get out of the car that day, and Greg Sacks finished the race for me. Like I said, that car and that team were capable of winning, but George Summers wasn't. I told everybody I was all done at the end of the year.

"I raced a couple more times, and then came a big NASCAR modified race at Oxford Plains, Maine. Well, I won the thing. Riding home, I said to [my wife] Maggie, 'Wouldn't it be nice if today had been my last race? It's too bad I promised Art I would go to the next show, the World Series at Thompson.' But we went to the World Series, and I won that race, too. It was one of the great days of my career, and my life, because the whole grandstand was going crazy. I've got a video of that race, and there wasn't anybody in the place sitting down for the last few laps. Everybody there knew the story, and they were all pumped up for me to win my last race.

The Home Stretch

"I knew I could never top that. And I remember thinking: I wish everybody who ever drove a race car got to retire just like this.

"Now, that doesn't mean it was easy to quit. I'll tell you, when it sunk in that I had driven my last race, it was like I had lost my best friend. I missed it more than I ever showed. But winning those last two races made it easier for me. And I think that's part of the reason guys like Bugsy, great drivers, didn't want to quit: They knew they could still win, and they wanted to get that one more victory.

"Of course, Bugsy did it a little different than I had done it. Once he got out of the modifieds, he still played around with the pro stocks at Seekonk. I knew how he felt about that, because I think he needed an outlet; everybody needs one. Mine was golf, and his was Saturday night at Seekonk Speedway. I went down there a few times in those years, and I'd always stop and talk to him.

"I mean, we went so far back together. I remember when he first showed up at Seekonk [in 1961], driving that number 28 car. He didn't win a lot right away, but he won some. And then once he got together with Lenny Boehler, he started winning at Seekonk and everyplace else: Thompson, Trenton, Martinsville . . .

"You know, as long as we raced, and as hard as we raced each other, we never really had any run-ins. There were times when we didn't agree on things, and times when one of us might have gotten a little bit mad at the other one, but that never lasted. Forget about roughing each other up on the race track, or throwing a fist at each other. We never even had a harsh word!

"Not so long ago, we were down in Florida, having a couple of beers and talking about the old times, all the nights we fought lap after lap, all the races when one of us won and the other ran second. Honestly, just talking about how much time we'd spent together over the years. And Bugsy said, 'You know, George, I feel like we've got a bond, like we're part of each other's lives.' That stayed with me, because I'd always felt the same way. It's like at my retirement party years ago, he gave me a rocking chair, and that meant so much just because it came from him. He's right: There really is a bond there.

"But, you know, I still remember that last race he ran in the modifieds, at Stafford [in 1987]. He was in Bob Garbarino's car, and he had that thing really going. I was sitting there, saying, 'Come on, Bugsy. *Come on!* You've got to win this thing.' Then I'd catch myself saying, 'Please, Lord, let him win this one last time, just like I did. Let him see how that feels. Give him that.' And, of course, he wasn't able to win that race, but I wanted that so bad for him.

"I still see him quite a bit, especially when we're in Florida. I just wish I could get him to come golfing with us. Ronnie Bouchard plays. Leo Cleary plays. Jerry Dostie has played with us, Bobby Santos. But Bugsy won't come out. And do you know why not? Because the sonofabitch knows he can't win, and he's the kind of guy who just can't finish second!"

The Home Stretch

The Home Stretch

If I'd been winning a lot of races, maybe it would have been easier to cope with some of the hard things I saw later in my career, like the crashes that killed Freddy and Richie. That might sound crazy if you've never raced, I'm sure, but winning has a way of making you look at everything differently. You look at the positives in your own situation instead of worrying about the negatives, and pretty soon the positives are all you can see. I guess race drivers have been thinking that way forever. It's a great way to block things out.

But in the first part of the eighties, and as the decade rolled along, I wasn't experiencing enough highs to offset those awful lows. Not only wasn't I winning like I used to, I wasn't winning much at all.

Oh, I had my days. In 1980 at Stafford, I was in the middle of a great fight with Richie in the Fall Final. I was driving Joe Brady's car,

Here's a tough loss. Richie Evans and I were having a heck of a fight in the 1980 Stafford Fall Final. Then my car overheated, and I had to watch from the infield as he crossed the line to win it. (Howie Hodge Photo/Courtesy of Speedway Scene)

Even as I got up into the second half of my 40s, I still had plenty of fight left in me. Joe Brady and I won the 1980 Westboro track championship, and that's me picking up the trophy from Dick Williams, the Westboro promoter. (Balser and Son Photo)

and Joe and I usually got outspent and out-powered at tracks like Stafford, but he had our car absolutely perfect that afternoon. Richie was good, too, and I could tell it was going to be a hell of a scrap for the win. Then we ended up overheating, and I had to watch Richie win the damn thing from the infield. That's a horrible feeling for a race driver; I don't mind seeing another guy win a race—especially a good friend and a clean racer like Richie—but I hated the idea that I never got the chance to make things tougher on him.

I had the exact same feeling in '81, on the infield track at Pocono, when I honestly felt like I was going to win the Race of Champions with Dick Armstrong's car. I ended up in the garage area with a broken set of spur gears after a bunch of us stacked up in traffic, and it was tough to climb out of what could very easily have been the winning car.

But that's just the way things were going for me back then. I'm telling you, the first half of the eighties was not an easy time for me. Just when it seemed like things were looking great, something would come along to mess it all up.

I was getting up there in age—I turned 46 in 1980—and I'm sure some people wrote me off as being over the hill. If you only saw the results, that was probably easy to do. But the results didn't show how fast we were that day at Stafford, or that day at Pocono. No matter what anybody else thought, *I* knew I could still get the job done.

A lot of people forget this, but early in 1982 I climbed into Bob Garbarino's car and ran off a string of wins at Seekonk; I mean, we were just about untouchable there, and that place was always a real driver's track. I was still getting to know Bob and his guys, and they were still getting to know me, but it seemed like we were building the

Bob Garbarino and I were awfully hot when we first teamed up. This shot was after we'd won a 200-lapper at Seekonk, where we had a bunch of success together. (Rick Nelson Photo/Courtesy of Speedway Scene)

kind of chemistry I mentioned earlier. It wasn't necessarily there yet, but it was beginning to jell. Then I broke my back in that Stafford crash, and we never seemed to hit our stride after that.

Bob was a good friend and terrific car owner who have me everything a driver could ask for. At the same time, I think I did everything Bob could have asked a driver to do. And yet the two of us were living proof that without a team meshing perfectly, winning is pretty close to impossible. Every now and then we'd hit it right, and we'd be quick. Even as late as 1986 we were good enough to win at Stafford, and that was saying something; a lot of the faces there had changed, but every Friday night you had to beat Reggie Ruggiero, Mike Stefanik, Charlie Jarzombek, and a bunch of other fast cats.

But we had a lot more nights that just frustrated the hell out of me. We'd miss the setup a little bit—which was just as much my fault

That's me on the inside, Mike Stefanik on the outside at Stafford in the mid-1980s. That was a tough period for me, because we were kind of hit-and-miss. (Courtesy of Speedway Scene)

202

as Bob's, because, as I've said, by that point in time a driver had to be a good chassis man—and I'd end up driving my ass off to finish sixth or eighth. I'd take the green flag thinking I had an honest shot to win, but within five laps I'd realize that we were just another car out there.

Maybe that's what I hated more than anything: being just another car. I had done an awful lot of winning in my life, and even when I wasn't winning I was usually somewhere in the picture. I could always live with losing, as long as I was *competitive*. Well, there were too many nights in the eighties when we just weren't competitive.

It was almost impossible to look at the positives, because there just weren't enough of them.

When you're struggling that hard, and then you pile all of this other shit on top of it—all these tragedies—it's pretty damn hard to stay motivated.

I mentioned the way I reacted when Richie was killed, and the anger I'd felt after losing both him and Freddy. Well, as hard as those two incidents hit me, it was probably Charlie Jarzombek's death at Martinsville in March of 1987 that first made me think about climbing out of the modifieds.

Charlie had crashed hard in the first turn – stuck throttle – and the officials red-flagged the race. Generally, when that happens, you roll around the track and you end up stopping just short of the crash site; I'd done it a hundred times, and most of those red flags had been for blocked tracks or wrecks which looked worse than they turned out to be. In this case, it just so happened that I was maybe the second car from the wreck when they stopped us, and it didn't take me long to figure out that this had been a really bad crash. They were pulling

Another old rival, another big loss. It was Charlie Jarzombek's death that probably clinched my decision to retire after the 1987 season. (Courtesy of Speedway Scene)

Charlie out through the top of the rollcage, and it was obvious that he was badly hurt, or worse.

I was 52 years old, and I remember saying—not to anybody else, but to myself—"You know, I'd like to see my grandkids grow up. I'd better get out before this stuff kills me, too."

That was a crazy thing for me to think, as much racing as I had done and as much as I still loved the sport. But I *did* think it, very clearly. It's something that probably came from deep inside me, from the inner soul.

Just a couple of months later, we lost Corky Cookman at Thompson. It was early in the race, and I was just a couple of cars behind him as we headed down the backstretch. I saw a quick shower of sparks as we got to the point where you start steering into the corner, and the next thing I knew, Corky's car was shooting up the banking, nose first. They had put a concrete wall around that place to prevent the kind of accidents that had launched me and Freddy DeSarro out of that place, and Corky hit that wall a ton.

It dawned on me at some point that all these incidents seemed to be happening somewhere near me. I'd been right behind Freddy DeSarro; I'd seen Richie go in; I was parked right there, staring at poor Charlie when they took from his car; and now I'd been just a car or two behind Corky.

This stuff was starting to take a toll on me.

But, like I said, I already knew by then that I was on my way out. Charlie's crash had started that, and Corky's death just sort of put the postage stamp on it. A bunch of my peers—George Summers, Jerry Cook, Maynard Troyer—had retired not long before that; Leo Cleary would hop into something every now and then, but his career was basically over; Eddie Flemke had gotten out in the early eighties and then died of a heart attack in '84. In a lot of ways, I felt like I was the last man standing, at least of the group I had spent so much of my life around. And I guess I just didn't feel like standing alone anymore.

I made up my mind that when the 1987 season ended, I'd retire as a modified driver.

I didn't ever discuss this with anybody. I didn't consult Doris or our kids or my friends. I didn't need to. Something in me said it was time, and I didn't need anybody else's opinion to confirm that.

There are people who think it's a bad idea to keep racing after you've already decided to quit. What they usually tell you is that you can't go fast if your heart's not in it anymore. Maybe I was the exception to that rule, because I honestly don't think it ever slowed me down in

*Even after I'd decided to quit, we still had some good nights. This was after we'd won the pole at a NASCAR Modified Tour show at Waterford in 1987.
(Courtesy of* Speedway Scene)

1987. I went to every race believing that as long as things jelled on that particular day or night, we could win.

I think about races like the NASCAR Modified Tour show at Waterford that summer. I was driving for Garbarino, and our car was a rocket in practice. I remember talking to Bob about the gear we were running, because I was afraid that if we didn't step it back a bit we might burn the rear tires off the thing; Waterford was the kind of place where you got a lot of wheelspin. Well, Bob and I discussed that for a while, and in the end we decided to leave it alone and stick with the gear we had. Sure enough, 75 laps later our right-rear was junk, and so was our day. Here I was, in good equipment at a track I loved, and for the rest of the race I was out there riding around, in the way.

Just another car.

I still hated that, which meant I still wanted to win.

My last modified race was supposed to come at Martinsville in October of '87. That would have been fitting, because I'd had so many wins and so many good times there; I think Martinsville's best days as a modified track and my best days kind of went hand in hand. But then the Fall Final at Stafford got postponed by weather, and the only sensible date to reschedule the thing was November 8, a Sunday afternoon. That was a lousy time for a race in Connecticut, but another fitting track for me. Over the years, Stafford and I had been awfully good to one another.

205

The gang at the Dutch Inn must have forgiven me for all the hell-raising I'd done there over the years, because they gave me this nice card before my last race at Martinsville.
(Berghman Family Collection)

For the most part, I treated that day as just another trip to work. It's not that I *tried* to think that way, necessarily; I guess that attitude had just become part of my makeup. I mean, I was obviously aware that it was going to be my last race in a modified—my last day on the job, you might say—but I didn't work myself into a frenzy over it.

For some reason, people don't want to believe that. They always say, "Come on, didn't you feel different going to the track that day? What was it like, driving from Rehoboth to Stafford one last time?" What they don't stop to think about is, I had been making that trip across Rhode Island and into Connecticut for more than twenty years. And in those twenty years, there were a lot of highs and lows, but I always made that same trip again the following week. You plug yourself in, and you go, because there's a race at Stafford and you're supposed to be there. That's the way I did it that day in November.

What I remember most about the race is that we were fast all day long, rock-solid fast. There were other guys running awfully well, too —Reggie Ruggiero, George Brunnhoelzl, Jeff Fuller—but I never got

206

the sense that anybody had us covered. If I wasn't up there rubbing nerf bars with 'em, it was only because it wasn't time to go just yet. It was a long race, 200 laps, and I had made a career out of being smart in those long races. It was pretty clear to me, early on, that we had a shot to win that thing.

What got us in the end was tires. There was a yellow flag with about 40 laps to go, and all the other fast cars pitted for new rubber. I wanted to come in when those guys did—in fact, I told my guys on the radio that I was sliding around, just about of tires—but Bob Garbarino thought we ought to stay out.

He said, "You can make it. You can make up the difference."

Bob's theory was that by the time the guys with fresh tires caught me, we'd be close enough to the end that I could hold 'em off. It was a gutsy call, and a lot of races have been won that way. But I didn't think this one would, and I was right. Ruggiero was the first guy to catch me, and he brought a pack of cars with him.

There's nothing that feels better to a race driver than fresh tires. You put a guy like Reggie on new rubber at a fast track like Stafford, and no amount of experience is going to beat him. I gave him all the fight I could, but passed me with probably 20 laps to go. By the end of the race we had slipped back to fourth, behind Ruggiero, Fuller, and Brian Ross.

I've seen a lot of pictures of me sitting in the car after that race, and from what I've always heard I stayed in the cockpit for a quite a while. But I've got to be honest: I've got no clear memory of what I was thinking, or why I sat there so long. I'm sure there was a reason, but it doesn't come to mind.

It took me a while to get out of the car after my last modified race at Stafford, but not because I was sad. I just really wanted to win that thing. (Mike Adaskaveg Photo)

207

That's Debra, our youngest, giving dear 'ole dad a hug after that last Stafford race.
(Mike Adaskaveg Photo)

I know everybody figures it was just a matter of the old man wanting to stay in that seat a while longer, and maybe that was part of it. After all, when you do anything as long as I had raced modifieds, and when it's as fun as I always made it, it's never easy to stop. But if I had to guess, I'd say I was probably just dejected.

Hey, the race is over. Might as well have a beer, right? On the left, you'll notice that PeePee Miguel, my old limo chauffeur, came out to see my big modified finale.
(Mike Adaskaveg Photo)

Because, see, I remember a lot of other people being around—my family, and a bunch of old friends—and there was a lot of emotion in the air. But their emotions were different from mine. Some of them were both happy and sad, crying about this being my last race. And yet the biggest emotion I felt was disappointment.

It broke my heart that I couldn't win that thing. I mean, wouldn't that have been a great way to go out, winning my last modified race, and doing it at Stafford?

I woke up the next day with the usual aches and pains. My back hurt, my neck hurt. But the biggest thing I remember feeling was relief.

I was happy it was over. Really.

My plan had never been to retire completely, just to step away from the modifieds. All along, the idea of playing around with a pro stock car on Saturday nights at Seekonk Speedway for a few more years really appealed to me.

I had my reasons.

The best reason was that I didn't see any way I could quit racing altogether. Just *stop*, right now. Most guys tend to retire cold turkey—just climb out of the car and never climb back in, the same way some people throw away their last pack of cigarettes—but I didn't think I was strong enough to do that. That would have been too abrupt a finish for me. I needed to wind down, to get racing out of my system in a more gradual way.

The second thing I found appealing about that pro stock deal was that Seekonk was so close to home. I could leave my house a half-hour before warm-ups and still be there in plenty of time; if I was at the salvage yard, same thing. It was almost *too* easy to go to Seekonk.

And as I started into that arrangement in 1988, it honestly *felt* easy. Climbing into that pro stock, there was never the same pressure I'd feel when I ran a big modified race, or when Lenny Boehler and I were chasing those NASCAR points all over the country. I think I looked at those pro stock races the way George Summers looks at his golf game, or the way Freddy DeSarro looked at his sailboat. It was a hobby, but a hobby I could pour a lot of heart and soul into.

Still, hobby or not, I went to Seekonk every Saturday with the idea that I could win that night. I still had a competitive spirit, and I damn sure didn't want to look bad, so I had to stay on top of my game.

In a lot of ways, running those pro stocks was a whole new ballgame. It's a late model car that's got more weight and less horsepower than a modified, so it has a much different feel; if you want to

For the most part, running a pro stock at Seekonk was a nice way to wind down. That's me in the 18, with John Rosati on the outside. (Courtesy of Speedway Scene)

measure the difference between a modified and one of those things, drive a Corvette for a while and then take a cruise in a Cadillac. And that's not putting down the pro stock, by any means, because you've still got to get in the damn thing and go as fast as you can. The car is different, but the objective is the same.

Seekonk in my pro stock days was a racey little joint, same as it had been with the Class A coupes in the early sixties and the modifieds in the late seventies. As long as that track exists, it's going to be the same deal: rough, tough, short-track racing, grinding it out on a little bullring.

My pro stock team was owned by Dick Del Sesto, who owned a commercial insulation outfit based right there in Seekonk, and he had good equipment: a Fred Rosner car, Nat Chiavettone engines. And we needed good stuff, because we had some pretty stiff opposition.

Seekonk was never easy, no matter which division you ran. A guy like Vinnie Annarrummo, who knew that joint like the back of his hand, could make you work your tail off. (Courtesy of Speedway Scene)

One of the things that makes Seekonk so competitive is that it's the kind of place some guys never leave. It's a little bit off the beaten path, and it's never really been part of any two-night or three-night circuit—at least not for long—so some drivers spend their entire careers there.

When you race at the same joint every Saturday night for 20 years, you *ought* to be one tough sonofabitch. And Seekonk had some tough sonsabitches.

Rick Martin, Vinnie Annarrummo, Joey Cerullo and Johnny Tripp were guys who had raced Seekonk long enough to know every inch of that joint; Eddie St. Angelo and George Murray were veterans who had branched out and done plenty of modified racing in the seventies and eighties, but by 1988 they had settled back in at Seekonk and were really tough in the pro stocks; and then there were guys like Jimmy Rosenfield, whose father Joe had been king of the hill at Seekonk when I got there in 1961.

There were good fields, good drivers, good crowds and good racing. Going home to Seekonk was a lot of fun.

I never really felt like I was anything special when I went back to Seekonk Speedway. The track people—from the Venditti family to the PR department—made a big deal out of having me back, and I guess

Just one of the guys. I always tried to keep things light in my pro stock days at Seekonk.
(Mike Adaskaveg Photo)

that made sense; I had made a pretty good name for myself over the years, and I probably helped them sell a few tickets every Saturday night. That was all right with me, just like it had been all right when Jack Arute and his people would use me and Ronnie Bouchard and Geoff Bodine and the rest to sell tickets at Stafford. If it was good for the race track, it was fine by me.

Some of the younger drivers seemed to treat me with a lot of respect; I didn't *ask* for that, but it was nice. I mean, when I was coming along, I always respected the guys whose names were bigger than mine, the guys who had paid their dues long before I'd come in.

But, naturally, there were also a few guys—not many, but a few—who seemed to resent the fact that I was there. Maybe it was a jealousy thing because of the attention I got, I don't know. But I'd hear things like, "Well, here comes the big shot." Hell, I was no big shot. I was just another dude pulling on his helmet, and trying to win the race. I couldn't understand where that attitude came from; I mean, if I was in their shoes, and along came a driver who put a few extra people into the grandstands every week, I'd have been happy to have him instead of whining about it.

I know one thing: I didn't *have* to be there. I didn't think I had anything to prove, and I sure wasn't racing for the money. I could have stayed home on Saturday nights, which wouldn't have helped their race track one bit. They should have thought about that.

Some of them apparently felt like they had to do a little extra banging and blocking with me, just to let me know I was on *their* turf now, I guess. But I made it clear right away that I was pretty capable

Dick Del Sesto always gave me good equipment at Seekonk, and we won the track championship in 1989. Not bad for a semi-retired old race driver. (Courtesy of Speedway Scene)

of banging and blocking right back. I never liked racing that way, but my outlook on that subject hadn't changed: I drove people like they drove me.

We got our act together pretty quickly, and won ourselves some races. That all goes right back to my theory about a driver being only as good as his mechanics; we had a guy named Tiny Levesque helping us, and ol' Tiny, who has since passed away, was as sharp a wrench as there ever was at Seekonk. He had worked on a dozen winning cars there over the years, and I was lucky to have him.

In 1989 we won the Seekonk Speedway pro stock title, which was great. Twenty-four years earlier, with Lenny Boehler, I had won the first track championship of my life right there at Seekonk.

I ran that pro stock for four seasons, and for most of that time we were competitive enough to keep me happy. But one of the really fun nights from that period happened on a night when we didn't run up front.

In 1991, the track brought Kenny Schrader in there for a regular Saturday-night show. He was running the Winston Cup race at Watkins Glen that weekend, and, like usual, he was looking to fit in a short-track race if he could. He flew in late, but after the heat races he came over to my car and we bullshitted for a few minutes. It was a natural thing, just a couple of race drivers talking. But we attracted quite a crowd; I remember people standing around, listening to the stories.

Kenny Schrader showed up at Seekonk to run a pro stock one night in 1991, and we found time for a good little bull session. (Bones Bourcier Collection)

Later on, I had a bunch of folks tell me that Kenny talked about having read my name for years in the racing papers, and that he enjoyed going to different parts of the country and getting to know guys who had been champions in those different areas. But he kind of caught me off guard when he said, "You know, I always wanted to meet you." That made me feel good.

The funny thing is, I always liked Schrader. He had won the pole a few times at Daytona, and had won the Busch Clash two straight times, and I remember being happy for the guy even though I didn't know him. He just struck me as a real racer.

The two of us started toward the back of the pack at Seekonk, and we ran together for a few laps, both of us trying to get to the front. But my car wasn't working very well, and Schrader, who was in one of Vinnie Annarummo's cars, was really rolling. I could tell in a hurry that I was pretty much holding him up. I didn't see any sense in jerking him around—that would have been no different than the treatment I'd gotten from the guys who resented me when I first went back there—so I gave him some room. No more room and no less room than I would have given Ray Hendrick or Eddie Flemke in the old days, but I gave him room. Schrader got next to me, got past me, and drove off.

And I thought to myself, Go on, Kenny. It's your night.

It sure was. He ended up winning the feature.

Packing up after another night at the office. Win or lose, I looked at Seekonk as a for of relaxation.
(Mike Adaskaveg Photo)

By the time the 1991 season ended, I was getting ready to quit that Seekonk ride, and, to be completely honest, I think Dick Del Sesto was getting ready to fire me. We both had the same reason: we weren't winning.

Looking back, I can pinpoint exactly why I think that was. Dick had gotten rid of Tiny Levesque; they'd had some silly dispute over Tiny buying a bump-steer gauge or something like that, and it got out of hand, and there went Tiny. Now I was back to being a jockey without a winning horse, the same as I had been too many times in my last few seasons in the modifieds.

My Saturday-night hobby—my golf game, my sailboat—wasn't as much fun as it used to be, and I just didn't see the point in going to the race track, even a race track right down the street, if it wasn't going to be fun.

I walked away from that pro stock, and, for all intents and purposes, that was the end of my active career as a race driver.

I say "active career" because I have climbed into race cars from time to time since then. I ran a few races in what's called a "Florida modified"—it's got a stock frame and a limited engine and narrow tires, nothing like the modifieds I used to run—for a guy out of New Smyrna named Charles Lashua, who a lot of racing people in New England know as "Buckwheat." He originally came from up around Fitchburg, Massachusetts, and for years he was always around the Bouchards and Pete Fiandaca and the rest of the gang from that area.

Once we started hanging around a little bit together in Florida, he was always after me to give his modified a run. I warmed it up a few times, but I never actually agreed to race it until one day a few years back at the Charlotte County Speedway, a little bullring in Punta Gorda.

That was a bad idea. It almost killed me.

We got to the track late, so we hustled to get ready for the last practice session. I was going to be the first car out, so I was parked and waiting to go. At Charlotte County, you pulled from the pits onto the track through a gate on the backstretch. When the previous warm-up ended and the cars rolled off the track, the official opened the gate and waved me out. I eased out the clutch and rolled out there. Well, some straggler from the previous practice session had been idling around, and now for some reason he came roaring out of turn two just as I got onto the race track.

I never saw a thing until the crash, but I damn sure heard him coming. The guy hit me wide open, T-boned me right in the driver's door. The impact turned my car, and then his car flew right over my hood. It was one hell of a hit. I can still see his entire front end—wheels, suspension, the whole shebang—flying right out of the track.

I must have been in shock. My car was still rolling, barely, so I drove it back to the pits with everything dragging and scraping along the pavement. Buckwheat came running over, saying, "Don't worry about a thing, Bugs. We can fix it for the feature. We'll just get us a set of headers, and straighten out the front end . . ."

I told him, "You go right ahead, Buck, but you won't be fixing it for me."

Seekonk Speedway, 1991.
(Mike Adaskaveg Photo)

It was about a week after that until I did anything but lie around the house, moaning. And thinking about the fact that after all the wrecks I'd survived when I was racing for real, it was pretty damn stupid of me to get banged up just playing around.

I never really officially retired. I just sort of stopped driving. But I'm done. I know that.

Still, that itch is there. Bobby Judkins, whose cars I'd raced against forever, moved down to Florida from Connecticut a few years back, and he lives not far from my winter place in Edgewater. Bobby also owns one of those Florida modifieds, and I've taken that thing out for a few practice runs at the Orlando Speedworld over the years, even as late as 2001. The last time out I went maybe 20 laps, and when I got back to the pits my tongue was hanging out. I was whipped, boy.

But you know what?

It was still a thrill. And if I did the same thing 10 years from now, it'd give me that same damn feeling.

Once a race driver, always a race driver, I guess.

Doris Berghman on Bugsy

Doris and Carl "Bugs Stevens" Berghman, Freetown, MA, 2002.
(Karl Fredrickson Photo)

Doris Berghman, AKA Mrs. Bugs Stevens: "Most of the time, I call him 'Bugs.' That was already his nickname when we met in Texas, so that's what I used. Later on, when we came back to Massachusetts, I started calling him 'Carl' because we were around his family, and that's what they called him. As time went on, I went back to 'Bugs,' or maybe 'Honey.' It's only 'Carl' every now and then, and maybe some other names if I'm mad!

"When the kids were small, I didn't go to very many races, but as they got older I started going more and more. But that doesn't mean I went with Bugsy. Most weekends, he'd take off early on a Friday, and I went with somebody else. See, Bugs had to be there for the warm-ups, and I had to worry about getting the kids ready after school or whatever else they were doing. But when the big races came up, like Martinsville, I'd sometimes go along for those trips. And at the end, when he was just racing the pro stocks at Seekonk, I'd go just about every week.

"Once he got out of the modifieds, I think the racing he did at Seekonk was a little bit of an outlet for him. It still gave him that weekly thrill, and it was less stressful for him than the modifieds. But for me, it was the same: Whenever he was out there, I wanted him to do well.

"Later on, once he quit for good, he pretty much stayed away from the tracks for a while. When he did go, it seemed like it bothered him to be there and not be driving. So many people there knew him, and of course they'd all want to talk about the days when he was racing. He was such a character back then—he still is, but he was really one when he raced—that I'm sure it had to be a big change for him.

Growing Old, Yes; Growing Up, No

"But, overall, I think he's adjusted pretty well to retirement. Oh, every now and then he'll start talking about the old days, and you can tell he really misses that life. I think that's why he loves going to that [New England Auto Racers] Hall of Fame dinner every year. He's got so many friends that go to it, and he enjoys talking racing with those people.

"He's still a joker. He's got to play around with everybody. Sometimes, people don't know how to take him at first—like, he'll start picking on a waitress, and she'll be embarrassed—but by the time we leave we're like old friends. I always say, 'He's been like this his whole life. He's not going to change now.'

"I guess we probably spend more time together now than we ever did. Back when he was chasing points, he'd leave home on a Thursday and then just blow in and blow out of the house all weekend long. He'd change clothes and then take off again, or maybe just stay long enough to take a nap. Now I've got to put up with him all week, and on weekends, too.

"Things are pretty casual for us these days. Of course, that doesn't mean it's always calm. I mean, he can make a race out of anything. We'll drive back and forth to Florida, and he's always got to get there quicker than he did last time. He's got to find the challenge in everything.

"When we're home in Massachusetts in the summer, I still work at the [salvage] yard, keeping busy, and Bugsy still messes around there, too. In Florida, I'll go out to the garden or maybe go to a yard sale, and he goes off and does his own thing, whether it's going to the races with Bobby Judkins or playing around with his boat. He's got a new pontoon boat he's been putting together, so that keeps him busy.

"We don't see the old racing crowd too much. When we're in Florida, sometimes people come around. We'll be sitting around, and somebody like Bob Garbarino might stop by. But it's funny; even if you only see those old friends once in a while, it's like you just saw them a week ago.

"We've been married since 1958, and it's been an interesting life. I'm sure we missed a lot of family-type things along the way, but Bugsy was always there when we needed him. And you know how I look at it? We got to go a lot of places, and see a lot of things, and meet a lot of people we wouldn't have met if it wasn't for racing. We have friends everywhere.

"We'll be walking along in Florida, and just when you think you're miles away from anybody we know, somebody will holler, 'Hey, Bugs.' And it'll be somebody who's seen him racing. That still amazes me, the places we go where people know him.

"You know what I've done all these years? I've just kind of stood off to one side, taking it all in, just watching everything that goes on. And I can tell you this: With Bugsy around, it's never been dull."

Growing Old, Yes; Growing Up, No

Growing Old, Yes; Growing Up, No.

THESE DAYS, I SPEND about half my year in Rehoboth, and the other half at the home we own in Florida. We've owned our place in Edgewater since about 1993. Down there, it's such a different life. For so many years, I was up early, heading for the salvage yard, going to work. When I'm in Florida, we start most of our days at noontime.

All those years of pressure—at the yard and at the race track—and now the only pressure I get is from Doris.

It's funny, the way a bunch of our old racing crowd ended up down there. Leo Cleary lives up around Ormond Beach; George Summers has a winter place in Port Orange; Ronnie Bouchard has a home over on the Gulf side of Florida, down near Naples. But I don't see those guys nearly as much as you'd think. George and Ronnie are big golfers, and every so often they'll call and ask me to play a round with them. But with all my old war injuries—my back, my knee, my shoulder, all the stuff I've banged up in wrecks over the years—I'm too tight to enjoy swinging the clubs. So I pass.

And, you know, that's probably a good thing. I mean, can't you see me, Summers and Bouchard racing from hole to hole on those karts? They'd throw us off the golf course.

Everybody from back home asks me what I do down there, how I spend my time. I tell 'em I work for Bobby Judkins, and that's partially true, because it seems like I spend an awful lot of time piddling around with him. I'll go to the races to help him sometimes—actually, I just sort of stand around and pretend I'm helping—and we see each other quite a bit during the week. We'll have lunch, and you never know where things might go from there. Lately, I've been hanging insulation and sheet rock in his new shop; Bobby put up a nice building behind his house, but once he got the outer walls and the roof up he was in such a hurry to move in his equipment that he never really finished the construction job. So a couple of us have been pitching in to get the place done.

Back home, Carl, my eldest son, is pretty much running the show at Freetown Auto Parts. Actually, he's been in charge for about ten years, and he's done such a good job with it that all I do is check in now and then. Little by little, I step more and more away from it.

When I'm home in Massachusetts, I hang around the house and maybe roam around town, visiting my friends. When I'm in Florida, I hang around the house and maybe roam around town, visiting my friends. I'm just wasting my life away. I love it.

Our place in Florida is right on the Intracoastal Waterway, and one of the things I've come to love is shrimping. I climb into my little boat, head out into the river, throw out my nets, and pull in a pretty good dinner. You can't get seafood any fresher than that.

There's a bit of a science to shrimping, or maybe an art. You don't just go out there when you feel like it; you have to operate according to the tides, and of course they're changing from day to day. We might shove off at three o'clock in the morning, and shrimp until the sun comes up. And you'd be surprised how many people are out there at that time: old men, old ladies, kids, all of 'em out there in their skiffs and pontoon boats.

It's hard work, working those nets and hauling them in when they get full, but it's also a great way to relax, floating down that river in the night air.

Whenever I can, I try to talk some of my old racing friends into going with me. Gene Bergin and Leo Cleary have been out on the water with me, and we've spent half the night shrimping and talking about our lives, which is kind of funny after all the years we spent racing our brains out together. Pete Zanardi, my old writer buddy, has been out there with me, too; Peter had a hell of a time, until Bergin walked off with his shrimp.

But it's funny: even doing something as simple as shrimping, I manage to work in a little danger sometimes. One night I fell overboard, and because the temperature was pretty cool I was wearing a heavy sweater, blue jeans, long johns and boots up to my knees. I was so waterlogged that I couldn't haul myself up into the boat. It was all I could do to hang on. Well, Red Peard, a good friend of mine from back home in Rhode Island—hell, a good friend of a bunch of us from those modified days—grabbed me by my belt and pulled me in. Saved my ass. Oh, it was something else.

I ended up cracking something in my ribs in that adventure. I'm pretty sure I broke one, and if anybody in America knows about broken ribs, it's me. I've walked out of a lot of pit areas feeling that pain. I just never expected to feel it at 60-odd years old, on some cold dark night, on a little boat in Florida.

This was a neat deal. When my son, David Berghman, won his first-ever feature in the Seekonk charger division, I got to give him a little high-five as I rolled out to run the pro-four mod race. (Courtesy of Speedway Scene)

I don't get to very many races anymore. My son David runs the NASCAR modified series, and I'll go to maybe a half-dozen of his races every season. He's done a good job, and he made me awfully proud by winning his first tour-type race at Waterford on May 11, 2002, which happened to be my 68th birthday. I was still in Florida at the time, but just hearing about that win was a nice birthday present. And the next day was Mother's Day, so it was like Doris got a gift, too.

I still enjoy seeing a hard, clean race, particularly a modified race. But, like any old driver can tell you, it's not easy to stand there and just *watch*. When I go to David's races, I get so wrapped up in what he's doing that it's almost like I'm driving the car myself. One time up at the New Hampshire International Speedway, the guys on his team let me have a radio, and I sat way up in the grandstands, hoping to help with the spotting. Well, I never said a word; I was watching him so closely, trying to plan every move he needed to make, that I forgot what I was up there to do. Of course, they all accused me of sitting up there and drinking beer instead of paying attention to the race, but the truth is, I was paying *too much* attention.

They haven't let me touch a radio ever since.

I've tried to help David with a little bit of advice here and there, but only to a point. The last thing I want to do is stand there like some old-timer who thinks he can tell all the young kids how to do things. It's his car, and I can't tell him how to drive it.

Another thing that's tough about going to the races is that I just

Here's another big moment, although I didn't get to be there. That's David after he won the NASCAR Featherlite Modified Series race at Waterford on May 11, 2002, my birthday. (Dave Mavlouganes Photo)

can't believe all the money involved. I mean, in the late seventies we all shook our heads over all the high-dollar equipment that was coming into modified racing, and today you'd look like an amateur if you ran that same caliber of stuff. Sometimes I wonder where it's all going, or how in the world today's version of the kid I used to be—you know, just a boy off the far—could ever get involved.

I don't know why I let that bother me so much. Money has always been an issue in racing, and I'm sure that's never going to change. I actually had a promoter tell me one time, "You know, Bugs, everybody complains about the purses, but the fact is, I don't really need to pay you guys at all. Hell, most of you would rent my track and haul your cars here anyway if that's what it took to race." He's probably right, but it's still a frustrating thing to see.

So instead of going to the races and getting all worked up over this stuff, I take the easy way out. I'll have a beer at four or five o'clock in the afternoon, and that's the end of me. I'll watch some sports thing on TV, and I'll be very content. Next thing you know, I'm falling asleep, and there goes another evening.

One last thing about the racing today: When I go, it sometimes occurs to me that half the people I used to talk to at the track aren't there anymore. And I miss a lot of those guys.

Where do you want to start? Fred DeSarro, Eddie Flemke, Fats Caruso, Ray Hendrick, Richie Evans . . .

How about Lenny Boehler?

When Lenny passed away in May of 2001, there went a big chunk of my racing career. Naturally, all the memories came back. You think of all the miles we went up and down the road, all the tracks we went to, all the races we won, and it'll make your head spin. But what I thought about most was the personal side of Boehler, the quirky side.

Anyone who knew Lenny can tell you how superstitious he was, and I've got a good example of that. We were at Darlington for the Southern 500 in 1970, trying to be Winston Cup racers, and Lenny was walking around in an old pair of shoes which were so worn out that one of the soles was hanging off. I mean, it was just flapping in the breeze. Well, one night I grabbed those shoes and tossed them into the Dumpster out behind the hotel. He had another pair with him, and I figured he'd just wear those instead. Wrong.

The next morning, Lenny refused to leave for the race track until I got those shoes back for him. They were his lucky shoes, he said. So there I was, rummaging around in that Dumpster. And two hours later, there was Lenny Boehler, strolling through the Winston Cup garage area with a flapping sole. That was beautiful.

In the winter of 1978, just after Freddy DeSarro died, Lenny got awfully sick. He had a problem with his lymph glands—some kind of cancer or blood disorder, I guess—and we almost lost him. He was down and out, and I think the only thing that really kept him going

There's Lenny Boehler in 1982, talking with his driver, Ronnie Bouchard. 'Ole Lenny was an original, all right.
(Mike Adaskaveg Photo)

was the fact that the guys on his crew insisted on finishing a new car he was building; Leo Cleary was right there with them, pushing Lenny along, and when they got that thing done Cleary won a bunch of races with it. At Seekonk, especially, he was really fast with that thing, and I think that pumped Boehler back up.

Still, Lenny was never really the same after that. He had a lot of racing left in him, and, as it turned out, a lot of winning: his cars won races with Ronnie Bouchard, Mike McLaughlin and Doug Heveron, and he won three straight NASCAR modified championships between 1994 and '96 with Wayne Anderson and Tony Hirschman. But you could tell that Lenny was pretty beaten up by his health problems, and when he got sick again a couple years back, it ended up being more than he could fight off. And that's saying something, because Lenny Boehler was a hell of a fighter.

All those guys were in my circle, and now they're gone. It really makes you think.

Ah, I'm probably getting a little too deep here. I mean, I'm not afraid of getting old. I'm not afraid of anything happening to me.

In fact, there's only been one time when I was actually afraid of death. A while back, I had some surgery done, just minor stuff. Later on, I was in the recovery room waking up, and there were these three fat ladies lying on gurneys, covered with sheets and not moving at all. I'm lying there thinking, Damn, did I really die? And what scared me the most was, when I looked at those women, it sure didn't seem like heaven to me

❖ ❖ ❖ ❖ ❖

I did an awful lot of racing in New York, and won my share of races out there, but I was kind of surprised when they stuck me into that New York State Stock Car Association Hall of Fame.
(John Grady Photo)

225

This is from the New England Auto Racers Hall of Fame dinner, 1998. (Dave Mavlouganes Photo)

Within the space of a couple of weeks in the spring of 1998, I got inducted into both the New England Auto Racers Hall of Fame and the New York State Stock Car Association Hall of Fame. That felt kind of strange; when I raced, I never thought that far down the road. A hall of fame? Come on. That was for old guys.

But, I have to admit, it was a pretty nice feeling, being honored like that.

Getting voted in by the New York club kind of surprised me. That was something I never expected; I guess I'd based myself in New England for so long that I started to overlook whatever I had done over there. But, looking back, I had an awful lot of good races at Albany-Saratoga, Utica-Rome, Plattsburgh and Shangri-La, at Freeport and Islip on Long Island, and even a few on the dirt at Fonda. In my point chasing days, I probably raced someplace in New York at least once a week. I never considered myself a New York State guy—that was Richie's turf, and Bill Wimble's, and Maynard Troyer's, and Lou Lazzaro's—but I guess I managed to turn a few heads out there over the years.

The NEAR induction wasn't as much of a shock, but it was still a thrill to be inducted in the very first class, at the Hall's inaugural dinner. And it was a hell of a group I went in with: Eddie Flemke, Pete Hamilton, Richie Evans, Ernie Gahan, Ron Bouchard, Rene Charland, Gene Bergin, Bill Slater and Ollie Silva among the drivers, plus Harvey

Here's a pretty good group at the first induction ceremony for the NEAR Hall. Top row, left to right: Bill Slater, Tara Evans (for her dad, Richie), Ed Flemke Jr. and Paula Flemke Bouchard (for their dad), Gene Bergin, Ron Bouchard, and Harvey Tattersall III (for his dad); bottom row, me, Ernie Gahan, Rene Charland, Florence Tattersall (for her dad) and Pete Hamilton. (Dave Mavlouganes Photo)

226

Tattersall, one of the great old promoters, and Bill Welch, who owned cars and promoted races and interviewed me a million times as a track announcer at different places.

Pete Zanardi gave my induction speech at the NEAR dinner, and he was his usual intellectual self. He's got to be a pretty sharp guy to make me sound so good. He talked about me being "New England's first auto racing media darling," and of course he talked about the free-spirited lives we all led in the sixties and seventies.

"We asked Bugsy Stevens to define what being a modified person was all about," Zanardi said. "And, damn it all, Bugsy gave us that."

I'm not nearly as articulate as Peter, so instead I talked about the time my good friend Gahan cut me off at Atlanta, and then I looked over at Charland's table and said, "Rene, I never had a chance to spin you out, but you probably deserved it." And I couldn't resist taking a shot at Jerry Cook: "The only guy I really did spin out—that I went after a few times—is not here. He's working for NASCAR now."

In other words, I was my usual self.

I've gone to the NEAR ceremony each year since that first dinner, and I hope to keep doing that. It's my way of paying my respects to the guys coming in. I mean, I raced for so long that it seems like at least a couple inductees every year have had direct connections to my career.

In 1999, Hop Harrington and Leo Cleary were inducted, and the three of us had fought so many battles; the late Anthony Venditti, who built and ran Seekonk Speedway, went in that same year; and they asked me to give the acceptance speech on behalf of Fred DeSarro, which made sense. It was a tough thing to do, to let my guard down and be personal about an old friend like Freddy, but I think it made sense to have me do it.

In 2000, they inducted Fats Caruso and Ron Narducci, two guys I'd run a lot of laps with, and Ralph Moody, who had done so much to help me when I was still thinking about Winston Cup racing. And my old friend George Summers, who raced with me forever, went in that same year, which was a great thing for me to see.

In 2001, Don MacTavish and Bobby Santos went into the Hall, and I had raced with those guys from Norwood Arena onward. Don Rounds, who I'd run with on the dirt at Stafford back in '65, also went in. And, speaking of Stafford, Jack Arute became a hall-of-famer that same year, and I took enough prize money out of his track over the years that attending his induction was the least that I could do.

In 2002, NEAR honored Bill Wimble and Ray Miller and Dick McCabe, three guys I'd raced with and been friends on three different circuits; Wimble was primarily a dirt man, Ray was an asphalt modified guy, and McCabe was a late model star with NASCAR North and

That's me and Jack Arute, the Stafford Motor Speedway owner and a guy who's been a friend forever. (Dave Mavlouganes Photo)

There was no way I could miss the 2002 NEAR Hall of Fame dinner, not with Sonny Koszela getting inducted. (Koszela Family Collection)

the American-Canadian Tour. They also inducted Ken Squier for his media work, but I remember Kenny most from all those Thursday nights when I raced at his Catamount Speedway and drank an awful lot of beer at his bar. And, probably most personally for me, Sonny Koszela also got inducted in 2002; how could I not be there after everything we'd done together?

That NEAR dinner has become a sentimental thing with me. Plus, it gives a lot of us old bastards one more chance every year to get together and raise a little hell.

A few years back, Georgie Summers, Gene Bergin and Leo Cleary and I flew up from Florida together for the NEAR ceremony. Isn't that something, after all the racing—all the hard, hard racing—we did? We landed in Boston, and then drove to George's home in Upton to spend the night. Once we got unpacked, the four of us went to some little pub down the road, and before long Cleary and Summers were arguing about some little incident at Westboro Speedway 25 years ago. Gene and I just sat there, listening and grinning.

While we're talking about halls of fame . . .

I always say that I'm still just a farm boy from Rehoboth, so it was really special for me to go into the Dighton-Rehoboth Alumni Athletic Hall of Fame in 2001. I was honored mostly for what I'd done in high school sports, but they also mentioned my college and Air Force football and baseball accomplishments, and, of course, the racing. I had most of my family there at the ceremony with me, which was nice.

I thanked my coaches and my teachers, talked about a couple of the great athletes I'd played with in my school days, and closed by summing up my outlook on the world in general: "I've raised the devil all my life. I was born that way. But I love people, and I love life. Life is short. I want to live every bit of it, and I want my friends to."

Then I said thanks, got a nice ovation, and started walking back to my seat. But I couldn't resist turning back to the podium for one last joke . . .

"I went through three years of having my mother in a nursing home before she passed," I said. "Well, this one little old lady used to run up and down the corridor in that nursing home. She used to lift her dress up and say, 'Super sex. Super sex.' She'd go to every door: 'Super sex.' After a while, nobody paid any attention to her.

"One day she goes up to this little old guy in a wheelchair at the end of corridor. She lifts up her dress and says, 'Super sex.' Then she looks at him, waiting for a reaction.

"Finally he looks up and says, 'I'll have the soup.'"

It took me about 30 years, but I finally got over the serious hell-raising. It just didn't feel right anymore, physically. When you're over 60,

Talk about a reunion! From left to right, that's Ronnie Bouchard, George Summers, Dave Humphrey, Seekonk Speedway's Irene Venditti, myself and Deke Astle. God knows how many Seekonk victories are represented in this shot. (Summers Family Collection)

you can't party like you did when you were 28. There comes a point when it just doesn't make sense.

Part of that, I think, is because I spend so much time in Florida, and when you're around that many retired people they have a way of slowing you down. You tend to smell the roses a little bit without even realizing it.

But, you know, I don't believe I *think* like most people my age. I still want to do crazy things. No, I don't take the same kinds of chances I used to, but in a lot of ways I feel like I still live on the edge.

Leo Cleary and I have that in common. Like me, he insisted on messing around with those Florida modifieds once he moved down there, but he took it a lot more seriously than I did. That's typical Leo; he always did everything flat out. Well, one night his car lost a radiator hose, and he slid hard into the wall. Leo broke some ribs and fractured his skull, and we all figured that, finally, he'd get over even thinking about driving anymore.

About a year later, the two of us were talking, and Cleary said, "You know, I'm about ready to race again." I said, "For Christ's sake, Leo, you're 68 or 69 nine years old. Last time you sat in one of those things, it almost killed you." And Cleary, as serious as can be, said, "I know, Bugs, I know. But it's *fun*."

What's crazy is, I knew how he felt.

Like I said: We're not like other people.

Not long before she died in 2000, I went to visit my mother. She was lying in bed, and I was clowning around, as usual. Right to the day we lost her, I was always trying to make her laugh.

She looked up at me and said, "Sonny, do you think you're ever going to grow up?" I said, "Well, Ma, I'm 65 years old. It might be a little too late for that."

I don't know if I ever *have* grown up. All I know is, every place I go, I'm the happiest guy in the room. I can't have dinner in a restaurant without kidding around with the waiter, or trying to get a rise out of the lady at the cash register.

Just the other day, I was driving around town with Doris, and I stopped at an auto parts place to pick up something for my granddaughter's car. The woman who works there started talking about old times at the race track. Before long, another guy jumped into the conversation. Then the parts manager cornered me, and we talked some more. I walked outside, and there was Doris, waiting in the car.

She said, "I thought you were going to be in and out? You've been gone 20 minutes!"

I shrugged and said, "Hey, they wanted to talk."

That's the way my life is. It was that way in every pit area on the East Coast for years and years, and it's that way still. I've spent a lot of time shooting the breeze, but I don't feel like that time has been wasted.

I've lived one hell of a good life.

I mean, really, what is life all about?

Is it about having somebody to love—family and friends—and having people who love you back? I have all that, and I've had it for a long time.

Is it about being happy, and having fun? I think it *should* be. And I've done my best to not miss out on any of that.

So far, it's been one hell of a ride.

(Mike Adaskaveg Photo)

(Mike Adaskaveg Photo)